The End of
Don't Ask
Don't Tell

THE IMPACT IN STUDIES

AND PERSONAL ESSAYS

BY SERVICE MEMBERS

AND VETERANS

EDITED BY

J. FORD HUFFMAN AND TAMMY S. SCHULTZ

Marine Corps University Press
3078 Upshur Avenue
Quantico, Virginia 22134
www.tecom.usmc.mil/mcu/mcupress

1st printing, 2012
PCN 10600008600

For sale by the Superintendent of Documents, U.S. Government Printing Office
Internet: bookstore.gpo.gov   Phone: toll free (866) 512-1800;   DC area (202) 512-1800
Fax: (202) 512-2104 Mail: Stop IDCC, Washington, DC 20402-0001

ISBN 978-0-16-090546-9

CONTENTS

About the Nomenclature

The terms "homosexual" and "gay" are used interchangeably in the essays and reports, depending on the historical, cultural, clinical, bureaucratic, or other context.

"Gay" includes men and women, and there are references to "gay service members" and "gay Marines," meaning both genders. "Gay men and lesbians" uses the adjective "gay" and the noun "lesbian."

Preface

by Tammy S. Schultz

"What about a class on 'Don't Ask, Don't Tell' [DADT]?" Colonel Michael F. Belcher, the director of the Marine Corps War College (MCWAR) at the time, asked me one February afternoon in 2009.

We were discussing potential "controversial issue" topics that would further enhance students' critical thinking. I cringed. I had deliberately avoided that topic for my entire professional career.

It was not that the subject lacked import or did not involve "hard" security issues, my main career focus. The issue of gay men and lesbians being free to serve their country openly checked the box on both counts. The reason I steered clear of DADT was the same reason I had not written about women in combat—as a lesbian, I felt critics could undermine anything I wrote simply because of who I was rather than the argument's merits (or lack thereof). I wanted no part in this type of pseudointellectual battle.

Furthermore, although my MCWAR colleagues knew I was gay, even that was a recent incarnation for me. I did not come out to my parents until I was 28. My professional career began with the U.S. Army War College in Carlisle, Pennsylvania, where who knew I was gay largely depended upon my verbal acumen on any particular day due to my desire not to lie or be fully open. The verbal gymnastics could be exhausting, although those who knew, including my colonel boss, treated me and my family like any other.

By the time I reached MCWAR, I was more comfortable in my own skin. My new personal policy entailed complete openness to colleagues, and honesty (if asked) to students. Most students did not ask. I did not tell. There was no reason to do so. Around this time, my then-partner had our second baby, Laken. I took some leave and Colonel Belcher announced the news to the students, who put together the fact that I did not look pregnant the last time they saw me. My baby "outed" me to that year's class, which brings me back to my cringe when Belcher mentioned holding a class on DADT.

I knew that Belcher's instincts were right (they usually were). It was the perfect topic given the contours of the upcoming presidential election and the statistics at the time showing a majority of military opinion against the repeal. Now, though, I knew how it might be perceived: the lesbian professor wants to hold a class about DADT. I immediately did two things. One, I invited Elaine Donnelly of the Center for Military Readiness (CMR), one of the most outspoken opponents of repealing DADT, to speak at MCWAR (as well as Aubrey Sarvis, president of the Servicemembers Legal Defense Network, an organization cofounded in 1993 by an essay author in this book, Michelle M. Benecke, whose mission includes bringing DADT to an end and supporting gay and lesbian service members). Two, I scheduled another meeting in Washington, DC, to ensure that I was not at the MCWAR event so that an open discussion could take place.

My understanding from some of those who were in class that day is that most of the opinion landed on the side against DADT's repeal. I never got a back brief, nor did I want one. But soon afterward, Air University Press at Maxwell Air Force Base had an open solicitation for book chapters on social issues in the military, such as DADT.

I did not know where I stood on DADT's repeal, having never systematically studied the issue. For the DADT class, I had assigned works against repeal—from Ms. Donnelly of CMR—and for repeal—from the Palm Center, a University of California research institute focused on gender, sexuality, and the military. I wanted to tear those studies apart. Having already dipped my toe into the DADT waters, I decided to write for Air University's book, landing wherever the research led me.

As a national security expert who has spent much time with members of the armed services, the last thing I desired was to make a recommendation that would harm the forces, especially during a time of war. And I did not consider DADT to be a civil rights issue, or at least that was not how I would approach it. For me, it came down to one basic question: would allowing homosexuals to serve openly hurt military readiness or not?

Frankly, being a lesbian against DADT's repeal would have garnered much more attention and notoriety had that been my goal. Yet, the more I researched, the more amazed I became at the lack of scholarly rigor by most repeal opponents, for example, quotations and statistics employed incorrectly and out of context, numerous logical fallacies, and facts used to barely mask the author's homophobia. The majority of opponents' work I saw in my research proved, at best, shaky.

All of the evidence pointed in the same direction: military readiness would not be harmed by the repeal, or at least it should not be in a professional force. The critics could not have it both ways: either we have the most professional force in the world, one that could handle the repeal as efficiently and effectively as other countries that had gone through the same process, as Nora Bensahel's report in this volume outlines, or we don't have a professional force. I obviously believe the former. After my book chapter was published,[*] I returned to writing, teaching, and speaking mostly on other issues.

Meanwhile, President Barack H. Obama promised the repeal of DADT would happen during his first year in office, and the debate began to heat up in Washington. Then, some Comprehensive Working Group numbers were leaked to the media. This 2010 Department of Defense study was established by Congress to determine the potential impact of DADT's repeal. The leaked poll statistics showed that out of all of the services, the U.S. Marine Corps was the least supportive of the repeal.

On 12 November 2010, I received an e-mail from Rachel Dry of the *Washington Post*, an editor with whom I had worked on another piece for their Outlook section. Greg Jaffe, a mutual friend and reporter for the *Post*, had mentioned to her that I was gay. Would I be willing to write for Outlook on the Marines' opposition to the repeal?

Coming out to my colleagues, friends, and family was one thing. Coming out to millions in the *Washington Post* was another matter entirely. Moreover, my sexual orientation would be a central part of the argument, one of the main reasons that I had never written about DADT in the first place.

The *Post* needed an answer right away. Although I always had complete academic freedom at MCWAR, I felt this was different. I was being asked to write

---

[*] Tammy S. Schultz, "The Sky Won't Fall: Policy Recommendations for Allowing Homosexuals to Serve Openly in the U.S. Military," in *Attitudes Aren't Free: Thinking Deeply about Diversity in the U.S. Armed Forces*, eds. James E. Parco and David A. Levy (Maxwell Air Force Base, AL: Air University Press, 2010), 179–98.

solely because of my byline, and because I was a gay woman. Unlike my procedure with other non-DADT op-ed articles I had written, I asked Colonel Belcher for permission since going ahead would potentially mean unforeseen consequences not only me, but also for MCWAR, the Marine Corps University (MCU), and potentially the Marine Corps. After making sure we were legally in the clear, Belcher put the ball right back in my court. "It's your call," he said.

That night I attended a church service with Carol, my surrogate mom (my second mom, who walked me down the aisle of my commitment ceremony when my parents did not attend), where the message of the sermon was having the courage to testify no matter the personal cost. All of the reasons I could think of for not writing—safety, privacy, professional branding, my MCWAR contract being up for renewal—came from selfish motivations. This was the opposite of the selfless service I so admired in the men and women I taught at MCWAR and had worked with throughout my career. I had to write the piece.

The *Washington Post* article argued that Marines held more resistance to DADT's repeal because of a culture imbued in masculinity, the warrior ethos, and the notion that every Marine is a rifleman (or ready to fight), much like two reports in this book by Major Darrel L. Choat and Major Alasdair B. G. Mackay.[*] Due to mostly false stereotypes of homosexuals not fitting the Marine self-perception of manliness (lesbians are an entirely different matter), some Marines essentially felt that homosexuals do not make good Marines—never mind that many gay men and lesbians were already honorably serving. I ended on a positive note, however, saying that the same Marine culture that seemed to push homosexual service away would also be the same culture that would mandate swiftly following the law after DADT's repeal.

The op-ed ran when my parents, both fundamentalist Christians, happened to be in town for a visit. I received hundreds of e-mails, having decided to print my Georgetown e-mail address so that any service member who wanted to reach me could do so at a non-".mil" address and understanding that this would also open the door for a flood of hate mail, which it did. The op-ed stayed number one on the *Post*

---

[*] Tammy S. Schultz, "Why Are the Marines the Military's Biggest Backers of 'Don't Ask, Don't Tell'?," *Washington Post*, 21 November 2010.

Web site's "most read" list for several days, receiving more than a thousand comments both for and against the repeal, my arguments, and me.

As I fielded media interviews, MCWAR and MCU shielded me from a backlash. At least one MCWAR student asked the dean for me to be disciplined or fired, and other calls came for the same from outside MCWAR to the university's then-president, Major General Robert B. Neller.

Although I suspected such fights occurred behind the scenes, it speaks volumes about the integrity, honor, and courage of Colonel Belcher, MCWAR Dean Robert J. Mahoney, Vice President of Academic Affairs Jerre W. Wilson, Vice President of MCU Darrell A. Browning, and President Neller that—to this day—I have heard only from others about the bullets that these men at the university took for me during this time. As importantly, I do not even know their position on DADT, which very well could be in opposition to (or support of) my own, but that was not the reason for their defense. They supported academic freedom whether they agreed with my position or not—the true test of a university.

Soon after the *Post* piece, several gay service members at MCU and elsewhere began contacting me. Many were not comfortable meeting me in my office, so we met elsewhere. Sometimes, I would be tracked down on the base away from my office. (I'm not hard to spot in a normal crowd, but definitely not at MCU, where I'm one of a handful of female civilian professors.) Each service member thanked me for writing what they could not, some choking up. Seeing some tough Marines—again, against the stereotype—show emotion when they were not used to doing so was humbling to me in a way that I will never forget. Other than these ongoing occasional meetings, however, I figured that had done my part on DADT.

During the 2010–11 school year, several MCU students wrote theses on DADT. Because I was known for the book chapter and for the *Post* commentary, each of the theses' authors had contacted me. One day, Colonel Belcher casually said, "Maybe we have enough solid, publishable papers for a DADT anthology."

I thought his was an interesting idea, but one that would require us to reach outside the university's walls. When I researched my scholarly chapter on DADT, I lamented the lack of a single volume on the services' desegregation that contained the voices, documents, and policy recommendations of that era, as noted in this book's introduction. If I were to put together a DADT anthology, I wanted the collection to be something as valuable to the modern policy maker as to the future historian or dissertation student.

This preface ends as it began—with Colonel Mike Belcher. He introduced me to the anthology's coeditor, J. Ford Huffman, without whom this anthology would be only an idea. When J. Ford and I met in June 2011 to discuss the idea for this book, I knew I had not only met the book's coeditor, but also a friend for life. J. Ford found most of the essay authors, performed the majority of the editing, and enabled us to complete something others thought was impossible.

But back to Colonel Belcher. As with many of my accomplishments at MCWAR, Belcher was front and center. Had it not been for his willingness to push MCWAR students, he would not have pushed this professor and for that I am grateful. J. Ford and I dedicate this anthology to him for his vision of *sapere aude*, the college's motto, "Dare to know."

Acknowledgments

The editors thank the authors of the essays and reports, without whom there would be no anthology. Most of the essayists share deeply personal events, and the courage they demonstrate is a core value of military service. Their bravery is on full display in this volume.

Thanks to the Marine Corps War College's (MCWAR's) dean, Robert J. Mahoney, and director, Colonel Jay L. Hatton, and to Marine Corps University's (MCU's) leadership, who provided Dr. Schultz with time and opportunity to work on this book.

Jennifer Van Horn runs the front office of MCWAR, and her assistance went beyond the call of duty, as always, in helping Dr. Schultz. Amy Cross of Northwestern University provided tenacious research assistance as well as timely editing. Second Lieutenant Adam P. Backsmeier, USMC, also provided support with good humor and skill.

A big thanks also goes to the Marine Corps History Division and Dr. Charles P. Neimeyer and his Marine Corps University Press staff, without whose expertise we could not have made such a professional product.

Dr. Schultz thanks the Servicemembers Legal Defense Network (SLDN), especially Aubrey Sarvis, president of this organization. There has never been a time when she reached out to Sarvis for assistance in which he and his organization did not step forward, and Dr. Schultz appreciates SLDN being on the frontlines of "Don't Ask, Don't Tell" since 1993.

Thanks to Marine Corps University Foundation (MCUF), especially President Thomas V. Draude, brigadier general, USMC (Ret.), and Chief Operating Officer John R. Hales, lieutenant colonel, USMC (Ret.). MCUF's support allows MCU to operate at an entirely different level of academic excellence, and their backing made this book possible.

Mr. Huffman thanks Mike Belcher, who offered an opportunity to work on this timely publication with Dr. Schultz.

Finally, thanks to all, gay and straight, who serve this nation.

Author Acknowledgments

"An Analysis of Opinion: The Impact of 'Don't Ask, Don't Tell,' Its Repeal, and the Proposed Plan to Implement the Repeal" by Major Darrel L. Choat, USMC

My deepest appreciation to Mr. Andre Lafleur, Ms. Erin Gallagher, Mr. James Gallagher, and Mr. Justin Anderson for their willingness to review and provide comments on initial drafts of the survey supporting this thesis as well as drafts of the thesis itself. Particular thanks to Ms. Lori Nathanson, who offered her knowledge and expertise in the discipline of statistics and in the methodology of developing and conducting a survey.

I recognize Dr. Jonathan Phillips, assistant professor, Command and Staff College, MCU, for his guidance, knowledge, expertise, patience, and most importantly, flexibility, as I circuitously found my way to complete this uncharacteristically long document just before the window of opportunity closed.

Most importantly, I thank the following individuals for their progressive professionalism and active recognition of the common humanity that bonds us all. The decision to move forward with this topic and conduct a survey of my peers, and subsequently maintain the resolve necessary to complete the analysis of the results and finalize this document, would not have been possible without their understanding and support:

> Rebecca J. Johnson, PhD, assistant professor of national security affairs, Command and Staff College, MCU; Tammy S. Schultz, PhD, director of security and joint warfare, MCWAR; Paoli G. Tripodi, PhD, head, ethics branch, Lejeune Leadership Institute, MCU; Colonel Michael F. Belcher, USMC (Ret.), director, MCWAR, MCU; and Colonel Mark A. Strong, USA, military faculty advisor, Conference Group 1, Command and Staff College, MCU.

* * *

"It's Time to Redefine the Marine Warrior" by Major Alasdair B. G. Mackay, USMC

I recognize these professionals for their guidance, knowledge, expertise, and patience in assisting me with my research that ultimately made this report possible:

Tammy S. Schultz, PhD, director of national security and joint warfare, MCWAR; Rebecca J. Johnson, PhD, assistance professor of national security affairs, Command and Staff College, MCU; Colonel Michael. F. Belcher USMC (Ret.), director, MCWAR; Colonel Scott A. Walker, USMC; Jay Goodwin, PhD, research psychologist, U.S. Army Research Institute; and Major Jason S. Freeby, USMC.

Introduction

by J. Ford Huffman and Tammy S. Schultz

The inspiration for this book came from some research Tammy Schultz conducted on the desegregation of the military. Finding African American and white voices from that era, as well as policy recommendations, proved a herculean task. Having all of these voices and recommendations in one place, she thought, would be a researcher's dream.

As noted in Dr. Schultz's previous research, "Don't Ask, Don't Tell" (DADT) is not analogous to desegregation of the U.S. military.[*] That said, for those researching the issues, policy makers desiring specific recommendations, or those simply wanting to learn more about the topic, the process of understanding is much the same. In some ways, getting voices on the record for DADT proved even more difficult because until 20 September 2011, one could not be openly gay or lesbian and serve in the U.S. armed forces. Nor could one tell by just looking at a soldier, sailor, airman, or Marine if he or she were gay—self-identification, something that goes against a culture that values the team above the individual, is necessary.

This book includes two parts in order to achieve its vision. The first part contains reports that shed light on the way forward for the services and policy makers. The second gives voice to those who have served under DADT, both gay and straight, and highlights their personal experience under this policy.

The reports begin with a piece by Dr. Nora Bensahel, deputy director of studies and a senior fellow at the Center for a New American Security. Dr. Bensahel, the one author included who is not in the armed forces, was asked to write because of her extensive research in this area with RAND Corporation, which she shares in her chapter. The United States is not the first country to allow homosexuals to openly serve—26 do, according to the Servicemembers Legal Defense Network. Through her analysis of foreign countries that allow homosexuals to openly serve, Dr.

---

[*] See "The Sky Won't Fall: Policy Recommendations for Allowing Homosexuals to Serve Openly in the U.S. Military" in *Attitudes Aren't Free: Thinking Deeply about Diversity in the U.S. Armed Forces* (Maxwell Air Force Base, AL: Air University Press, 2010), 192.

The End of Don't Ask, Don't Tell

Bensahel concludes that while there are some lessons to be learned, the policy change proved to be a nonevent overall. Indeed, her work shows that because the law changed via the legislature versus the courts and that the U.S. military's positive opinion of a policy reversal is far higher than it was in other countries before they removed their bans, the change could be much smoother in the United States.

The reports then dive into U.S. policy with a piece by Colonel Thomas Dolan, USMC, and Commander Randall J. Biggs, USN. Taking a slightly different perspective than Dr. Bensahel, the authors suggest that DADT's repeal left much work to do, specifically because the Defense of Marriage Act (DOMA) is still on the books, which will impact commanders' abilities to provide a truly ready force. In short, commanders provide a ready force for the nation, and that includes family readiness. Dolan and Biggs address the fact that DOMA does not allow many federal rights to be extended to same sex couples, which will make these families less ready to support their military member both stateside and deployed. Ultimately, Dolan and Biggs look toward the Civil Rights movement for answers, where some troops realized desegregation was not enough—the military should advocate for a change in federal law similar to the one that allowed African Americans and their families to be treated the same as their white counterparts.

The final two reports by two USMC majors, Darrel L. Choat and Alasdair B. G. Mackay, examine the views and culture of the armed forces and USMC toward DADT, with recommendations for the way ahead. Choat's piece uses extensive survey data he gathered while a student at Command and Staff College in Quantico, Virginia. Although not a scientific survey, his data remarkably mirrors that gathered by the Pentagon's *Report of the Comprehensive Review of the Issues Associated with a Repeal of "Don't Ask, Don't Tell,"* issued in November 2010, that surveyed over 600,000 individuals.[*] Choat's data shows a bias in the Marine Corps against homosexual service, which he attributes to Marine Corps culture. He believes that this bias can be overcome when stereotypes are replaced with actual experience with homosexual service members, a realization that DADT compromises Corps

---

[*] U.S. Department of Defense, *Report of the Comprehensive Review of the Issues Associated with a Repeal of "Don't Ask, Don't Tell": Support Plan for Implementation* (Arlington, VA: Department of Defense, 2010).

values such as integrity, and a Marine Corps leadership that embraces all service regardless of sexual preference.

Mackay identifies a Marine Warrior Paradigm (MWP) that, at its core, includes such traits as being in the combat arms, masculine, white, and heterosexual. Drawing upon Marine Corps doctrine, demographics, history, and other sources, Mackay first shows how this MWP permeates the Corps. He then analyzes the implications that the MWP will have on DADT's repeal, specifically for the Marine Corps. Given the perception of homosexual males as not being masculine, false though this stereotype may be, Mackay argues that homosexuals falling outside the core MWP will mean that gay service members will have a harder time integrating into and being respected by the Corps. Like Choat, Mackay argues that leadership could help overcome this cultural disposition by widening what the core MWP includes. Using Marine General Alfred M. Gray Jr.'s move toward maneuver warfare as a case study, Mackay shows how what it means to be a Marine can be expanded and altered, demonstrating that a shift is once again possible to include both women (who are also outside the MWP) and gays into the core warrior paradigm.

These reports achieve one part of the editors' vision for this book: to include policy recommendations and ways of looking at this change that will help smooth the repeal's implementation for the force. Frankly, we see this as having practical implications in the present day, but also as having historical import in the future when scholars wonder what the major impediments to change were, and what were some of the proffered solutions. Furthermore, as Dr. Schultz advises students at the Marine Corps War College, it is not enough to simply write into a vacuum solely for a professor or two in order to get a grade. The officers in this book have decades of experience, their ideas have merit, and they deserve a wider audience. Many ideas that have changed the world began in universities, and we believe strongly that only by starting a debate, or engaging in one, does change become possible.

The book's second half provides service members with the opportunity to speak for themselves. These personal essays peel back the curtain of the shame, uncertainty, homophobia, anger, fear, and other emotions of living under DADT. These are the views, recollections, and words of the authors alone. Unlike normal scholarly works or op-eds, the normal "fact checking" on these pieces many times proved impossible. When pushed on certain parts of essays, authors added details (e.g., the issue had already been investigated) or assurances that they were willing to testify under oath regarding their experiences. As the reader will note from reading the essays, many of the events herein clearly have become part of the public record.

The quality of the reports and essays compiled exceeded the editors' expectations, and will benefit policy makers, historians, researchers, or simply someone who wants to know more about DADT and its repeal.

Part One
The Reports

After Repeal: Lessons from Foreign Militaries
by Nora Bensahel

This chapter analyzes the experiences of five foreign militaries after they repealed poli-cies that had excluded gay men and lesbians from service. In these countries, predic-tions about implementing new policies proved incorrect; military benefits were not provided immediately; coming out was personal, not public; complaints involving sex-ual orientation are very rare; defense ministries strive to be seen as diversity employ-ers of choice; chaplains work effectively with gay and lesbian personnel; and integrating women has been a harder challenge. Although no other country is exactly like the United States, there are several reasons to expect that the repeal of "Don't Ask, Don't Tell" will proceed just as smoothly as it did in these countries.

On 20 September 2011, the "Don't Ask, Don't Tell" (DADT) policy was repealed and gay men and lesbians will be allowed to serve openly in the military for the first time. But what happens next?

Effectively implementing any important policy change involves a process that unfolds and adjusts over time, as issues arise—or anticipated issues fail to arise. The Department of Defense has already acknowledged this by calling for "follow-on review and ongoing monitoring of implementation of repeal, in order to make adjustments to implementation" as necessary.[1]

What implementation issues will the U.S. military face after repeal? Although precise predictions always pose challenges, we can learn a lot from the experiences of other countries. Several U.S. allies that once barred gay men and lesbians from serving in the military have allowed them to serve openly for years and even decades. Their experiences with implementation were remarkably similar despite their national differences, and as argued below, are likely to be similar in the United States as well.

This report draws heavily on research conducted by the author for a report pub-lished by the RAND Corporation about five countries that experienced a clear pol-icy change: Australia (1992), Canada (1992), Germany (2000), the Netherlands

(1974), and the United Kingdom (2000).[2] It identifies seven common findings from these cases, and concludes by arguing that the United States is likely to be even more prepared to effectively manage the implementation process than these five countries were.

Predictions about Implementation Proved Incorrect

Anecdotal evidence suggests that military personnel in all five countries predicted that allowing gay people to serve openly would harm military effectiveness, re-cruiting, and retention, among other areas. Yet none of these consequences actu-ally occurred. For example, one scholar found that the Australian policy change did not lead to mass resignations from the Australian Defense Force (ADF) or an increase in gay bashing as had been predicted.[3] Survey data from Canada and the United Kingdom (UK) reinforce this point.

In 1986, a task force created by the Canadian chief of Defense Staff surveyed members of the Canadian Forces (CF) for their views on allowing gay troops to serve. The survey revealed extensive opposition, with 87 percent agreeing that ho-mosexuals should not be enrolled in the CF. Eighty percent of men and 47 percent of women who identified themselves as heterosexual said that allowing gay people to serve would reduce military effectiveness, while fewer than two percent overall said that military effectiveness would improve. Twenty-seven percent of male and 16 percent of female recruits and officer candidates said that they would not have joined the CF if there had been a policy in place allowing homosexuals to serve, and only one percent of all service members who identified themselves as heterosexual said that they would be more likely to recommend joining the CF if such a policy existed.[4] Based on these results, the task force concluded that there would be "se-vere problems integrating known homosexuals into the CF," that allowing gay men and lesbians to serve would have an "overall negative impact on recruiting" and would "cause some service members to leave the CF," and that the anticipated problems with cohesion and morale would "constitute a serious threat to military effectiveness."[5]

None of these predictions came true. The CF changed its policy in October 1992 after choosing to settle a lawsuit challenging the policy rather than trying to continue defending it in court. A 1993 report by the U.S. General Accounting

Office (GAO) found that the CF did not experience any problems in the first six months after the policy changed.[6] According to the GAO, Canadian officials said that "mass resignations, lower recruitment, morale and cohesiveness problems, gay-bashing incidents, and more open displays of homosexual behavior—the major problems that had been predicted—have not materialized."[7] Nor have any of these issues arisen since, even as the Canadian military moved beyond the focus on peacekeeping that characterized the 1990s. The Canadian military has conducted intensive combat operations in Afghanistan during the past several years, where it suffers from one of the highest casualty rates of any troop contributor. Today, the only significant debate about sexual orientation focuses on whether it is fair that the military pays for gender reassignment surgery but does not pay for Lasik vision correction surgery.

The British survey data demonstrates this point even more clearly. In 1996, the Ministry of Defence (MOD) created the Homosexuality Policy Assessment Team (HPAT) that, among other things, surveyed serving military personnel about whether gay people should be allowed to serve. The results were overwhelmingly negative. Eighty-two percent of the men and 63 percent of the women surveyed agreed or strongly agreed that "[t]he MOD's policy on homosexuality should re-main unchanged," with only small minorities disagreeing.[8] Seventy-three percent of men and 46 percent of women agreed or strongly agreed that "[h]omosexuals should be excluded from the military because their presence would damage com-bat effectiveness," and 68 percent of men and 50 percent of women agreed or strongly agreed that "permitting homosexuals to serve in the military would dam-age recruiting."[9] Largely on the basis of this survey, the final HPAT report con-cluded that it was "evident that in the UK homosexuality remains in practice incompatible with service life if the armed services, in their present form, are to be maintained at their full potential fighting power."[10]

Meanwhile, two lawsuits challenging the government's policy were working their way through the legal system. After the British High Court and Appeals Court found in favor of the government, the plaintiffs filed suit with the European Court of Human Rights (ECHR), which enforces the 1950 Convention on the Protection of Human Rights and Fundamental Freedoms. On 27 September 1999, the ECHR ruled in favor of the plaintiffs, finding that their rights had been violated under Articles 8 and 13 of the Convention.[11] The MOD spent several weeks preparing for the policy change, and officially allowed gay people to serve in the military in January 2000. Several people who worked in the MOD at the time later said "the world did not end" when the policy changed, as many had feared, and one said that the policy change was "like flipping a light switch."

Six months later, the British MOD reviewed the policy change to see if any problems had arisen. A summary of the review stated that there was "widespread acceptance of the new policy" and a "marked lack of reaction." It found "no reported difficulties of note concerning homophobic behavior amongst service personnel" and stated that the new policy "had no discernible impact, either positive or negative, on recruitment."[12] Two years later, the MOD commissioned a thorough review of the policy. The report of the review, released in December 2002, found that commanders from all three services "generally concur that there has been no tangible impact on operational effectiveness, team cohesion, or service life."[13] Despite continuing reluctance from some officers, including warrant officers and senior noncommissioned officers, all of the services reported that there had been no significant problems in implementing the new policy.[14] Perhaps most remarkably, the report concluded that "[n]o further formal review of the armed forces policy on homosexuality is currently judged to be necessary."[15]

Military Benefits Were Not Provided Immediately

None of the five militaries examined in this report provided benefits for same-sex partners when they changed their policies because none of these countries recognized civil partnerships or allowed gay marriage at the time. Instead, they generally modified their policies as national laws changed.

In the Netherlands, gay people were allowed to serve openly in 1974 but civil partnerships were not legalized until 1998 and gay marriage became legal in 2001. In Canada, military benefits were provided in 1996, four years after the policy change, when a federal tribunal ruled that same-sex partners of all federal employees—including military personnel—had to receive the same benefits as heterosexual common-law couples. In Germany and the UK, military benefits were provided one year later (2001) and four years later (2004), respectively, when laws provided civil partners of any gender with the same rights as married couples.

Australia is the only country that did not follow this path. The Australian Department of Defence, which had allowed people to serve openly since 1992, chose to provide equal benefits to same-sex partners of military personnel before civilians had legal rights to benefits at the national level. Civilians gained these rights three years later, in 2008, when the benefits of heterosexual "de facto" relationships (which had long been recognized as similar to a common-law marriage) were extended to same-sex "de facto" relationships. This means that gay couples today receive essentially the same rights and benefits as married couples, even though gay marriage remains illegal.

Coming Out Was Personal, Not Public

In all five countries, there were fears that the policy change would lead gay service members to come out immediately and behave flamboyantly. Neither fear proved true. According to one German observer, there was no "earthquake" of people coming out; instead, it involved a gradual process that unfolded over time, depending on individual preferences. In these countries, many gay service members chose not to reveal their sexual orientation for weeks, months, and even years after the policy change, and some still choose to keep it private. Furthermore, coming out is not a one-time event for these personnel; each time they take a new assignment, they must decide whether to reveal their sexual orientation. Sometimes this decision is even more complicated. For example, one member of the Dutch military who taught month-long training classes said that she faced this decision every time a new class arrived.

Those who choose not to reveal their sexual orientation immediately often wait until they have proved that they are good at their jobs and they have earned the respect of their peers, so that they will be seen first and foremost as good soldiers rather than gay soldiers. Those who do come out often choose to simply stop hiding their private lives—by putting up pictures of their loved ones or mentioning their names during conversations—rather than actively announcing their sexual orientation to members of their units. Some reveal their sexual orientation only by filing for partner benefits, in which case only those who process the paperwork will know. And some choose not to come out at all because they believe that their sexual orientation is irrelevant to their job performance and prefer to keep their professional and private lives separate.

Complaints Involving Sexual Orientation Are Rare

All five militaries have a formal complaints procedure that can be used to report numerous types of problems, including harassment and discrimination, but very few complaints involve sexual orientation. In the Netherlands, for example, no soldier has been discharged from the military for discriminating against gay personnel for at least 15 years. In the UK, a 2009 survey of military personnel showed that 12 percent said they been discriminated against during the previous 12 months, but that only one percent of those said that this discrimination was based on sexual orientation. Similarly, six percent reported having been harassed during the previous 12 months, but only one percent of those said this harassment was based on sexual orientation.[16]

Data from the formal complaints processes in Canada and Germany support this point. The complaints tracking system used by the Canadian forces includes no formal complaints related to sexual orientation since the tracking system was established in 2000. Between 2000 and the summer of 2009—the most recent period for which data was available—there were no courts-martial for either sexual misconduct involving gay or lesbian personnel, or for inappropriate behavior toward gay personnel.[17] In Germany, military personnel have the right to directly file any type of question or complaint with the Parliamentary Commission on the Armed Forces (commonly abbreviated as PC), which is entirely independent from the military.[18] The PC has received approximately 60,000 complaints since 2000, when the policy change allowed gay people to serve openly, but only 50 involved sexual orientation. Of those, the PC reports that only 22 cases involved discrimination or bullying, and only a small number of those involved physical abuse or another form of severe harassment.[19]

Informal complaints can always be discussed through the chain of command, and many countries train designated members of individual units to advise others on how to handle their complaints and also to serve as a resource for commanders. In Canada, trained harassment advisors, who provide information and can advise commanders who are addressing informal complaints, serve in every unit. In the UK, all units include an equality and diversity advisor, who helps advise commanders on how to resolve informal complaints and can also advise unit personnel on whether to file complaints formally, informally, or submit them to independent mediation. In Germany, every unit includes an equal rights representative who serves in the same way.

Because informal complaints are by definition not formally tracked, there is no way to determine how effectively they are addressed. But wide spectrums of personnel in all five countries reported that they generally trusted the complaints processes. Some of the gay personnel interviewed said that some harassment persists at the unit level and that commanders do not always do enough to prevent this behavior, but none reported any serious cases that were not addressed either through the formal or informal complaints processes. This suggests, along with the extreme rarity of formal complaints, that complaints related to sexual orientation are generally addressed effectively at the unit level. While individual experiences may vary depending on the unit commander and the specific dynamics of each unit, existing procedures seem capable of handling most of the issues that arise and prevent issues related to sexual orientation from becoming a systematic policy problem.

Defense Ministries Strive to Be Seen as Diversity Employers of Choice

None of these countries treats sexual orientation as a protected category that should be tracked, as is often the case with gender, race, ethnic background, and so on. The militaries therefore do not know how many personnel identify as gay, and there are no recruiting or retention targets for gay personnel. However, the defense ministries in these countries reach out proactively to gay people in the same way that they reach out to other people, in order to demonstrate that they are a diversity employer of choice. They want to promote the message that citizens from all backgrounds are welcome in the military, so they attract as much talent as possible and truly reflect the societies they represent.

In recent years, some defense ministries have chosen to reach out to gay men and lesbians by allowing uniformed military personnel to participate in gay pride parades—a visible signal of support. Many defense ministries resisted this for years and even decades, even as they undertook other outreach initiatives, because they feared that participating personnel would behave in ways that undermined respect for the uniform. The UK was the first country to change this policy, when the Royal Navy allowed its personnel to march in uniform in the London Gay Pride parade in 2007. No incidents occurred, and in 2008 the other services allowed their personnel to march in uniform as well. Canada has been sponsoring recruiting booths at gay pride parades for several years before deciding in 2008 to allow its personnel to march in uniform. In 2009, the Dutch military allowed uniformed personnel to participate in Amsterdam's Canal Parade (where participants float on boats through the city's canals rather than march), and in 2011, the Ministry of Defense sponsored its own boat for the first time.[20]

Some defense ministries also participate in broader initiatives designed to promote lesbian, gay, bisexual, and transgender (LGBT) personnel in the workplace. The Australian Department of Defence is a founding member of Pride in Diversity, which helps employers include LGBT personnel and address their concerns.[21] In the Netherlands, the Ministry of Defense and the Foundation for Homosexuals in the Armed Forces (known by the Dutch acronym SHK) joined Company Pride Platform, a membership organization for LGBT employee networks and others that promotes visibility and acceptance at work and throughout society.[22] In the UK, the MOD and the three individual services work closely with Stonewall, which lobbies for equality and works with British employers on LGBT issues.[23] The MOD and the services belong to Stonewall's Diversity Champions Program, which provides a number of benefits including seminars, networking opportunities, and listings in its annual recruiting guide. Stonewall also publishes an annual Workplace Equity Index, which lists the top 100 employers for LGBT personnel. In 2010, the MOD and each of the services were ranked either in or very close to the top half of the 352 companies that applied to be included in the index. In 2011, the Royal Air Force was ranked at number 97.[24]

Chaplains Work Effectively with Gay Personnel

Before gay service members were allowed to serve openly, there were some concerns that chaplains would be required to act in ways that would conflict with their denominational beliefs. In all five countries today, chaplains work effectively with both homosexual and heterosexual military personnel.

In Canada, for example, chaplains were concerned that allowing gay people to serve openly would require them to bless same-sex civil unions, and after such marriage became legal in 2005, to perform those marriages also. But Canadian chaplains, like those in the other four countries and the United States, are required to comply with all denominational teachings. This means that they cannot be required to perform same-sex civil unions or marriages if their denomination does not allow it, and they may individually refuse to do so even if their denomination does allow it. In any case in which a chaplain cannot meet someone's needs, he or she is required to provide a referral to someone who can. This ensures that the chaplains' denominational beliefs are respected while they still care for the spiritual needs of all military personnel.

Anecdotal evidence suggests that very few chaplains resigned their positions when gay troops were first allowed to serve in the military. Government and military officials in four countries could not recall any such resignations, while one British official reported that one chaplain resigned because of the new policy. Chaplains in some of these countries were screened for their ability to work in diverse environments even before the policy change, since they must work with personnel from a wide variety of denominations (including agnostics and atheists). Today, the chaplain screening process in Australia includes an explicit question about how a prospective chaplain would handle a soldier who is gay. In the Netherlands, all chaplains must sign a statement at the end of the training process that says that they accept diversity, including sexual orientation, within the force.

Integrating Women Has Been a Harder Challenge

Government and military officials in some countries believe that integrating women into the military has been much more difficult than integrating gay service members. In Canada, for example, women were first allowed into the Canadian forces in 1988, three years before gay people were. Complaints arose each time women were allowed to serve in new specializations, along with concerns about fairness and facilities. Today, harassment complaints between men and women occur regularly, while as argued above, same-sex harassment remains extremely rare. Officials in the UK made the same observation. They also noted that in exit surveys, women identify sexual harassment as one of the main reasons they choose to leave the military, while few if any exit surveys mention any issue related to sexual orientation. Officials in Canada and Germany speculated that integrating women into the force may have unintentionally made it easier to integrate gay service members, since they posed very few problems by comparison. Some of this may be due to the fact that gay men and lesbians can choose to keep their sexual orientation private, while women cannot hide their gender in the same way.

Drawing Lessons for the United States

No other country is exactly like the United States. In 2010, the United States spent 692.8 billion dollars on its military—263.6 billion more than the next nine countries combined. Different countries have different attitudes about the role of gay people in society that may affect the implementation process. While the experiences of other countries do not automatically apply directly to the United States, there are at least three reasons to expect that implementing DADT repeal will be at least as straightforward, if not even more so, than it was in Australia, Canada, Germany, the Netherlands, and the UK.

First, foreign militaries may not operate in the same cultural context as the U.S. military, but U.S. police and fire departments do. These departments share many common features with the military, including relying on hierarchies, task cohesion and readiness, and volunteer forces, and they are also predominantly male. Some U.S. federal agencies also deploy civilian personnel abroad, sometimes to serve alongside military forces in combat zones. In 2010, RAND studied several federal agencies and police and fire departments in six cities across the United States— Charlotte, Chicago, Houston, Oklahoma City, Orange County (California), Philadelphia, and San Diego—to understand their experiences integrating gay men and lesbians. The study found that their experiences were very similar to the experiences of foreign militaries identified above: the presence of gay personnel did not undermine performance and may have enhanced it in some ways, gender and race posed greater problems than sexual orientation, and many personnel chose to keep their sexual orientation private.[25] Based largely on this research, the Department of Defense's report on implementing DADT repeal concluded that

> as with racial and gender integration of the military, the process of integrating gay men and lesbians into these municipal and Federal organiza-

tions ultimately laid many fears to rest. The experience of municipal law enforcement agencies and Federal agencies has been that the integration of gay and lesbian personnel has not negatively affected institutional or individual job performance.[26]

Second, the United States is changing this policy through the legislative branch of government, not the judicial or executive branches. Canada and the UK were required to change their policies after losing court cases. In Australia, the prime minister and his cabinet decided to change the policy. The German decision did include a legislative dimension but it involved European legislation instead of German legislation. The German minister of defense chose to change the policy while a court case was still pending, in anticipation of a new European Union (EU) directive prohibiting employment discrimination on the basis of sexual orientation. By contrast, Congress voted last year to change the law through the normal democratic process, the same way that it changes laws on education, the environment, health care, and so on. Individuals may strongly disagree with that change but few question the legitimacy of the process itself. That makes it much more likely that U.S. military personnel and the American people more broadly will support the policy change than if it had been forced through a court decision or imposed unilaterally by the president.

Finally, U.S. military personnel are far more ready to accept gay service members than their foreign counterparts were. Last year, DOD surveyed the force and found that 69 percent of respondents believe that they have served with someone who was homosexual during their career, and 36 percent believed that they were currently serving with someone who was homosexual.[27] Eighty percent said that repeal would have a positive, mixed, or no effect on unit effectiveness on a day-to-day basis, and 70 percent said that repeal would have a positive, mixed, or no effect on their unit in intense combat or crisis situations.[28] Only 23 percent said that their willingness to recommend military service to a close friend or family member would be negatively affected by repeal, and only 13 percent believed that they would leave the service earlier than planned.[29]

Views among ground combat personnel were consistently less positive. Forty-seven point five percent of the Army combat personnel and 57.5 percent of the

Marine combat personnel surveyed believed that working with a service member who has said that he or she is gay or lesbian would negatively or very negatively affect how unit members work together to get the job done, and 35.1 percent of the Army combat personnel and 43.5 percent of the Marine combat personnel surveyed said that the readiness of their immediate unit would be negatively or very negatively affected by working with a service member who has said that he or she is gay or lesbian.[30] Yet these percentages are much lower among those who believe that they are already serving with someone who is homosexual. According to DOD,

while a higher percentage of service members in warfighting units predict negative effects of repeal, the percentage distinctions between warfighting units and the entire military are almost nonexistent when asked about the actual experience of serving in a unit with someone believed to be gay. For example, when those in the overall military were asked about the experience of working with someone they believed to be gay or lesbian, 92 percent stated that their unit's "ability to work together" was "very good," "good," or "neither good nor poor." Meanwhile, in response to the same question, the percentage is 89 percent for those in Army combat arms units and 84 percent for those in Marine combat arms units—all very high percentages. Anecdotally, we heard much the same. As one special operations warfighter told us, "We have a gay guy [in the unit]. He's big, he's mean, and he kills lots of bad guys. No one cared that he was gay."[31]

Since this survey was taken, all U.S. military personnel have received specific training on the policy changes resulting from the repeal of DADT, which may have addressed some of their concerns. Some U.S. military personnel undoubtedly still oppose repeal, however, and some may oppose it quite strongly. Yet as discussed above, military personnel in Canada and the UK opposed allowing gay people to serve in the military by far larger majorities. If repeal proceeded smoothly there despite much stronger opposition, there is no reason to expect that it will proceed any less smoothly in the United States.

In the five countries examined in this report, most junior military personnel have never known a time when gay people were not allowed to serve—and in Australia, Canada, and the Netherlands, gay people have been allowed to serve since before the youngest military personnel were even born. Most simply accept this, and the few who think about this issue at all wonder why so many people opposed letting men and women serve together. Someday soon, U.S. soldiers, sailors, airmen, and Marines will wonder the same thing.

Notes

1 U.S. Department of Defense, *Report of the Comprehensive Review of the Issues Associated with a Repeal of "Don't Ask, Don't Tell": Support Plan for Implementation.* (Arlington, VA: Department of Defense, 2010), 3. This document identifies three different stages of the implementation process: prerepeal, implementation, and sustainment. This quotation describes efforts that should be taken during the sustainment stage.

2 See "The Experience of Foreign Militaries," in National Defense Research Institute, *Sexual Orientation and U.S. Military Personnel Policy* (Santa Monica, CA: RAND, 2010), 275–320. The RAND report also studied Israel and Italy, but those countries did not experience a clear policy change and so are less useful here. All information not otherwise cited comes from this report.

3 Hugh Smith, "The Dynamics of Social Change and the Australian Defence Force," *Armed Forces & Society* 21 (1995): 546.

4 Major R. A. Zuliani, "Canadian Forces Survey on Homosexual Issues," in 2 Charter Task Force, *Final Report* (Ottawa: Canadian Department of National Defence, 1986), 26–28, 36, 40. This document reports selected findings from the survey but does not include the original data.

5 Ibid., 36, 43, 45.

6 U.S. General Accounting Office, *Homosexuals in the Military: Policies and Practices of Foreign Militaries*, GAO/NSIAS-93-215 (Washington, DC: General Accounting Office, 1993), 27.

7 Ibid., 31–32.

8 United Kingdom Ministry of Defence, *Report of the Homosexuality Policy Assessment Team* (London: Ministry of Defence, 1996), G-28, Q73G2-8.

9 Ibid., Q 83–84.

10 Ibid., 233.

11 Richard Kamm, "European Court of Human Rights Overturns British Ban on Gays in the Military," *Human Rights Brief 7* (2000); Raymond Psonak, "'Don't Ask, Don't Tell, Don't Discharge,' At Least in Europe: A Comparison of the Policies of Homosexuals in the Military in the United States and Europe after Grady v. United Kingdom," *Connecticut Law Review* 33 (2000). The ECHR decisions for both cases include identical sections that state, "to the extent that they represent a predisposed bias on the part of a heterosexual majority against a homosexual minority, these negative attitudes cannot, of themselves, be considered by the Court to amount to a sufficient justification for the interferences with the applicants' rights outlined above any more than similar negative attitudes towards those of a different race, origin, or colour." See Council of Europe, *Case of Lustig-Prean and Beckett v the United Kingdom*, Strasbourg, 1999, Section 90; Council of Europe, *Case of Smith and Grady v the United Kingdom*, Strasbourg, 1999, Section 97. *Lustig and Beckett v the United Kingdom* available at http://www.macalester.edu/courses/intl245/docs/lustig-prean.pdf.

12 Mark Newton, "Review of Armed Forces Policy on Homosexuals," United Kingdom Ministry of Defence, 31 October 2000.

13 United Kingdom Ministry of Defence, *Tri-Service Review of the Armed Forces Policy on Homosexuality and Code of Social Conduct*, SPB 12-02, Ministry of Defence Service Personnel Board (London: Ministry of Defence, 2002), 12.

14 Ibid., 14.

15 Ibid., 9–10, 12.

16 Deputy Chief of Defence Staff Personnel, *Armed Forces Continuous Attitudes Surveys* (London: Ministry of Defence, 2009), 218, www.parliament.uk/deposits/depositedpapers/2011/DEP2011-0260.pdf.

17 Nathanial Frank, *Gays in Foreign Militaries: A Global Primer* (Santa Barbara, CA: The Palm Center, 2010), 60, http://www.palmcenter.org.

18 The PC was founded in 1965 to protect the constitutional rights of all members of the German military and to prevent any recurrence of the abuses that occurred during the Nazi period. The parliamentary commissioner is elected every five years by the Bundestag, the lower house of Parliament. It has always elected someone who is currently serving as a member of the Bundestag, who then immediately resigns his or her seat to take the position.

19 Nine additional cases involved service members stating that they had been disadvantaged based on their sexual orientation but were not confirmed after the subsequent investigation. Of the remaining 19 cases, seven involved issues with receiving partner benefits; five asked for additional resources or support; four complained that they were suspected of being gay or lesbian but were not; and three involved issues related to security clearances.

20 Arthur Max, "Dutch Military Joins Gay Pride Parade for 1st Time." Associated Press, 6 August 2011, http://www.huffingtonpost.com/huff-wires/20110806/eu-netherlands-gays-in-the-military/.

21 For more information, see http://www.prideindiversity.com.au/.

22 For more information, see http://www.companyprideplatform.org/home.

23 For more information, see http://www.stonewall.org.uk/.

24 Stonewall, *Stonewall Top 100 Employers 2011: The Workplace Equality Index* (London: Stonewall, 2011), 7.

25 See "The Experience of Domestic Agencies: Police, Fire, and Federal Agencies," in National Defense Research Institute, *Sexual Orientation*, 321–49.

26 U.S. Department of Defense, *Report of the Comprehensive Review of the Issues Associated with a Repeal of "Don't Ask, Don't Tell."* (Arlington, VA: Department of Defense, 2010), 96.

27 Ibid., 71.

28 Ibid., 65–66.

29 Ibid., 69.

30 Forty-seven point five percent of the Army combat personnel and 57.5 of the Marine combat personnel surveyed believed that working with a service member who has said that he or she is gay or lesbian would negatively or very negatively affect how unit members work together to get the job done. However, this does not necessarily mean that these personnel believe the unit *cannot* get the job done.

31 DOD, *Report of the Comprehensive Review*, 6.

The Case for Military Family Readiness: Support for the Committed Same-Sex Partners and Families of Gay Service Members

by LtCol Thomas Dolan, USMC, and Cdr Randall J. Biggs, USN

The repeal of "Don't Ask, Don't Tell" (DADT) was only a half-measure in ending dis-crimination based on sexual orientation. The federal law known as the Defense of Marriage Act restricts the U.S. military from providing the committed same-sex part-ners of homosexual service members equal access to pay, benefits, and support serv-ices enjoyed by heterosexual service members and their spouses.

Yet, the president as commander in chief has identified military family readiness as a strategic interest, and benefits and support services are important elements of the support provided to military families. Thus, the U.S. military has been placed in an awkward position of implementing a change in policy that allows homosexuals to serve openly while denying their families fair and equal treatment.

In addressing this inconsistency, this report examines the role of the U.S. military in the racial integration of the armed forces and in ensuring equal treatment for its services' members and their families in both the military and civil society. With DADT's repeal, military and political leadership are not only responsible for the health and welfare of all service members but must identify and address barriers to the fair and equal treatment of all service members and their families regardless of sexual ori-entation.

During his 27 January 2010 State of the Union address, President Barack H. Obama pledged that he would work with Congress and the military to "repeal the law that denies gay Americans the right to serve the country they love because of who they are."[1] Referring to the policy concerning homosexuality in the armed forces,[2] also known as "Don't Ask, Don't Tell" (DADT), the president sought a re-peal of the federal law that bans homosexuals from disclosing their sexual orien-tation in order to serve in the armed forces. Following nearly a year of discussion, inquiry, and review, the Department of Defense released *The Report of the*

The End of Don't Ask, Don't Tell

Comprehensive Review of the Issues Associated with a Repeal of "Don't Ask, Don't Tell" on 1 December 2010, that advised that the "risk of repeal . . . to overall military effectiveness [was] low."[3] Reinforced by this assessment, Congress voted in favor of repeal and on 22 December 2010, and the president fulfilled his pledge by signing the DADT Repeal Act of 2010.[4]

In a press conference held the same day, ABC News correspondent Jake Tapper asked the president whether it was "intellectually consistent to say that gays and lesbians should be able to fight and die for this country but they should not be able to marry the people they love?"[5] The question addresses the inconsistency between hailing the repeal of DADT as ending discrimination based on sexual orientation while ignoring the Defense of Marriage Act (DOMA),[6] which prevents the U.S. military from providing homosexual service members and their committed same-sex partners the same rights and benefits enjoyed by married heterosexual service members. The president's answer—that he believed in "a strong civil union that provides them the protections and the legal rights that married couples have"— was in support of extending benefits to committed same-sex couples, his caveat that "this is going to be an issue that is not unique to the military—this is an issue that extends to all of our society, and I think we're all going to have to have a conversation about it" highlighted the limits of the DADT Repeal Act and the lack of a plan to address equal treatment and opportunity for gay service members and their families.[7] This inconsistency amounts to an important military family readiness concern with potential impact on military readiness.

Conceived prior to DADT's repeal, this report's intent was not to argue for or against the DADT policy but to address an element missing in the debate about the impact of a change to that policy. The focus of the debate, and the review commissioned to examine the potential impact on the military, limited its assessment to the risk posed to military effectiveness. No attention was paid to the impact DOMA would have on the military effectiveness of a postrepeal force that includes openly serving gay men and lesbians. With the repeal of DADT, the military is responsible for not only enacting a change in policy, but supporting the military readiness of its homosexual service members, of which family readiness plays an important role. Thus the U.S. military finds itself in the awkward position of removing the barriers to military service based on sexual orientation while denying the ability to support homosexual service members and their families in the same manner as heterosexuals. In looking for a possible approach to reconcile the illogic between allowing gay people to serve while denying support for their families, this report also examines the role of the U.S. military in racial integration of the armed forces and in ensuring equal treatment and opportunity for its service members in military and civil society.

DOMA's Background and the Half-Measure It Creates

Though hailed as an accomplishment by the administration, repeal of DADT was only a half-measure in ending what the president termed a "[violation of] fundamental American principles of fairness and equality," that is, discrimination based on sexual orientation.[8] Another barrier is DOMA, which produces the same discrimination that the president decried. Signed into law in 1996 by President William J. Clinton, DOMA was a reaction to debates about the rights of gay citizens and concerns over proposed state legislation to legalize same-sex marriage.[9] DOMA is codified in two locations in the federal code. Section 2 of DOMA identifies the state as holding jurisdiction in decisions involving marriage law, to include that no state shall be required to recognize a same-sex marriage of another state.[10] Section 3 of DOMA provides a federal definition of the word *marriage* as "only a legal union between one man and one woman" and the word *spouse* as "only [referring] to a person of the opposite sex."[11] While DADT's repeal allows gay troops to serve openly, the definition of "marriage" and "spouse" that DOMA establishes prohibits the U.S. military from recognizing their committed same-gender partners, regardless of marriage, civil union, or domestic partnership status.

DOMA's impact on gay service members and their families is more apparent in view of the president's military family readiness initiative. Released on 24 January 2011, the result of Presidential Study Directive 9 (entitled *Strengthening Our Military Families: Meeting America's Commitment*) outlines the president's initiative to "better coordinate and strengthen the Federal government's support for military families."[12] Family readiness, defined by the president as "a matter of national security [since] . . . the readiness of our armed forces depends on the readiness of our military families," is dependent upon federally regulated marriage-based benefits currently available only to heterosexual couples, due to prohibitions of

DOMA.[13] DOMA has been referred to as a "major roadblock for a military policy that attempt[s] to recognize same-sex marriage for the purpose of partner benefits," but worse, as a major barrier to supporting the family readiness of gay service members,[14] a barrier that will affect the military effectiveness of the unit in which they serve.

In describing military family readiness in terms of national security, the president has identified it as a strategic concern. *The National Military Strategy of the United States of America 2011* (NMS) echoes the president's message.[15] In introducing the NMS on 8 February 2011, Chairman of the Joint Chiefs of Staff Admiral Michael G. "Mike" Mullen emphasized the importance of leadership and declared that the NMS "places a clear priority on our people and their families as they are truly indispensable elements of any strategy."[16] Leadership is responsible for promoting this strategic interest by caring for the health, welfare, and readiness of its service members and their families. However, DOMA stands in opposition to supporting family readiness by limiting the U.S. military's ability to "reduce the strain on military families" of gay service members.[17]

It is counterintuitive to think that the U.S. military, ordered to implement the repeal of DADT, would be prohibited from fully supporting the family readiness of gay troops. However, the DADT Repeal Act of 2010 contains a savings clause stating, "nothing in this section . . . shall be construed to require the furnishing of benefits in violation of . . . [DOMA]."[18] In effect, the U.S. military has been given an impossible assignment: to end unlawful discrimination of service members based on sexual orientation but to ignore the lawful discrimination of their families based on DOMA. With the U.S. military beginning to implement a change in policy that allows homosexuals to serve openly, and understanding the importance of supporting service members and their families, leadership must identify and attack barriers that stand in opposition to these goals. Only by reconciling the inconsistency that exists between allowing homosexuals to serve while denying pay and benefits to the families that support them can the military effectively fulfill its responsibility to its soldiers, sailors, airmen, and Marines.

Since DOMA was enacted, most states have either included DOMA language in their state legislation or passed constitutional amendments prohibiting same-sex marriage.[19] Currently five states plus the District of Columbia permit same-sex marriage.[20] Eight other states allow some form of civil union or domestic partner-ship that provides certain state-level spousal rights.[21] However, even if a same-gen-der couple is joined by marriage or civil union under the laws of a particular state, that status is not recognized under federal law. Therefore, gay service members and their same-sex partners are prohibited from receiving federal marriage-based ben-efits. Further, the military's definition of "dependent"—for the purpose of provid-ing certain benefits and support services—is tied to the words "marriage" and "spouse," further complicating the issue of support for the families of homosexual service members.

As stated, based on DOMA, no state is required to recognize a same-sex mar-riage legally performed in another state. Given how frequently military service members transfer, whether a state recognizes a committed same-sex relationship may create hardships that will affect family readiness. Another issue is that of over-seas assignments and another nation's laws on homosexuality. Based on military regulations and status of forces agreements, gay service members would receive no support from the U.S. military for a committed same-sex partner.[22] Specifically, travel is not funded nor is command sponsorship, which provides host-nation legal protection to military family members. [23] In the United States, however, DOMA has been challenged as unconstitutional in the courts under both the full faith and credit clause that establishes that states will recognize the laws of other states, and the due process clause and its equal protection principle.

In a recent challenge to the constitutionality of DOMA in the courts, a federal employee and her same-sex spouse applied for and were denied federal marriage-based benefits.[24] In defending DOMA, the federal government said the law was es-tablished to provide a consistent definition of *marriage* between the states in order to establish eligibility for federal marriage-based benefits. In the court's opinion, there was no reason to define marriage since the federal government already rec-ognizes heterosexual marriage.[25] And if DOMA exists only to define marriage as the legal union between one man and one woman, then it does not exist to clarify but to restrict same-sex couples from enjoying the federal marriage-based benefits offered to other married couples.[26]

Additionally, the government argued that DOMA provides relief to federal agencies by reducing the "administrative burden" required to navigate individual states' marriage laws.[27] The court disagreed, stating that there was no "administrative burden" on federal agencies because each state maintains jurisdiction of its laws and the federal government is required only to provide benefits to "those couples that have already obtained state-sanctioned marriage licenses."[28] Hence, the administrative process to change a heterosexual couple's status to married is no more complex than that required for a same-gender couple. The court said, "DOMA seems to inject complexity into an otherwise straightforward administrative task" by creating a distinction between those marriages eligible and those not eligible for federal benefits.[29]

While the example points to one challenge to the constitutionality of DOMA, the federal government has found it increasingly difficult to defend DOMA against other legal attacks. In a statement released on 23 February 2011, Attorney General Eric H. Holder noted that President Obama had instructed the Department of Justice not to defend the constitutionality of DOMA in court.[30] The attorney general stated that the "legal landscape has changed over the past 15 years since Congress passed DOMA," pointing to the repeal of DADT and Supreme Court decisions that laws criminalizing homosexuality are unconstitutional.[31] Thus, the attorney general recommended and the president concluded that given "a documented history of discrimination, classifications based on sexual orientation should be subject to a more heightened standard of scrutiny [and] that Section 3 of DOMA, applied to legally married same-sex couples, fails to meet that standard and therefore is unconstitutional." [32]

Forecasting the "inevitable" repeal of DADT in November 2010, Secretary of Defense Robert M. Gates expressed his uncertainty about whether Congress or the courts would end DADT.[33] With court activity surrounding DOMA and partisan division over the topic, the best bet for the demise of DOMA is in the courts vice legislative action. However, unlike Secretary Gates' concern that a decision to end DADT by the courts would limit the military's ability to prepare for a change in policy, court action to end DOMA would open the door for the military to provide benefits to gay service members and their partners. It is important that the military begins to plan for the eventual end of DOMA, especially in light of legal challenges and the statement of White House Press Secretary Jay Carney, who said the president believes that DOMA "is an unnecessary and unfair law [and that] he supports the repeal of the law."[34]

The Importance of Supporting Military Families for Readiness

Lesser noted than the president's pledge to repeal DADT, though equally important to the military, was his 2010 State of the Union statement that service members need to know "that they have our respect, our gratitude, our full support" and that the administration was focused on forging "a national commitment to support military families."[35] Outlining the 2011 priorities and strategic objectives of the joint force, Admiral Mullen says the "health-of-force priorities are to care for our people and their families, and restore readiness."[36] The message is clear: family readiness is important to military readiness and overall military effectiveness.

Gates, in a memorandum dated 2 March 2010, appointed a "working group [to] examine the potential impacts of a change in the DADT law on military effectiveness . . . and other issues crucial to the performance of the force."[37] The working group, called the Comprehensive Review Working Group (CRWG), was directed to conduct a review of how any change to DADT could potentially impact military readiness, military effectiveness, unit cohesion, recruiting, retention, and family readiness. According to the CRWG, family readiness "is the military family's ability to successfully meet the challenges of daily living in the context of military life including deployments and frequent relocation. Programs and benefits provided by the services play a key role in helping service members and their families through deployment-related stresses."[38] The secretary outlined the objectives and directed the working group to recommend changes to existing policies and regulations, including personnel management, pay and benefits, and family programs and support services.[39] A report, to include a plan for implementation, was delivered on 30 November 2010.

The CRWG produced a model to aid its review of the repeal's impact on military effectiveness.[40] The model shows how the six issues (military readiness, military effectiveness, unit cohesion, recruiting, retention, and family readiness) in

Gates' memorandum interrelate and depicts military effectiveness as the overarching concern, with military readiness and unit cohesion considered subsets. Family readiness and personal readiness (including recruiting and retention) were parsed by the CRWG as subordinate elements of military readiness, which was defined as "the ability of forces to fight and meet the requirements of the National Military Strategy."[41] In this way the CRWG shows how family readiness is linked to the military's ability to conduct missions.

The CRWG was directed to consider how a repeal of DADT would potentially affect family readiness. However, the CRWG limited its focus on family readiness within the context of a heterosexual military and the impact a repeal would have on heterosexual service members and their spouses. In a single, unsupported statement, the CRWG predicted "that there would likely be a substantial positive effect on family readiness for gay and lesbian service members and their families" following repeal of DADT.[42] Otherwise, the CRWG did not address how the denial of marriage-based pay, benefits, and support services would affect the family readiness of newly recognized gay service members. The review did little more than identify DOMA as the rationale for denying these marriage-based benefits and recommend that this issue be re-examined later. DOMA, by denying support to all military families, may affect military readiness by forcing the commander to focus on the unsupported needs of an individual or a small portion of his unit to the detriment of the whole.

In a survey of spouses designed to "collect information about community life and potential impact of a repeal of 'Don't Ask, Don't Tell' on family readiness," CRWG focused on how respondents felt about homosexuals and their families and whether a change in policy would affect their participation in social events and their use of benefits including base housing, support groups, and family programs.[43] By posing only questions on family readiness that established an understanding of the prevailing attitudes and concerns of straight families, the survey failed to address what potential concerns would arise for gay families in the event of a change in policy. Thus, the CRWG evaluated the impact on family readiness as low because CRWG failed to provide insight into family readiness concerns of gay service members. Also missing in the survey was the point that heterosexual families would continue to receive the support they valued but a committed same-sex couple would not be able to live next to them in base housing because they would be denied equal access.

This oversight is notable because CRWG cites an e-mail from a military spouse and family readiness program volunteer said to capture the foundation of the CRWG's assessment.[44] The e-mail speaks to a belief that despite the challenges, repealing DADT is important and necessary to fulfilling the country's egalitarian principles.[45] With the CRWG's endorsement of this altruistic message in mind, the question remains: Why did the report avoid addressing fair and equal support for gay service members? The report points out that DOMA denies gay couples federal marriage-based benefits but does not identify this as a family readiness concern with a potential impact on overall military readiness. It is difficult to understand this omission in light of the president's intent to "(end) this discriminatory policy (DADT) once and for all,"[46] a policy that not only required an act to allow gay people to serve openly but also begged for a review and plan to address the feelings of heterosexuals and, also, the needs of homosexuals. Essentially, in building its strategic assessment, the CRWG addressed the impact of a potential repeal on the current force but avoided the subsequent impact on a U.S. military that includes same-sex military families that do not receive equal pay and benefits.

There were times during the DADT debates when the plight of the homosexual service member was considered. Admiral Mullen said in his congressional testimony that "no matter how I look at this issue, I cannot escape being troubled by the fact that we have in place a policy which forces young men and women to lie about who they are in order to defend their fellow citizens."[47] With the repeal act now signed and the military preparing to implement this change, it is troubling that the implementation plan is focused on re-educating the force on professional standards and harassment policies at the expense of defining the barriers to implementation and providing leadership the tools necessary to ensure equal treatment and opportunity for gay troops and their families.

While the DOD "Support Plan of Implementation" (SPI) of the comprehensive review includes an appendix entitled "Frequently Asked Questions and Vignettes" that "address[es] some of the areas of concern . . . and illustrates approaches to a sample of issues" such as pay and benefits for homosexual service members and their families, the report and the plan stop short of noting how restrictions on certain benefits affect family readiness and the overall military readiness of those service members.[48] Moreover, the manner in which the subject is covered and dismissed based on DOMA places the burden on military leadership to explain why fair and equal treatment for gay service members ends at equal access to compensation and support.

In order to minimize the impact of a potential repeal of DADT, the CRWG recommended that homosexual service members and their partners should not be afforded the same pay and benefits enjoyed by heterosexual couples. However, it is not only important that the concerns of service members who already participate openly in the military are addressed, it is important that those who have been denied this right are provided fair and equal treatment, to include pay and benefits. Providing this support is not only about ensuring fairness and equality but is of strategic importance in ensuring the health and welfare of the force. With DADT now repealed, the DOD should support a repeal of DOMA to allow military leadership to fulfill their responsibilities to all military families regardless of sexual orientation. The next section of this report highlights issues concerning the pay, benefits, and support services available or denied to gay service members.

Unequal Pay, Benefits, and Support Services

While researching this report, specifically when asking questions about eligibility of pay and benefits, the authors routinely encountered difficulty in getting answers from agencies. The difficulty was not in the form of officials refusing to answer questions but from individuals not knowing or understanding their organization's official stance or policy regarding same-sex spouses. In most cases when the authors asked questions, the representative had to push the questions up the chain of command. Sometimes the question was pushed up three to four echelons before it was answered—usually after referring to the legal department. This is not an indictment of the individuals for not knowing their jobs but it amplifies the point that training about how DOMA affects service members needs to be conducted at all levels—especially for service providers.

There are many benefits for military spouses, ranging from monetary provisions to rights pertaining to medical decisions. According to the Government Accountability Office (GAO), "as of 31 December 2003, [their] research identified a total of 1,138 federal statutory provisions classified to the United States Code in which marital status is a factor in determining or receiving benefits, rights, and privileges."[49] Once a service member produces a marriage certificate, he or she is eligible to receive benefits provided to military spouses. As a legal spouse of an active duty service member, there is no need to fight for these benefits because they are automatically provided by policy. Eligibility to benefits for same-sex couples is more complex and may require same-sex couples to petition for the benefits. Under CRWG recommendations there is an argument that service members can assign a beneficiary who is not a dependent, so spouses in same-sex couples will have access to some benefits that are "member designated," such as service member group life insurance (SGLI). However, if the service member with a same-sex partner fails to name a beneficiary or there is an administrative error, the partner will not automatically become the beneficiary as in the case of a heterosexual spouse.

Benefits are provided to members of a service member's family if they are eligible to be claimed as a dependent. In the case of the Marine Corps, for instance, Marine Corps Order (MCO) P1751.3F states: Eligible dependents include spouse, parent(s), parent(s)-in-law, stepparent(s), adoptive parent(s), in loco parentis, legitimate child(ren), stepchild(ren), incapacitated child(ren), adopted child(ren), pre-adopted child(ren), child(ren) from the age of 21 to the date of their 23rd birthday who are enrolled in a full-time course of study in an institution of higher education, dependent child(ren), and court-appointed wards.[50]

When it comes to marriage recognition, MCO P1751.34F directs commanding officers to approve NAVMC Form 10922 (marriage recognition form) when a service member brings in documentation supporting a marriage in one of the following cases:

- U.S. ceremonial marriages: marriages within the United States or its territories by a legal civil or religious ceremony
- Foreign marriages

- Indian tribunal marriages: in states that recognize Indian tribal law and custom, such marriages and divorces are acceptable provided both are members of Indian tribes
- Common-law marriages: informal marriage recognized as valid in some states and in some foreign countries. A common-law marriage, if valid where contracted, is valid elsewhere
- Proxy and telephone marriages[51]

The MCO does not reference same-sex marriages or civil unions, owing to the provisions of DADT. However, with DADT's repeal, the issue will need to be addressed because of the provisions in DOMA.

In addition to filing a NAVMC form 10922, service members enroll a spouse in the Defense Enrollment Eligibility Reporting System (DEERS). Once enrolled as a dependent, the spouse is eligible for benefits from not only the component service of their sponsor but from other government agencies such the Department of Veterans Affairs (VA). Specifics about VA benefits are discussed later in the report.

Here is a look at some of the benefits normally provided to spouses and dependents, and how they may apply to same-gender spouses:

Base Allowance for Housing

Base Allowance for Housing (BAH) is based on geographic duty location, pay grade, and dependency status. The intent of BAH is to provide uniformed service members accurate and equitable housing compensation based on housing costs in local civilian housing markets and is payable when government quarters are not provided. Service members with a dependent receive a higher BAH rate than those without dependents. Service members who have a same-sex partner are not eligible to claim them as a dependent and will not receive the higher "with dependent" rate. However, if the service member has a housemate—a "spouse" recognized under state law but not federal law (because of DOMA)—who is dependent upon the member for more than half of his or her support, the service member can petition to claim their partner as a dependent. In theory this may work but could create an incentive for the partner not to seek employment, and produce inequities for other couples where the nonmilitary member is not dependent upon his spouse for more than half of his support.

Due to the inability to receive the BAH "with dependent" rate, service members may not be able to afford housing off-base. The alternative to off-base housing is on-base housing in which the service member no longer receives BAH but is provided living quarters based upon rank and number of dependents. For single service members, on-base housing is provided in the form of bachelor's quarters that are similar to dormitory living, in which rooms are shared. With the exception of single general officers, base commanders, and chaplains, rarely do single service members receive on-base housing that is suitable for a family.

When a same-sex couple has a child and the service member lists the child as a dependent, the service member will be able to apply for base housing based on the child's status as a dependent. However, the spouse may not be allowed to take residence in the housing on a permanent basis because of the rules in base housing contracts. Most rules state that the residents of the housing are limited to service members and their dependents. Guests are allowed for up to two weeks. In a situation in which the guest must stay longer than two weeks, the service member needs to request an extended stay Administrative Action (AA) form.

The extended-stay process is used in cases in which a family member is assisting the service member because of physical limitations or sickness; for example, a service member's spouse has a broken leg and will be in a cast for months. The service member requests permission for someone to stay at his home in order to assist his spouse and take care of a child until the spouse's leg heals. These requests are usually approved with a specific end date based on the medical prognosis. In the situation in which a service member lives on-base with his child, the same-sex spouse is not authorized to live with the family on a permanent basis. A same-sex couple could submit an extended-stay request to provide child care but there is no consistent policy suggesting that such a request would be approved.

Another aspect of housing for same-sex couples will arise when the service member is a junior service member (E-5 and below). As codified in Title 37, Section 403 of U.S. Code, "a member without dependents who is in a pay grade above pay grade E–6 and who is assigned to quarters in the United States or a housing facility under the jurisdiction of a uniformed service, appropriate to the grade or rank of the member and adequate for the member, may elect not to occupy those quarters and instead to receive the basic allowance for housing prescribed for the member's pay grade by this section."[52] Service members below the pay grade of E-6 and "without dependents" are directed to live in the bachelor enlisted quarters. They can, however, request BAH in order to live off-base. When the barracks reach capacity, the area commander will offer service members the opportunity to move out of the barracks but, if the barracks has space, the request for BAH will not be approved. (Each base has different vacancy percentage guidelines.) If an E-5 has a same-gender spouse, he may not be able to afford to live off-base with his spouse because he will not receive BAH. However, commanding officers have some flexibility when it comes to approving BAH. There are no provisions supporting BAH for service members in a same-sex marriage, but there are also no regulations forbidding it. DOMA forbids making the spouse a dependent, but there is the opportunity for commanders to work around this situation by approving BAH for the service member. However, the BAH will be at the "without dependent" rate, which is lower than the "with dependent" rate.

The CRWG identified that commanders and bases do have leeway regarding the housing issue but ultimately issued the following opinion:

> We do not, however, recommend that military family housing be included in the benefits eligible for this member-designated approach. Permitting a service member to qualify for military family housing, simply by designating whomever he chooses as a "dependent" is problematic. Military family housing is a limited resource and complicated to administer, and such a system would create occasions for abuse and unfairness.[53]

What was argued was that it is unfair for a service member to be able to designate a dependent rather than having to follow the normal protocol. Specifically, a heterosexual has to marry in order for their partner to get the benefits afforded to a dependent. However, this line of logic does not support the scenario in which the gay service member is legally married to a same-gender partner or is in a civil union.

On-base support activities such as the commissary, post-exchange (PX), auto-service centers, gas stations, and other stores and services tied to the PX system are another issue. These activities provide products and services available off-base but at a cheaper rate. (Many service members who live off-base shop on-base.) Access to these facilities requires military-issued identification cards based on dependency status. Unless the partner can be claimed as a dependent based upon fiscal dependency, same-sex spouses will not receive identification cards and will be excluded from using the establishments.

Day care is another support activity provided for families on-base. Like the PX system, child care on-base is more affordable than off-base. For a same-sex couple with a child, the service member can enroll the child in day care and authorize the spouse to be allowed to drop off and pick up the child. However, if the spouse does not have a dependent identification card, there are occasions in which he or she may have a difficult time getting on the base (a base lockdown, for example), requiring the service member to have to pick up the child. In such a situation the service member may be involved with duties relating to the security situation, further complicating matters.

Health care benefits also become an issue for homosexual couples. Active-duty service members are covered through the government and their dependents are covered through TRICARE. Same-sex spouses will not receive government-sponsored health care. The exclusion of health care for same-sex spouses represents a significant financial strain.

Financial instruments that service members have access to include SGLI, Thrift Savings Plan (TSP), and Survivor's Benefit Plan (SBP). The CRWG identified that service members in a same-sex marriage can designate their beneficiary for these plans. The CRWG recommended that service members should receive training in beneficiary designation to ensure their loved ones receive the funds. But the heterosexual spouse of a heterosexual service member who failed to designate a beneficiary will receive the benefits by law. A homosexual service member who fails to designate a beneficiary will have benefits paid via the same law but the same-sex spouse will receive nothing. If the service member did not select an SGLI beneficiary, the law requires the insurance be paid in the following order of precedence: spouse, children in equal shares, parent or parents in equal shares, an executor or administrator of the estate, and the next-of-kin entitled to payment under the law of the service member's state of residence.[54] If the same-sex spouse is not considered a spouse per the DOMA definition and the service member failed to list a beneficiary, there can be a confusing legal situation.

In conjunction with SGLI there is a supplemental insurance program called Family Servicemember's Group Life Insurance (FSGLI). Under FSGLI a service member can insure a spouse or children for up to $100,000 coverage in the event of the death of the spouse. The program is linked to the SGLI, and offers economical rates when compared to commercial life insurance. Since eligibility for the supplemental insurance is based on dependency status, DOMA may bar coverage for same-sex spouses.

In the event of the service member's hospitalization or death, the CRWG noted that service members can designate in their Record of Emergency Data (RED) whomever they wish for visitation, access, or decision-making rights. Service members can use estate-planning vehicles such as a will, living will, power of attorney, or the like to arrange their affairs. The law provides a safety net for straight service members that does not exist for gay service members. Initially, this seems like the same-sex spouses of service members are supported and have rights. However, as with the beneficiary issue for SGLI, the law will not support the same-sex spouse if there is a problem with the paperwork.

This can be demonstrated by a worst-case scenario: a service member is in a catatonic state at a military hospital and a decision needs to be made about continuing life support. If there is no living will, the protocol is for the spouse to state the service member's wishes. If no spouse, the decision goes to the children who are not minors; if no children, the parents are consulted. In this case a heterosexual spouse is protected by the law and has a voice but the same-sex spouse may not have a voice. This thread can be continued down to decisions regarding the service member's funeral and burial. Such decisions are the responsibility of the Person Authorized to Direct Disposition of Human Remains (PADD). All service members are required to name a PADD on their RED. According to the rules, the PADD must be the spouse, a blood relative of legal age, or adoptive relatives of the deceased member.[55] Same-sex spouses may not be eligible to be the PADD under DOMA.

Following the loss of a spouse, the same-sex spouse will have more stress by not having the rights afforded to a heterosexual spouse. In order to have their concerns addressed, the same-sex spouse may have to retain legal counsel for assistance that would have been provided to a heterosexual spouse as a matter of course. If the issue involves any federal activity and funds, then the provisions of DOMA will be a hurdle that might not be overcome.

Higher education is one of the major recruiting tools for the military, specifically the educational benefits during time of service and postservice in the form of the Post 9/11 GI Bill. One of the provisions in the bill is that service members can transfer their eligibility to one of their dependents or be divided among multiple dependents. In the case of transferring eligibility to the spouse, the spouse will receive 100 percent tuition cost and BAH at the E-5 rate for 36 months if they are attending a public university in their resident state. If they attend a private school or university in another country the coverage is capped at $17,500. According to the VA, eligibility for the program is limited to spouses and dependents that are listed in DEERS as dependents of the service member. Because same-sex spouses will not be listed as a dependent in DEERS they are not eligible for receiving benefits from the GI Bill.

Survivor benefits, or taking the steps necessary to ensure loved ones are provided for in case of the death of a breadwinner, is a major issue as well. Service members are eligible for enrollment in the Survivor's Benefit Plan (SBP). The SBP is a DOD program that provides up to 55 percent of a service member's retired pay to an eligible beneficiary upon the death of the member. The program provides no-cost, automatic coverage to members serving on active duty and reserve component members who die of a service-connected cause while performing inactive duty training. In addition, active duty members can purchase coverage upon retirement and reserve component members can elect coverage when they have 20 years of qualifying service for Reserve retired pay.[56]

There are two major aspects to SBP: (1) death of service member while on active duty; and (2) insurance on a retired service member's pension, in which he can pay a monthly premium after retirement that will transfer 55 percent of his retirement pay to a recipient when he dies.

The second aspect is easily remedied for the service member who has a same-sex partner. At retirement he fills out a document stating whether he wants to enroll in SBP. If yes, he names his same-sex partner as the beneficiary. The eligible beneficiaries for the SBP are the spouse and/or dependent children, a former spouse and/or dependent children, or a natural person with an insurable interest, providing they meet certain eligibility requirements.[57] The same-sex partner probably falls in to the "natural person with an insurable interest" category but must be proven at the time the retiree has to make a decision on whether to choose the SBP annuity insurance.

The first aspect is where a service member who has a same-sex spouse runs into a problem. When a service member dies on active duty, his dependents automatically receive SBP coverage that equates to 55 percent of what his retirement pay would have been had he medically retired at that time at the 100 percent disability rate. Since same-sex partners normally cannot be claimed as dependents, they probably will not receive SBP. The same-sex partner will have to petition the DOD to try to receive SBP, possibly arguing that they fall into the "natural person with an insurable interest" category. DOD regulations state that, in the case of a member who dies on active duty and no other beneficiary is eligible to receive an annuity, a person who is, as determined by the secretary concerned, a dependent of that member as defined in Title 10, United States Code, Section 1072(2) is considered an eligible person.[58] Section 1072(2) lists dependents as previously noted: spouse, children, family members who are listed as dependents owing to medical conditions, etc. It does not apply to same-sex spouses because of DOMA's definition of spouse. The same-sex survivor of a service member can petition to receive SBP but there is no guarantee of success.

In addition to SBP, dependents of service members who die while on active duty are eligible for the VA-provided Dependents Indemnity Compensation program (DIC). The DIC provides surviving dependents $1,154 per month and the total can be split among multiple dependents. Eligibility for DIC is available only to dependents; the VA determines eligibility through DEERS. Owing to the previously discussed fact that same-sex couples will not be entered into DEERS, the VA may not provide the benefit to the same-sex spouse.

In addition to benefits that have been in place for years, since 11 September 2001, benefits have been added for families coping with the stress of war. In a 2010 speech about supporting military families, President Obama stated, "We're going to help spouses to get that degree, find that job or start that new business . . . we want every company in America to know our military spouses and veterans have the skills and the dedication, and our nation is more competitive when we tap their incredible talents."[59]

An example of the new benefits to military spouses is unemployment benefits. Four more states recently approved the change in policy:

> According to the Defense Department, 21 states now allow trailing military spouses to receive unemployment benefits. Eight states deny such benefits outright; the rest consider such requests on a case-by-case basis. The Pentagon is working this issue hard. Since defense officials launched a "USA 4 Military Families" state partnership program three years ago, 13 states have changed their policies to let spouses get unemployment compensation.[60]

This DOD effort reinforces its stance on the importance of supporting military families. However, it is unclear if the unemployment benefits will be extended to same-sex partners.

Other support services that focus on spouses and are offered through DOD include the Army's Warrior Transition Program and counseling and education programs when a service member returns from a deployment. The Warrior Transition Program (WTP) is designed to support soldiers who were wounded in combat. One aspect of the program is directed at training spouses of wounded soldiers about how they can serve and help the spouse. Understanding that the spouse will have stress because of the injury, the WTP offers get-away weekends in which spouses receive training and relaxation opportunities at an off-base site. In order to attend, the spouse has to be identified as the "spouse" through the DOD. Same-sex spouses may be ineligible to attend.

Another program for family members is the Survivors and Dependents Educational Assistance Program (DEA), offered through the VA. The DEA offers up to $6,000 to spouses and children of service members who died on active duty or are missing in action. The money can be used for any educational or vocational training. As with the DIC, the VA establishes eligibility through DEERS; same-sex partners may not be eligible.

There are other tangential benefits afforded to spouses via organizations such as the United Services Organization (USO), which provides support services ranging from access to airport facilities to assistance in finding off-base day care facilities—if the dependent has an ID card. Thus the USO is another support service denied to committed same-sex partners of gay service members because of DOMA.

Recognizing the importance of pay, benefits, and support services in support of family readiness, it is difficult to understand how the CRWG assessed the risk to family readiness and overall military effectiveness as low. The historical record of racial integration offers a lesson in how an integrated force allowed to fester in inequalities can affect morale.

Lessons from Desegregation for Today's Military

Drawing comparisons between the concerns expressed about racial integration to those expressed about the repeal of DADT, the CRWG notes that the opposition to racial integration of the armed forces was based on "what we know now to be blatant stereotype."[61] The CRWG goes on to postulate that the military experienced difficulty in integrating because society was generally opposed to racial integration in the 1940s, yet today's society is more accepting of homosexuality, which will ease the transition.[62] The CRWG posits that the concerns expressed about the repeal of DADT are unsupported by history because, despite similar concerns over racial integration, when the military received the order to integrate, integration was accomplished.[63]

Further, the CRWG states that service members are more tolerant of homosexuals serving in the military today than they were with racial integration in the 1940s. This conclusion was reached by comparing the results of a 1946 survey of white officers and enlisted men to a survey of service members conducted as part of the comprehensive review. These surveys show that while 80 percent were opposed to racial integration in 1946, only 30 percent of military respondents predicted a negative impact from a repeal of DADT.[64] However, federal and state laws still serve as barriers to equal treatment and opportunity for gay service members. This places the military in the position of leading social change because civil society cannot, or will not, make this change on its own. Civil society is still considering the issue of same-gender rights and relationships, and consensus has not been attained.[65]

Arguments against using the military to advance a social agenda are found in the debates about racial integration and the repeal of DADT.[66] However, the military, given the lead, is often ahead of society in facilitating integration efforts.[67] In the case of racial integration, the comprehensive review report states that the "military did serve as a social experiment . . . for the rest of American society."[68] Racial integration of the armed forces was a change in policy that was executed by the military "in advance of American society."[69] According to the CRWG, however, this is where the parallel ends. While the military led the effort to end racial discrimination, the repeal of DADT would only serve to bring parity with that of the civilian community.[70]

Following the Senate's vote to repeal DADT, Secretary Gates—echoing the CRWG—stated he was "convinced that the U.S. military can successfully accommodate and implement this change, as it has others in history."[71] Gates' sentiment is supported by a racial integration study cited by the Palm Center,[72] in which the military is highlighted as an institution ahead of society in its ability to carry out unpopular or challenging transitions.[73] The military is suited for this mission based on its command structure, professionalism, and discipline that ensure the success of integration efforts they are ordered to execute. This point is supported by Admiral Mullen, in his statement that notwithstanding the repeal of DADT being "a complex social and cultural issue . . . at the end of the day . . . we in uniform have an obligation to follow orders."[74]

In 1948, President Harry S. Truman effectively ordered the U.S. military to integrate by directing in an executive order "that there shall be equality of treatment and opportunity for all persons in the armed service,"[75] a change in policy that was implemented by the military in six years—while civil society continued to lag behind. Racial integration of the military was accomplished well before the civil rights movement succeeded in ending laws that stood in conflict with the fair and equal treatment of African Americans. By 1954 the armed forces were integrated while discrimination against African American service members was still prevalent in local communities, and society supported federal and state laws that maintained segregation and prohibited interracial marriage well into the 1960s.[76] These laws were noted for the negative impact they had on the morale and military readiness of African American service members and their families.[77] To be sure, friction and obstruction to integration took place in the military but history shows that the military was integrated long before society took steps to end legal racial discrimination.

The DOD also responded to continued community-based discrimination. In 1962 President John F. Kennedy announced the formation of a committee to investigate what should be done to "improve current policies and procedures in the services and . . . equality of opportunity for service members and their families in the civilian community."[78] The committee said continued "discrimination affected . . . morale and military efficiency" and recommended that not only should more be done by the commanders on-base but, when necessary, they also should engage with the local community to end discriminatory practices.[79] Opponents countered that the military should not be used to enforce a social issue in the civilian community because it was outside the military's responsibility and a "usurpation of state sovereignty and a threat to civil liberties."[80]

While the committee was not recommending a military-led civil rights movement, they did believe that the military as a "symbol of American society had to be a leader in the quest for racial justice . . . [therefore] social reform . . . where it affected servicemen . . . was a legitimate military function."[81] The subsequent DOD directive released by Secretary of Defense Robert S. McNamara assigned military commanders responsibility for "oppos[ing] discriminatory practices affecting [their] men and their dependents," with an "emphasis placed on . . . achieving voluntary compliance [in the community] with the department's equal opportunity policies."[82] Thus, under the leadership of Secretary McNamara, the DOD established a policy to address discrimination against African American service members in the civilian community and expanded the limits of the military's responsibility for the welfare of all service members.[83] In 15 years the U.S. military had gone from carrying out an executive order to integrate the armed forces to promoting equal treatment, opportunity, and rights for its service members in society at large.

Similar to this example from history is the military's effort in leading social change to end discrimination based on sexual orientation. While there is a risk in looking to history for answers because one may oversimplify a complex and multifaceted issue in order to make or prove a point, history suggests options and identifies possible solutions.

Homosexuals are allowed to serve openly in the military, while federal and state laws remain that discriminate against sexual orientation. The military's ability to achieve its goal is hindered by societal limitations beyond the military's control; the military may only influence developments in the civil sector. The question is to what degree should military leadership, professionalism, and respect for all service members compel the military to prevail upon political leadership to finish the effort they began with the repeal of DADT? Therefore, as this report says history suggests, the DOD must champion the attainment of fair and equal treatment for all of its service members.

The dynamics of the DADT debate during 2010–11 not only led to the repeal of DADT but have also served to rekindle debate over DOMA. As a result, the military again finds itself the chosen agent of social change. Further, the military— while maintaining its focus on the current fight—must not only implement DADT's repeal but must also champion further policy changes that are necessary to fulfill responsibility to its service members. The military must ensure that DOMA's impact on military readiness remains a point of discussion with political leadership because political leadership is also responsible for the welfare of all military service members regardless of race, gender, religion, and, now, sexual orientation. When leadership finds that a service member is being denied equal treatment or opportunity, it is their responsibility to correct this injustice or seek resolution.

Notes

1 Office of the Press Secretary, "Remarks by the President in State of the Union Address," transcript, 27 January 2010, http://www.whitehouse.gov/the-press-office/remarks-president-state-union-address.

2 U.S. Code [U.S.C.], title 10, section 654.

3 U.S. Department of Defense, *Report of the Comprehensive Review of the Issues Associated with a Repeal of "Don't Ask, Don't Tell"* (Arlington, VA: Department of Defense, 2010), 3, www.defense.gov/home/features/2010/0610_dadt /DADTReport_FINAL_20101130(secure-hires).pdf.

4 Don't Ask, Don't Tell Repeal Act of 2010, Public Law 111-321, 22 December 2010, http://thomas.loc.gov/cgi-bin/bdquery/ z?d111:h2965:.

5 Office of the Press Secretary, "News Conference by the President," transcript, 22 December 2010, http://www.whitehouse.gov/the-press-office/2010/12/22/ news-conference-president.

6 Codified in U.S.C. title 1, section 7, and U.S.C., title 28, section 1738C.

7 "News Conference by the President," 22 December 2010.

8 Office of the Press Secretary, "President Obama on the DOD Report on 'Don't Ask, Don't Tell,'" transcript, 30 November 2010, http://www.whitehouse.gov/ blog/2010/11/30/president-obama-dod-report-don-t-ask-don-t-tell.

9 Alliance Defense Fund, "Federal Defense of Marriage Act (DOMA)," http://www.domawatch.org/ about/federaldoma.html.

10 Codified in Title 28, Section 1738C of U.S. Code, Section 2 of DOMA asserts: No State, territory, or possession of the United States, or Indian tribe, shall be required to give effect to any public act, record, or judicial proceeding of any other State, territory, possession, or tribe respecting a relationship between persons of the same sex that is treated as a marriage under the laws of such other State, territory, possession, or tribe, or a right or claim arising from such relationship. See http://www.law.cornell.edu/uscode/text/28/1738C.

11 Codified in Title 1, Section 7 of U.S. Code, Section 3 of DOMA states: In determining the meaning of any Act of Congress, or of any ruling, regulation, or interpretation of the various administrative bureaus and agencies of the United States, the word "marriage" means only a legal union between one man and one woman as husband and wife, and the word "spouse" refers only to a person of the opposite sex who is a husband or a wife. See "U.S. Code: § 7. Definition of 'mar-

riage' and 'spouse'," Cornell University Law School, Legal Information Institute, 1 February 2010, http://www.law.cornell.edu/uscode/1/7.html.

12 President Obama, Strengthening Our Military Families: Meeting America's Commitment, January 2011, http://www.defense.gov/home/features/2011/ 0111_initiative/Strengthening_our_Military_January_2011.pdf; Office of the Press Secretary, "Background on the President's PSD Event Today with the First Lady and Dr. Biden," 24 January 2011, http://www.whitehouse.gov/the-press-office/2011/01/24/background-presidents-psd-event-today-first-lady-and-dr-biden.

13 Office of the Press Secretary, "Remarks by the President, Mrs. Obama, and Dr. Biden on the Presidential Studies Directive: Strengthening Our Military Families," transcript, 24 January 2011, http://www.whitehouse.gov/the-press-office/2011/01/24/remarks-president-mrs-obama-and-dr-biden-presidential-studies-directive-.

14 Matthew P. Cashdollar, "Not Yes or No, But What If: Implications of Open Homosexuality in the Military," in *Attitudes Aren't Free: Thinking Deeply about Diversity in the US Armed Forces*, ed. James E. Parco and David A. Levy (Maxwell Air Force Base: Air University Press, 2010), 174.

15 Joint Chiefs of Staff, *The National Military Strategy of the United States of America 2011: Redefining America's Military Leadership* (Arlington, VA: Joint Chiefs of Staff, 2011), http://www.jcs.mil//content/files/2011-02/020811084800_2011_NMS_-_08_FEB_2011.pdf.

16 Joint Chiefs of Staff, *The National Military Strategy 2011*, CJCS introduction.

17 The White House, "Defense," 30 July 2009, http://www.whitehouse.gov/ issues/defense.

18 "Bill Summary & Status, 111th Congress (2009–10), S.4023." Library of Congress, 13 December 2010, http://thomas.loc.gov/cgi-bin/bdquery/z?d111:S4023:.

19 Alliance Defense Fund, "Federal Defense of Marriage Act (DOMA): Issues by State," DOMAwatch.org, http://www.domawatch.org/stateissues/index .html.

20 National Conference of State Legislatures, "Same Sex Marriage, Civil Unions, Domestic Partnerships," 14 July 2011, http://www.ncsl.org/ de-fault.aspx?tabid=16430.

21 Ibid.

22 DOD, Comprehensive Review, 147.

23 Ibid.

24 Gill v. Office of Personnel Management, No.1:09-cv-10309-JLT (D. Mass. 2010), 1–39.

25 Ibid., 34.

26 Ibid.

27 Ibid., 35.

28 Ibid.

29 Ibid.

30 Office of Public Affairs, "Statement of the Attorney General on Litigation In-volving the Defense of Marriage Act," transcript, 23 February 2011, http://www.justice.gov/opa/pr/2011/February/11-ag-222.html.

31 Ibid.

32 Ibid.

33 Scott Wong, "Robert Gates: 'Don't Ask Repeal Inevitable," Politico.com, 10 November 2010, http://www.politico.com/news/stories/1110/44937.html.

34 Office of the Press Secretary, "Press Briefing by Press Secretary Jay Carney, 2/24/2011," transcript, 24 February 2011, http://www.whitehouse.gov/the-press-office/2011/02/24/press-briefing-press-secretary-jay-carney-2242011.

35 Office of the Press Secretary, "Remarks by the President in State of the Union Address."

36 ADM Mike Mullen, "CJCS Guidance for 2011," 05 January 2011, www.dtic.mil/dtic/tr/fulltext/u2/a535131.pdf.

37 Secretary Robert Gates, "JCS Speech: Testimony Regarding DOD 'Don't Ask, Don't Tell' Policy," transcript, 02 February 2010, http://www.jcs.mil/speech.aspx?id=1322.

38 Secretary of Defense, "Comprehensive Review on the Implementation of a Repeal of 10 U.S.C. §654," 02 March 2010, http://www.defense.gov/news/CRTOR.pdf.

39 Ibid.

40 DOD, Comprehensive Review, 97.

41 Ibid., 107.

42 Ibid., 115.

43 U.S. Department of Defense, *Report of the Comprehensive Review of the Issues Associated with a Repeal of "Don't Ask, Don't Tell": 2010 Department of Defense Survey of Spouses* (Arlington, VA: Department of Defense, 2010), www.defense.gov/home/features/2010/0610_dadt/DADTReport_FINAL_201011 30(secure-hires).pdf.

44 DOD, Comprehensive Review, 120.

45 Ibid.

46 Jesse Lee, "President Obama on the DOD Report on Don't Ask, Don't Tell," The White House Blog, 30 November 2010, http://www.whitehouse.gov/blog/2010/11/30/president-obama-dod-report-don-t-ask-don-t-tell.

47 ADM Mike Mullen, "JCS Speech: Testimony Regarding DOD 'Don't Ask, Don't Tell' Policy," transcript, 02 February 2010, http://www.jcs.mil/speech.aspx?id=1322.

48 U.S. Department of Defense, *Report of the Comprehensive Review of the Issues Associated with a Repeal of "Don't Ask, Don't Tell": Support Plan for Implementation* (Arlington, VA: Department of Defense, 2010), 69–75, www.defense.gov/home/features/2010/0610_dadt/DADTReport_FINAL_20101130(secure-hires).pdf.

49 "Defense of Marriage Act: Update to Prior Report," 23 January 2004, http://www.gao.gov/products/GAO-04-353R.

50 Commandant of the Marine Corps, Dependency Determination and Basic Allowance for Housing (BAH) Manual, MCO P1751.3F, 24 December 2003, 5, www.marines.mil/unit/hqmc/hqbat/Documents/BAH%20Manual.pdf.

51 Ibid., 5–6.

52 U.S.C. title 37, section 403.

53 DOD, Comprehensive Review, 154.

54 U.S. Department of Defense, A Survivor's Guide To Benefits: Taking Care Of Our Families (Arlington, VA: Department of Defense, 2011), 17.

55 Ibid., 9.

56 Undersecretary of Defense, Personnel, and Readiness, "Survivor Benefits Program," http://militarypay.defense.gov/Benefits/SBP.html.

57 U.S. Department of Defense, Department of Defense Financial Management Regulations (FMR), DOD 7000.14-R, 2001, vol. 7B, chap. 44, sec. 4401, http://comptroller.defense.gov/fmr/.

58 Ibid., chap. 44, sec. 440205, para. C.

59 Elaine Wilson, "Obama Announces 'Unprecedented Commitment' to Military Families," Armed Forces Press Service, 24 January 2011, http://www.defense.gov/ /News/NewsArticle.aspx?ID=62554.

60 Karen Jowers, "Four More States Offer Benefits to Spouses Forced to Quit Jobs," Army Times, 02 October 2007, http://www.armytimes.com/benefits/family_resources/military_spousejobs_071002w/.

61 DOD, Comprehensive Review, 82.

62 Ibid., 84.

63 Ibid., 85.

64 Ibid., 83, 119.

65 The state legislatures of Hawaii and Maryland have both recently approved bills allowing same-sex unions. The state of Iowa has repealed a law that allowed same-sex marriage and New Hampshire's legislature is considering doing the same.

66 Reference the comments of current and former homosexual service members surveyed during the Comprehensive Review as well as the statement of General George Marshall in 1941. See DOD, Comprehensive Review, 6, 82.

67 In her study, Margot Canaday cites that "throughout the twentieth century, the American military has brought together cultural, religious, and racial groups even when civilian life has been characterized by considerable prejudice towards such groups. Indeed, military integration has often proceeded at a faster pace than civilian integration." See Margot Canaday, "U.S. Military Integration of Religious, Ethnic, and Racial Minorities in the Twentieth Century," Palmcenter.org, 01 May, 2001, http://www.palmcenter.org/publications/dadt/u_s_military_integration_of_religious_ethnic_and_racial_minorities_in_the_twentieth_century.

68 DOD, Comprehensive Review, 84.

69 Ibid.

70 Ibid.

71 Office of the Assistant Secretary of Defense, "Statement by Secretary Robert Gates on Senate Vote to Repeal 'Don't Ask, Don't Tell,'" news release, 18 December 2010, http://www.defense.gov/releases/release.aspx?releaseid=14154.

72 Palm Center is a research organization affiliated with the Institute for Social, Behavioral, and Economic Research at the University of California, Santa Barbara.

73 Canaday, "U.S. Military Integration."

74 Admiral Mike Mullen, "DOD News Briefing with Secretary Gates and Adm.

Mullen from the Pentagon," transcript, 30 November 2010, http://www.defense.gov/transcripts/transcript.aspx?transcriptid =4728.

75 President Harry Truman, "Executive Order 9981," Harry S. Truman Library and Museum Web site, 26 July 1948, http://www.trumanlibrary.org/9981a.htm.

76 Morris J. MacGregor Jr., *Integration of the Armed Forces 1940–1965* (Washington, DC: Center of Military History, U.S. Army, 1985), chap 24, http://www.history.army.mil/books/integration/iaf-fm.htm.

77 Ibid.

78 Ibid.

79 Ibid.

80 Ibid.

81 Ibid.

82 Ibid.

83 Ibid., chap 1.

An Analysis of Opinion: The Impact of "Don't Ask, Don't Tell," Its Repeal, and the Proposed Plan to Implement the Repeal

by Maj Darrel L. Choat, USMC

The "Don't Ask, Don't Tell" (DADT) law has created an "anti-intellectual" climate surrounding the issues of sexuality and military service. This has contributed to a lack of understanding of DADT's compromise of military values such as justice and integrity as well as a lack of understanding of the illusory nature of DADT's purported benefits to unit cohesion and mission accomplishment.

Gay service members' view of DADT and its repeal contrast sharply to that of service members generally and of Marines in particular. Gay service members overwhelmingly believe DADT compromises their integrity and civil rights while providing no attendant benefits to the all-volunteer force. Gay service members also believe the DADT repeal will have a decidedly positive impact on all factors considered by this report, while Marine respondents in particular predict a neutral to negative impact. Non-Marine respondents believe repeal will have a neutral to slightly positive impact on these same factors. The difference in perspectives between the three populations, and in particular that of the Marines, can partially be explained by the low awareness of gay service members among Marines and statements of senior Marines that predict negative consequences of open service.

The seeds of this project were sown on 12 August 2010, when outgoing Commandant of the Marine Corps General James T. Conway addressed the 2010–11 Command and Staff College class. In response to a question about DADT, Conway told the assembled students that "90 percent to 95 percent of you believe DADT is working" and change to the law was not necessary. I did not believe his statement was accurate, and Conway did not poll the assembled students but instead told them what they thought. I began to consider how to determine an accurate statistic for Conway's statement, and I began developing an online survey that could help answer the question. As the debate about the repeal in Congress moved forward and the Pentagon review of DADT was released, the survey was modified to maintain relevance. I developed a three-part survey: (1) opinion regarding DADT; (2) opinion regarding DADT's repeal; and (3) opinion and recommendations regarding the Pentagon's proposed implementation plan. Survey data was collected from mid-January to mid-February 2011.

> *You gain strength, courage, and confidence by every experience in which you really stop to look fear in the face. You are able to say to yourself, 'I lived through this horror. I can take the next thing that comes along.' . . . You must do the thing you think you cannot do.*
>
> —Eleanor Roosevelt, *You Learn by Living*[1]

A Busy Year, 2010, and What Followed

On 22 December 2010 President Barack H. Obama signed H.R. 2965, the "Don't Ask, Don't Tell" Repeal Act of 2010, creating Public Law 111-321. This law repeals 10 United States Code §654, commonly known as "Don't Ask, Don't Tell" (DADT), 60 days after "the president transmits to the congressional defense committees a written certification signed by the president, secretary of defense, and chairman of the Joint Chiefs of Staff stating" that:[2]

(1) They have reviewed a report of the repeal of DADT on the impact on military readiness, military effectiveness and unit cohesion, recruiting/retention, and family readiness;

(2) The Department of Defense (DOD) has prepared the necessary policies and regulations to effect the repeal; and

(3) The repeal of DADT is consistent with the standards of military readiness, military effectiveness, unit cohesion, and recruiting and retention of the Armed Forces.

Throughout the following spring and summer, DOD and the Marine Corps complied with the above by preparing training materials and directing commanders to provide DADT repeal training to all Marines, soldiers, sailors, coast guardsmen, and airmen.[3] On 22 July 2011, President Obama, Secretary of Defense Leon E. Panetta, and Chairman of the Joint Chiefs of Staff Admiral Mike Mullen fulfilled the requirements of Public Law 111-321 and started the 60-day clock that would repeal DADT on 20 September 2011.

The RAND Corporation describes the DADT repeal and the consequent open service of homosexuals as analogous to the integration of African Americans into the military. Yet, desegregation of the armed services was begun by presidential directive, without congressional action and without formal input from active military members on 26 July 1948, when President Harry S. Truman signed Executive Order 9981.[4]

The most recent DADT repeal debate began in earnest on 27 January 2010 when President Obama said in his State of the Union address that he would "work with Congress and our military to finally repeal" DADT.[5] The 2010 debate in many ways resembled the 1993 debate that created DADT, with DADT proponents predicting dire consequences to unit cohesion and mission accomplishment in the event of repeal while repeal proponents insisted that action to respect the civil rights of gay Americans was long overdue.

A significant difference in the 2010 debate quickly became apparent as the leading advocates of repeal included Secretary of Defense Robert Gates, Chairman of the Joint Chiefs of Staff Mike Mullen, and Senate Armed Services Committee Chairman Carl M. Levin. In 1993, while then-Secretary of Defense Les Aspin supported President Bill Clinton's attempt to allow homosexuals to serve, he did so ineffectually. Secretary Aspin was sidelined by the allied opposition of Chairman of the Joint Chiefs of Staff Colin L. Powell and Senate Armed Services Committee Chairman Samuel A. Nunn. They controlled the terms of the debate and ultimately achieved approval of legislation that removed presidential discretion to integrate homosexuals into the armed services.

In 1993, the Clinton administration was unprepared for congressional Democrats to join the armed services' uniformed leadership in strident opposition to the open service of homosexuals. In an effort to avoid a replay of 1993, Secretary Gates executed a sophisticated and deliberate strategy that began with the 2 March 2010 appointment of Jeh Charles Johnson and General Carter F. Ham to conduct a review of issues associated with DADT's repeal. In unprecedented DOD action and in contrast to Truman's action to desegregate the armed services, by 30 November, the views of 115,052 active and reserve component service members had been collected and analyzed. The review concluded "the risk to repeal of DADT to overall military effectiveness is low."[6] This exhaustive review effort, aided by key congressional allies, injected momentum into the repeal effort during Congress' "lame duck" session in late 2010.

Litigation provided extra impetus for congressional action in 2010. Two federal appellate courts and the Central District Court of California required the government to show a heightened scrutiny standard to defend DADT rather than the "rational basis" standard that federal courts had accepted prior to 2003.[7] On 12 October the U.S. District Court of the Central District of California ruled the government did not demonstrate an "important governmental interest" to justify gay discharges and issued a worldwide injunction prohibiting DADT enforcement. Openly homosexual applicants were accepted at DOD's recruiting offices until this injunction was stayed on 20 October.[8] This court action further supported the Obama administration's argument for Congress' approval of an orderly transition to full repeal, as it became clear that legislative inaction would likely lead to court ordered integration of homosexuals.

Although President Obama, Secretary Gates, and Admiral Mullen clearly articulated their belief that the policy was discriminatory and unjustified, significant percentages of Marines, particularly the retired cadre, rallied behind the opposition of Army Chief of Staff General George W. Casey and the 34th and 35th Commandants of the Marine Corps—Generals James T. Conway and James F. Amos, respectively—to seek DADT's retention. The effect of this opposition on armed services culture, and in particular Marine Corps culture, is addressed below.

The thesis of this study is the DADT law allowed an "anti-intellectual" climate to pervade thinking surrounding the issues of sexuality and military service. This absence of critical thinking hindered understanding of DADT's compromise of values such as justice and integrity as well as promoted belief in the illusory nature of DADT's purported benefits to unit cohesion and mission accomplishment.

The "official" embrace of homophobia that DADT prompted within the armed services has granted a harmful prejudice unchallenged legitimacy in military culture. This occurred despite long-standing experience of successful integration of homosexuals into the militaries of U.S. allies; the successful integration of gay people into police and fire departments, the Central Intelligence Agency, the State Department, and Federal Bureau of Investigation; the absence of any scientific or empirical studies that found that homosexuals harmed unit cohesion; and the findings of multiple studies conducted since the 1957 Crittenden Report[9] that concluded that homosexuals were not a threat to national security and would not harm unit cohesion.

Research in this chapter will demonstrate that, despite the lack of evidence, unjustified fears of homosexuals permeate the Marine Corps and, if not addressed, will diminish the justice and respect that gay Marines, soldiers, sailors, airmen, and coast guardsmen have earned. Further, these strong beliefs exist in sharp contrast to the actual experiences of Marines who have served with known homosexuals and with the experiences of gay Marines.

This chapter begins with a brief review of the history of sodomy laws and the service of homosexuals in the armed services. In order to test the thesis, an online survey was developed to assess active duty service members' opinions regarding DADT, the repeal, and the Pentagon's Support Plan for Implementation.[10] Full survey results are online at http://www.mcu.usmc.mil/pages/dadt.aspx.

> *Naval tradition? Monstrous. It's nothing but rum, sodomy, religion and the lash.*
>
> —Winston Churchill, *The Harold Nicolson Diaries*[11]

A History of Sexuality and the Armed Services

In 1916, administrative and sodomy provisions of military law were revised for the first time in 100 years to preclude service of homosexuals for mental or physical fitness reasons.[12] Prior to that time, the notion of "homosexual" identity did not exist and the service of "homosexuals" was not at issue. Sex that was not reproductive was socially proscribed, and any exhibition of "perverted" or "unnatural" acts such as heterosexual or homosexual sodomy was prohibited by military law. This prohibition followed the mores of Western society.[13]

The 1916 update reflected an evolution in the understanding of human sexuality. In the late 1880s, the European "sexologist" movement first included homosexuality as a "deviant" practice and by the late 1800s, "pathological models of homosexuality were standard." In 1952, the American Psychiatric Association (APA) published its first *Diagnostic and Statistical Manual of Mental Disorders* and included homosexuality as a mental disorder, reflecting an understanding of (or bias toward) homosexuality as a disease, neurological defect, or mental illness. This classification was considered controversial because research had not established any scientific or empirical basis for these diagnoses.[14]

The "mental disorder" view was officially retained by the psychiatric community until 1973, when the APA removed homosexuality from its listing of mental disorders.[15] In the accompanying position statement on *Homosexuality and Civil Rights*, approved by APA's board of trustees and assembly in 1973, the APA stated that "homosexuality per se implies no impairment of judgment, stability, reliability, or general social or vocational capabilities" and "deplore[d] all public and private discrimination against homosexuals in such areas as employment, housing, public accommodation, and licensing, and no burden of proof of such . . . shall be placed upon homosexuals greater than that imposed on any other persons." The position statement also recommended civil rights legislation be enacted to protect homosexuals and repeal all discriminatory legislation that singled out homosexual acts between consenting adults.[16] The APA and the American Psychological Association now consider same-sex sexual and romantic attractions, feelings, and behaviors to be normal and positive variations of human sexuality.[17]

The U.S. armed services approach to homosexuality in the twentieth century has, albeit with a time lag, followed the medical and psychiatric community's evolving view of sexuality that has led to today's notions of homosexuality, heterosexuality, and bisexuality. The nascent science of "sexology" led to World War I–era revisions, and as the United States geared up for World War II, concerns about mental health prompted attempts to screen out homosexuals through the use of pseudoscientific stereotypes such as effeminacy and an interest in interior decorating or dancing. In 1949, the new Department of Defense issued a regulation that stated gay men and lesbians were "unsuitable for military service," and banned homosexuals whether or not evidence of homosexual conduct was present. In 1950, Congress adopted the Uniform Code of Military Justice (UCMJ), which criminalizes homosexual and heterosexual sodomy.[18]

In the 1970s, court cases challenged the homosexual exclusion policy and identified wide implementation disparities across the services. To achieve consistency and solidify the legality of the exclusion, the Carter administration proposed and the Reagan administration implemented a new policy in 1982. This DOD directive standardized treatment of homosexuals across the services, deemed homosexuals "unsuitable" for military service, declared homosexuality "incompatible with military service," and mandated separation.

To provide a rationale for the ban, the "gay menace list" first appeared in DOD Directive 1332.14, Enlisted Administrative Separations of 28 January.[19] Paragraph 1a of the below directive provided the "legitimate government interest," i.e., impairment of the accomplishment of military mission, to justify discrimination against homosexuals.[20] This language represented a shift in justification for homosexual discharges from one of physical or mental unfitness to one of negative consequences on mission accomplishment, discipline, good order, and morale. No empirical or scientific evidence was available or cited to support it.[21]

<u>Homosexuality</u> (Part 1, Section H)

1. Basis

    a. Homosexuality is incompatible with military service. The presence in the military environment of persons who engage in homosexual conduct or who, by their statement, demonstrate a propensity to engage in homosexual conduct, seriously impairs the accomplishment of the military mission. The presence of such members adversely affects the ability of the military services to maintain discipline, good order, and morale; to foster mutual trust and confidence among service members; to ensure the integrity of the system of rank and command; to facilitate assignment and worldwide deployment of service members who frequently must live and work under close conditions affording minimal privacy; to recruit and retain members of the military services; to maintain the public acceptability of military service; and to prevent breaches of security.[22]

The legislative findings of 10 United States Code §654, commonly known as the 1993 DADT law, followed the pattern of this directive and created 15 assertions:[23]

(1) Congress has the exclusive authority to raise and support the military as well as establish qualifications and conditions of service.

(2) There is no constitutional right to serve in the armed forces.

(3)–(13) Eleven statements regarding the purpose of military service; the sacrifices of service; the unique nature of military service; the need for high morale, good order and discipline, and unit cohesion; the criticality of unit cohesion to combat capability; the differences between military and civilian life such as the critical role of unit cohesion and restrictions on personal behavior unacceptable in civilian life; that military standards of conduct are pervasive and apply 24 hours per day; that worldwide deployment requires working and living conditions that are spartan, primitive, and that provide little privacy; and the armed forces must exclude those who create an unacceptable risk to morale, good order and discipline, and unit cohesion.

(14) The prohibition against homosexuals is a long-standing element of military law required by unique circumstances of military service.

(15) The presence of persons who demonstrate a propensity or intent to engage in homosexual acts creates an unacceptable risk to morale, good order and discipline, and unit cohesion.

In "additional views" submitted into *Congressional Record* during the 9 September Senate debate of DADT, Senator Edward M. "Ted" Kennedy (D-MA) rebuts points 2, 14, and 15, noting no scientific evidence or studies were presented or cited during the hearings to support them or homosexual exclusion in general. Further, Senator Kennedy not only disagreed with the findings, but he also stated that the committee chose to ignore evidence found in the 1993 RAND study, two Personnel Security Research and Education Center studies,[24] two General Accounting Office (GAO) studies,[25] the experience of NATO allies, and the experience of police and fire departments that proved the exact opposite.[26]

Lieutenant General R. Minter Alexander (who in 1993 was directed by then-Secretary Aspin to chair a military working group to make recommendations on homosexual service),[27] Colonel Om Prakash (in an October 2009 article in *Joint Forces Quarterly*),[28] and Aaron Belkin (in a summer 2003 *Parameters* article)[29] each state that there was no empirical or scientific evidence presented or available in 1993 to support the ban. Prakash says, "The stated premise of the law (DADT)—to protect unit cohesion and combat effectiveness—is not supported by any scientific studies."[30] They also state that simple leadership could adequately address any challenges that may arise due to openly gay service members. The RAND study commissioned by DOD in 1993 also found no evidence or studies to support the 1983 "gay menace list," and its 2011 update found no studies or empirical evidence had been completed in the interim to support the homosexual exclusion.[31]

In *Unfriendly Fire*, Nathaniel Frank charges that Samuel A. Nunn Jr. actively suppressed information during the 1993 hearings that would have supported the open service of gay men and women. Specifically, Nunn withdrew an invitation to testify sent to former Republican Senator Barry M. Goldwater after learning the conservative icon would advocate for the service for open homosexuals, and he declined to include any researchers who participated in the RAND or GAO studies.[32] Senator Kennedy states that his suggested witnesses, who would have provided views in support of open service, were not included in the hearings.[33] Belkin says retired Army Colonel Lucian K. Truscott III was deleted from a witness list after Nunn learned he would provide positive examples of openly serving gay soldiers.[34]

Nonetheless, federal officials charged with defending DADT against constitutional challenges have consistently used the 1993 congressional findings to argue the military necessity of the ban. Accepting the argument that military life is fundamentally different from civilian life, courts have granted the military broad latitude in "matters relating to military service, organization, and personnel." So long as the U.S. military could demonstrate a "rational basis" standard in discriminating in accession and retention policies by referencing the 1993 findings, the courts accepted the military practice.[35]

The hurdle faced by gay service members in challenging the ban became even more significant with passage of DADT in 1993, as they were now required to disprove the legislative findings as well as prove that DADT serves no rational military interest. The legal landscape began to change in 2009, however, when two federal appellate courts held that the "rational basis" standard was not appropriate and required the government to defend DADT under a heightened level of scrutiny. The U.S. Court of Appeals for the First Circuit found DADT constitutional under heightened scrutiny, while the Ninth Circuit found that DADT did not "'significantly further' an 'important governmental interest.'" On 9 September, the Central

California District Court found that the "government failed to show that DADT significantly furthers the government's interest in military readiness or unit cohesion," officially acknowledging what DADT opponents had known since 1993.[36]

The political significance of DADT's findings was also demonstrated in 2009–10 discourse by its proponents. For example, in a 12 January 2010 *Washington Times* commentary, former Marine Commandant Carl E. Mundy cites no facts or evidence to support DADT other than the 1993 legislative findings.[37] General Mundy also refers to support for DADT expressed by a 2009 "Open Letter to The President and Members of Congress" that was signed by more than 1,160 retired general and flag officers. As prima facie evidence of the danger of homosexuals, the letter cites as evidence only the assertions found in DOD Directive 1332.14 and in DADT's legislative findings.[38]

Retired Army General John M. Shalikashvili, chairman of the Joint Chiefs of Staff from 1993 to 1997, in a 19 June 2009 *Washington Post* commentary, rebuts the letter by stating, "Not only is there no evidence to support these conclusions, but research shows conclusively that openly gay service members would not undermine military readiness." He chides the letter's signatories: "My colleagues made claims as if no new knowledge has been acquired over past decades, during which time Israel and Britain joined more than 20 other nations to allow openly gay individuals to serve without overall problems." General Shalikashvili warns that "for such a large group of retired senior officers to oppose the inevitable could cause the very disruptions they predict."[39]

As recently as 14 December 2010, the current Marine Corps Commandant, General James F. Amos, also acknowledged there was no empirical basis for the claims that open homosexuals would harm unit cohesion. Despite this acknowledgement, he was firm in his opposition to repeal. From a roundtable discussion, *Stars and Stripes* reported,

> When pressed to explain exactly what a breakdown of "unit cohesion" could look like and why it would endanger Marines in combat, or the larger war effort, Amos said he was "unsure" but that the significant concern of breakdown was good enough for him. . . . "I can't explain what the expectations are. I can't explain what they think might happen."[40]

As Dr. Lawrence J. Korb, who served as assistant secretary of defense for manpower, reserve affairs, installations, and logistics during the Reagan administration and who was in charge of implementing the exclusion policy in 1982, stated in 2010, "Every study done by or for the Pentagon going back to the 1957 Crittenden Report, which was done for the secretary of the Navy, shows that allowing openly gay people to serve does not undermine military readiness. In fact, those studies prove the opposite."[41] Dr. Belkin, associate professor of political science at San Francisco State University, suggests that political and military leaders who remain unwilling to join most of the rest of NATO (in allowing homosexuals to serve) "should at least have the integrity to admit that current American policy is based on prejudice, not on military necessity."[42]

Survey Structure

The survey included three major sections:

(1) Historical effect. This report's survey sought a solid measure of DADT's support or opposition and perceived impact in the targeted population by asking opinion of DADT's effect on 15 characteristics such as honesty, integrity, unit cohesion, and mission accomplishment. Respondents were asked if they had served with a "known homosexual" to determine if a correlation existed with support or opposition to DADT and, in subsequent questions, to explore whether service with a "known homosexual" caused a moral dilemma for the respondent.

(2) Effect of repeal. This survey sought a solid measure of the support for or opposition to DADT repeal in the targeted populations. Questions explored the respondent's support or opposition to repeal by asking opinion of repeal's impact on the 15 characteristics.

(3) Proposed implementation plan. Six key sections of the plan were summarized to gain the respondents' opinions and comments. Questions explored the level of discomfort or challenge that serving with an openly gay subordinate or superior would cause the respondent.

Surveyed Populations

Respondents of this survey are composed of four distinct populations (descriptions of each population are in this chapter's appendix):

(1) Volunteers from the U.S. Marine Corps Command and Staff College (CSC)

student body. Respondents who agreed to participate received an electronic link to the survey. Out of 101 Marines and 58 non-Marines (Army, Navy, Air Force, and Coast Guard), 53 CSC students agreed to complete the survey. Of the 50 CSC students who completed the survey, 32 were Marines, 16 were non-Marines, and 2 were civilians. Three did not complete the survey.

(2) Volunteers from the Expeditionary Warfare School (EWS) student body. Out of 193 Marines and 27 non-Marines (Army and Air Force service members), 58 EWS students agreed to complete the survey. Of the 50 who completed the survey, 46 were Marines, and 4 were soldiers. No Air Force students agreed to participate. Eight volunteers did not complete the survey.

(3) Active duty Marines and service members known by the author, and service members they recommended. A request to participate was sent to 192 service members (Marine, Army, Air Force, Navy, and Coast Guard). The service affiliation of the 94 respondents was 79 Marines, 4 soldiers, 2 airmen, 3 sailors, and 6 coast guardsmen. Ninety-eight recipients did not respond.

(4) Volunteers from a Facebook group ("Outserve") that includes only gay active duty service members. The service affiliation of the 166 gay service members who took the survey was 35 Marines, 34 soldiers, 62 airmen, 33 sailors, and 3 coast guardsmen. A link to the survey with an explanation and request to participate was posted on the site.

Significant effort was made to draft the requests in a neutral tone to achieve participation from across the spectrum. The first survey question was written to provide those with opinions at either extreme the opportunity to register their opinion and to create a neutral tone. The survey results contain opinions at both extremes, indicating some success at achieving a neutral tone. The support for DADT among surveyed Marines was 58 percent, within the range of responses from the professionally and randomly administered Pentagon survey of service members. No claim is made that the survey sample is random or representative of the Corps or other services. However, the survey results can provide insight into the thinking of some service members at a "snapshot" in time.

The analysis compares and contrasts the results from three respondent groups: "All Marine," "Non-Marine," and "Gay Service Members." The all-Marine results combine the responses of all Marine respondents from surveyed populations 1, 2, and 3. The non-Marine results are the Army, Navy, Air Force, and Coast Guard respondents from surveyed populations 1, 2, and 3. The all-gay results are from surveyed population 4.

All of the survey's supporting documentation and data are available on-line at http://www.mcu.usmc.mil/pages/dadt.aspx. To preserve the ability of future scholars to access this information, the Gray Marine Corps Research Center in Quantico, Virginia, also houses several electronic and hard copies of the survey data.

> *How does one determine when a law is just or unjust? A just law is a man-made code that squares with the moral law or the law of God. An unjust law is a code that is out of harmony with the moral law. To put it in terms of St. Thomas Aquinas: An unjust law is a human law that is not rooted in eternal law and natural law. Any law that uplifts the human personality is just. Any law that degrades human personality is unjust. All segregation statutes are unjust because segregation distorts the soul and damages the personality. It gives the segregator a false sense of superiority and the segregated a false sense of inferiority.*
>
> —Martin Luther King Jr., "Letter from Birmingham City Jail"[43]

Opinion Regarding the Effect of DADT

The analysis of survey results illustrates a trichotomy of views. Aggregated Marine responses consistently cluster at one end, "all-gay" service member responses consistently fell at the other end, and non-Marine respondents consistently fell between.

This trichotomy is illustrated by Table 2.1, in which 57.9 percent of Marine respondents agreed or strongly agreed that open homosexuality was incompatible with military service in contrast to 35.2 percent of non-Marines and 2.1 percent of gay service members. The opinion distribution of the three populations in subsequent questions, while sometimes more subtle, consistently follows this pattern.

Table 2.2 summarizes the responses that explore DADT's impact on leadership traits and principles and intangible factors such as camaraderie, mission accomplishment, and war-fighting capability. Table 2.2 provides a weighted average of

The End of Don't Ask, Don't Tell

Table 2.1 How much do you disagree or agree with the following:

In my opinion and irrespective of the repeal of the DADT law, open homosexuality is incompatible with military service.

Respondents	All Marine		Non-Marine		All Gay	
Answer Options	Response Count	Response Percent	Response Count	Response Percent	Response Count	Response Percent
Strongly Disagree	20	13.2%	11	32.4%	128	87.7%
Disagree	44	28.9%	11	32.4%	15	10.3%
Total Disagree	64	42.1%	19	64.8%	143	98.0%
Agree	34	22.4%	6	17.6%	1	0.7%
Strongly Agree	54	35.5%	6	17.6%	2	1.4%
Total Agree	88	57.9%	10	35.2%	3	2.1%
Answered Question	152		34		146	

responses for each group and illustrates the views of each.

Gay service members indicated a belief that DADT was discriminatory (88 percent) and wasted resources (48.2 percent). The most similar response of gay service members and Marines, 16.3 percent and 23.6 percent, respectively, was the percentage responding that DADT had a neutral effect on unit cohesion and mission accomplishment. Nearly twice the percentage of Marine versus non-Marine responses indicated a belief that DADT served a valuable purpose (52.2 percent vs. 32.3 percent) and protected unit cohesion and mission accomplishment (47.1 percent vs. 27.8 percent).

While 27.8 percent of non-Marines responses indicated DADT was appropriately repealed, this outcome was more than two times larger than the 13.4 percent of Marines who responded that DADT was appropriately repealed. Not surprisingly, 88.0 percent of gay service members believe DADT was appropriately repealed.

The summarized values provided for each sampled population, or "rating average" are a weighted average. For example, the weighted average of the 157 all-Marine responses to the first question, "What was DADT's effect on the moral character of military service?" was 3.29. Since "3" is equivalent to "neutral/no effect" and "4" is equivalent to "positive," the weighted average of Marine responses to this question was on the positive side of neutral. In other words, the average

Table 2.2 In my opinion, the "Don't Ask Don't Tell" (DADT) law:
(Check all that apply.)

Answer Options	All Marine		Non-Marine		All Gay	
	Response Percent	Response Count	Response Percent	Response Count	Response Percent	Response Count
Served a valuable purpose and should have been retained.	52.2%	82	33.3%	12	0.0%	0
Protected unit cohesion and furthered mission accomplishment.	47.1%	74	27.8%	10	3.6%	6
Neither supported nor harmed unit cohesion and mission accomplishment.	23.6%	37	36.1%	13	16.3%	27
Wasted resources and was appropriately repealed.	8.3%	13	13.9%	5	48.2%	80
Was discriminatory and was appropriately repealed.	13.4%	21	27.8%	10	88.0%	146
Answered Question		152		34		146
Skipped Question		5		2		20

Marine response regarding DADT's effect was on the positive side of neutral for all characteristics except "honesty between service members." At a weighted average of 2.87, the collective Marine responses indicate DADT's effect on honesty was on the negative side of neutral. Marine respondents' most positive ratings of DADT's effect were on combat effectiveness, unit cohesion, mission accomplishment, and warfighting capability. The weighted average of these responses was over 3.50, indicating that Marine respondents collectively believe DADT's effect on these three characteristics was more positive than neutral.

The weighted averages of non-Marine responses to DADT's impact were consistently within plus or minus 0.5 of "3," or "neutral/no effect," with one exception. The weighted average of non-Marine responses of DADT's effect on "honesty between service members" was 2.47. This means non-Marines as a whole rated DADT's effect on honesty just slightly more negative than neutral. The second lowest response for non-Marines was DADT's effect on "justice" at 2.61. This response indicates non-Marines as a whole rated DADT's effect on justice slightly more neutral than negative.

The weighted averages of gay service members' responses illustrate a view in sharp contrast to the other surveyed populations. Gay respondents rated DADT's impact on seven of the fifteen characteristics between very negative and negative. Of the remaining eight characteristics, six were rated more negative than neutral. The remaining two characteristics, combat effectiveness and mission accomplishment, were rated at 2.51 and 2.46 respectively, meaning gay respondents saw DADT's effect on these characteristics just slightly more neutral than negative. The characteristics gay service members indicated were most negatively affected by DADT were "honesty between service members" and "justice" with a weighted average of 1.53 and 1.61 respectively.

Table 2.3 What was DADT's effect on the following:

Answer Options	Very Negative	Negative	Neutral/ No effect	Positive	Very Positive
Numeric Rating Scale	1	2	3	4	5
Survey Population	All Marine		Non-Marine		All Gay
	Rating Average		Rating Average		Rating Average
The moral character of military service	3.29		3.03		1.89
The warrior ethos of military service	3.45		3.36		2.17
Trust between service members	3.31		2.94		1.74
Honesty between service members	2.87		2.47		1.53
Integrity of the chain of command	3.27		2.92		1.83
Combat effectiveness	3.61		3.25		2.51
Loyalty to the Marine Corps (or Service)	3.33		3.17		2.24
Communication between service members	3.05		2.89		1.88
Loyalty to peers and subordinates	3.30		3.06		2.05
Camaraderie	3.46		3.28		1.99
Unit cohesion	3.63		3.44		2.20
Mission accomplishment	3.54		3.28		2.46
Recruiting and retention	3.29		2.92		1.99
Justice	2.98		2.61		1.61
Warfighting capability of U.S. forces	3.52		3.28		2.39
Answered Question	157		36		166

Table 2.4 also illustrates a sharp contrast between Marine respondents and gay service members. Respondents were asked to indicate how much they agreed or disagreed with six questions that suggested possible DADT impacts with a value of "1" assigned to "strongly disagree" and "4" assigned to "strongly agree."

The weighted averages of Marine responses to five of the six questions fell between "disagree" and "agree." The only question where the weighted average of Marine responses fell between disagree and strongly disagree, at 1.78, was "DADT increased workplace tension." At 2.48, the only question with which Marines barely agreed was "DADT forced some service members to compromise their integrity or gave the impression of compromised integrity."

Non-Marine responses were slightly less equivocal than Marine responses. At 2.86, or nearly agree, the highest weighted average non-Marine response was to the statement "DADT forced some service members to compromise their integrity or gave the impression of compromised integrity." Non-Marine respondents evenly split on whether DADT had a negative or positive effect on civil rights and agreed more than disagreed that DADT was based on prejudice and stereotypes, and compromised the chain of command.

Responses of gay service members were the most straightforward. The weighted average of the responses to five of the six questions was between agree and strongly agree and the remaining average fell between strongly disagree and disagree. The three responses with the strongest agreement: DADT compromised integrity, compromised civil rights, and was based on prejudice and stereotypes. The one question in which gay service members' responses fell between strongly disagree and disagree was "DADT was based on strong evidence that homosexuals would harm mission accomplishment."

Gay service members view DADT as a policy that compromises civil rights and integrity. Their honorable service demonstrates to gay service members that they do not harm mission accomplishment and that the policy is based on prejudice and stereotypes. Marines, in part because of their low awareness of gay service members among them (illustrated in Table 5.2), are the least likely to recognize the inherent prejudice in DADT.

Table 2.4 How much do you agree or disagree with the following statements?

Answer Options	Strongly Disagree	Disagree	Agree	Strongly Agree	
Numeric Rating Scale	1	2	3	4	
Surveyed Population	All Marine		Non-Marine		All Gay
	Rating Average		Rating Average		Rating Average
DADT forced some service members to compromise their integrity or gave the impression of compromised integrity.	2.48		2.86		3.82
DADT compromised the civil rights of homosexual service members.	2.19		2.50		3.74
DADT was based on solid evidence that open homosexuals would harm mission accomplishment.	2.35		2.44		1.69
DADT increased work place tension.	1.78		2.17		3.19
DADT was based on prejudice and stereotypes.	2.12		2.60		3.69
DADT contributed to harmful suspicions or negative perceptions of some service members.	2.14		2.47		3.61
DADT compromised the chain of command when homosexuality appeared to be selectively overlooked or investigated.	2.32		2.62		3.46
Answered Question	157		36		166

> *When a subject people moves toward freedom, they are not creating a cleavage, but are revealing a cleavage which apologists of the old order sought to conceal.*
>
> —Martin Luther King, Jr., *Stride Toward Freedom: The Montgomery Story*[44]

Impact of DADT Repeal

This section examines opinion regarding DADT's repeal.[45] For Marine respondents, Table 3.1 shows the highest weighted averages were 2.85 and 2.79 for DADT's repeal on integrity and justice, meaning Marine respondents believe the repeal would have the most neutral effect (rather than negative) effect on integrity and justice. These highest averages among the populations correlated to the greatest number of Marines that believed the repeal would have a positive effect on integrity (26.3 percent) and justice (19.1 percent) as compared to any other factor. In a near-mirror image to Table 2.1, Marine respondents believe the repeal's most negative impacts will be on combat effectiveness, camaraderie, and unit cohesion. These averages indicate the greatest number of Marines believe repeal will have a negative effect on unit cohesion (67.1 percent), and the second and third greatest number of Marines believe repeal will have a negative effect on camaraderie (58.5 percent) and combat effectiveness (57.2 percent).

The weighted average of non-Marine responses regarding repeal again fell on both sides of neutral/no effect with a positive effect expected for nine of the traits and a barely negative effect predicted for six of the traits. While of a different absolute value, non-Marines predict the most positive effect would be on the same two characteristics as Marines, that of integrity and justice, with a value of 3.41 for each.

Gay service members predict that the repeal will have a positive to very positive effect on 10 of the 15 characteristics, demonstrating a slightly less enthusiastic expectation of the repeal as compared to their more strongly negative sentiment regarding DADT's actual effect. While gay service members predict the "least" positive impact of the repeal on warrior ethos, prestige, combat effectiveness, mission accomplishment, and warfighting capability, this is a logical response for service members who do not believe their presence has negatively impacted these factors. Although still a "positive" prediction with weighted averages just under 4.0, gay service members predict DADT repeal will have the least positive impact on these characteristics.

Similar to the results of Table 2.1, in which gay service members believed DADT had the most negative impact on the moral factors of service such as honesty and integrity, gay service members also indicate their belief that repeal will have the greatest positive impact on moral factors. Gay service members predict the repeal will have the greatest impact on integrity and justice, with weighted averages of 4.42 and 4.32 respectively. While the absolute values differ, Marine, non-Marine, and gay service members believe the repeal's effect will be most positive on integrity and justice.

Table 3.1 What effect do you think the DADT
repeal will have on the following:

Answer Options	Very Negative	Negative	Neutral/ No effect	Positive	Very Positive
Numeric Rating Scale	1	2	3	4	5
Surveyed Population	All Marine		Non-Marine		All Gay
	Rating Average		Rating Average		Rating Average
The moral character of military service	2.49		2.97		4.07
The warrior ethos of military service	2.38		2.82		3.74
The prestige of military service	2.36		2.82		3.84
The honor of military service	2.58		3.06		4.12
The integrity of service members	2.85		3.41		4.42
Combat effectiveness	2.28		2.94		3.73
Loyalty to the Marine Corps (or Service)	2.70		3.15		4.08
Service members' ability to focus on their primary mission	2.36		2.97		4.08
Loyalty to peers and subordinates	2.53		3.18		4.10
Camaraderie	2.28		2.82		4.08
Unit cohesion	2.15		2.79		4.03
Mission accomplishment	2.47		3.06		3.79
Recruiting and retention	2.61		3.26		4.20
Justice	2.79		3.41		4.32
Warfighting capability of U.S. forces	2.48		3.06		3.81
Answered Question	152		34		146
Skipped Question	5		2		20

With a weighted average of 1.12, gay service members most strongly disagreed with the statement, "The repeal of DADT will prompt me to voluntarily separate from my service earlier than I had previously planned." Marine respondents showed the least commitment to continued service after DADT's repeal with a weighted average of 1.79. Consistent with previous trends, non-Marine respondents fell between the extremes.

The weighted average of gay service members' responses predominantly fell between agree and strongly agree that DADT repeal would positively impact recruiting and retention decisions, increase honor and integrity in decision making, increase integrity of professional relationships, and increase justice in recruiting, retention, and evaluation decisions. Gay service members also expect DADT repeal to create opportunities to rebuild cooperation with universities that have declined to host ROTC programs. The one exception to the positive responses was the weighted average of 1.89, indicating that gay service members strongly disagree to disagree with the statement that DADT repeal would harm cooperation with religious institutions that support service members.

Marine respondents' weighted averages of 2.55 and 2.49 indicate their collective opinion that the repeal will have an essentially neutral effect on cooperation with religious institutions and with universities that have declined to host ROTC programs. Weighted averages between 2.06 and 2.18 indicate Marines believe the repeal will have a neutral to slightly negative effect on honesty and integrity of decision making, integrity of personal relationships, justice in evaluation, recruiting and retention decisions, and integrity between service members and their chain of command.

Non-Marine weighted averages again fell between the Marine and all-gay results with one exception: non-Marines predict that the repeal will have a more negative effect on religious cooperation than do Marines.

While the lukewarm Marine responses to DADT repeal are consistent with expectations and consistent across the survey, the responses to questions regarding the impact of DADT repeal on integrity warrants examination, specifically, the collective disagreement of Marines with two statements: "the repeal of DADT will increase the integrity of professional relationships between service members" and "the repeal of DADT will increase integrity between service members and their chain of command."

If DADT required gay service members to create the impression among coworkers that they were heterosexual, even if coworkers knew or suspected otherwise, then, as Mullen stated, honesty and integrity suffer in multiple ways. It seems counterintuitive to assert that removal of an absolute prohibition on com-

Table 3.2 How much do you disagree or agree with the following statements related to the repeal of DADT? The repeal of DADT will . . .

Answer Options	Strongly Disagree	Disagree	Agree	Strongly Agree	
Numeric Rating Scale	1	2	3	4	
Surveyed Population	All Marine		Non-Marine		All Gay
	Rating Average		Rating Average		Rating Average
Prompt me to voluntarily separate from my service earlier than I had previously planned.	1.79		1.36		1.12
Allow recruiting and retention decisions to be based on qualifications, conduct, and performance to a greater degree.	2.32		2.65		3.52
Enhance the honor of military service by increasing the honesty and integrity of military decision making.	2.06		2.68		3.59
Harm cooperation with religious institutions that provide chaplains to support service members.	2.55		2.35		1.89
Provide opportunities to renew cooperation and build public support for the Armed Services, for example, among academic communities that barred ROTC units.	2.49		2.88		3.49
Increase the integrity of professional relationships among service members.	2.10		2.69		3.53
Increase respect for military service by enhancing the perception of justice in evaluation, recruiting, and retention decisions.	2.13		2.69		3.52
Increase integrity between service members and their chain of command.	2.18		2.78		3.55
Answered Question	152		34		146
Skipped Question	5		2		20

munication and resultant obfuscation would not have a positive impact on integrity. Marines' collective responses, however, indicate a belief that not only would repeal have no *positive* impact on integrity, but 67.7 percent either disagreed or strongly disagreed with the statement that DADT repeal would increase the integrity of personal relationships between service members. Sixty-one point one percent either disagreed or strongly disagreed with the statement that DADT repeal would increase integrity between service members and their chain of command. Respective percentages of non-Marines who disagreed or strongly disagreed with these two statements were 44.1 percent and 38.3 percent, a respective difference of 23 percentage points in both cases. Of note is not only the absolute strength of Marine disagreement, but the relative difference between Marines and non-Marines.

While many explanations could be suggested to explain this absolute and relative level of disagreement, this report suggests only two: (1) A significant segment of Marine respondents are so implacably opposed to the service of open homosexuals that they reflexively refuse to acknowledge any negative effect of DADT and any corresponding benefit of repeal, and (2) Marine respondents' low awareness of gay service members leads to a lack of awareness of the negative consequences of a policy that prevents open and honest communication.

Table 3.3 demonstrates a surprising result. Gay service members and non-Marines have greater confidence in the capability of the UCMJ to handle issues of proper personal relationships, public displays of affection, and harassment that may arise due to the repeal of DADT than do Marines. While 49.3 percent of Marines do not believe the UCMJ will be adequate, only 24.7 percent of gay service members and 29.4 percent of non-Marines agree.

In contrast, 75.4 percent of gay service members and 70.6 percent of non-Marines have confidence in the UCMJ to handle issues that may arise due to the repeal but only 50.7 percent of Marines do. This could be an example of Marine fear of change and fear of the unknown. The higher percentages of Marines that have not served with someone they knew to be gay and that do not know civilians that are gay may have been manifested as greater fear of change or of the unknown.

Table 3.3 How much do you disagree or agree with the following:

The UCMJ provides the chain of command the necessary tools to address issues of proper personal relationships, public displays of affection, and harassment that may arise due to the repeal of DADT.

	All Marine		Non-Marine		All Gay	
Rating Average	2.40		2.97		2.99	
Answer Options	Response Count	Response Percent	Response Count	Response Percent	Response Count	Response Percent
Strongly Disagree	31	20.4%	5	14.7%	14	9.6%
Disagree	44	28.9%	5	14.7%	22	15.1%
Total Disagree	**75**	**49.3%**	**10**	**29.4%**	**36**	**24.7%**
Agree	57	37.5%	14	41.2%	56	38.4%
Strongly Agree	20	13.2%	10	29.4%	54	37.0%
Total Agree	**77**	**50.7%**	**24**	**70.6%**	**110**	**75.4%**
Answered Question	152		34		146	
Skipped Question	5		2		20	

I have served with homosexuals since 1968 . . . everybody in the military has, and we understand that.

No matter how I look at the issue, I cannot escape being troubled by the fact that we have in place a policy which forces young men and women to lie about who they are in order to defend their fellow citizens. For me personally, it comes down to integrity—theirs as individuals and ours as an institution.

—Chairman of the Joint Chiefs of Staff
Adm Mike Mullen, 2 February 2010[46]

Moral Conflict

Admiral Mullen's testimony before the Senate Armed Services Committee moved the repeal debate beyond the State of the Union address and discussions among gay and Democratic activists and into the congressional realm. Mullen's framing the problem of DADT as an integrity issue not only for gay service members but for the DOD as a whole represented a significant change in the dialogue.

Mullen's statement highlighted the problematic nature of the policy, which forces heterosexual and homosexual troops into a moral conundrum about integrity. To explore this question, respondents were asked if they had served with a "known" homosexual.[47] Respondents answering affirmatively were directed to two more questions that explored whether they believed this knowledge created a conflict between an obligation to follow all laws and regulations and personal loyalty to a gay service member or their personal principles of justice.

Question 3.3 was designed to explore the moral dilemma that DADT created for those members who served with someone that they "knew," as opposed to "suspected," was gay. DADT did not require service members to act on suspicions and forbade them from asking questions that would provide a definitive answer to the nature of someone's sexuality. Proximity, camaraderie, and a variety of circumstances often lead to knowledge, as expressed by Admiral Mullen, that prompts a service member to know of the orientation of another service member. The survey results indicate that, at minimum, "purposeful ignorance" of the presence of homosexuals is common.

Table 4.1 indicates slightly more than 46 percent of Marine respondents served with someone they knew to be homosexual. This contrasted with 65 percent of non-Marine respondents who indicated they had served with a homosexual and just over 98 percent of gay respondents who indicated they had served with a homosexual service member. The overwhelming response of gay service members could indicate the prevalence of gay service members was much higher than that perceived by heterosexual service members.

Table 4.1 Have you served with a U.S. service member that you knew to be homosexual?

Answer Options	All Marine		Non-Marine		All Gay	
	Response Percent	Response Count	Response Percent	Response Count	Response Percent	Response Count
Yes	46.2%	72	63.9%	23	98.1%	159
No	53.8%	84	36.1%	13	1.9%	3
Answered Question		156		36		162
Skipped Question		1		0		4

Of Marine respondents who served with a "known" homosexual, 30 percent either disagreed or strongly disagreed with the statement "prior to the December 2010 repeal, I faithfully executed my duty to enforce DADT when confronted with knowledge of a DADT violation" (Table 4.2). Further, 41.4 percent of this subset of Marine respondents agreed or strongly agreed with the statement "DADT created situations where I felt I had to either compromise my sense of justice to a fellow service member or my duty to comply with the law." More gay respondents found themselves confronted with this dilemma as 67.5 percent indicated they did not execute their duty to enforce DADT, and 73.3 percent indicated DADT created situations in which they believed they either had to compromise their sense of justice to another service member or comply with the law.

Table 4.2 How much do you disagree or agree with the following:

Respondents	All Marine				All Gay			
Answer Options	**Strongly Disagree and Disagree**		**Strongly Disagree and Disagree**		**Strongly Agree and Agree**		**Strongly Agree and Agree**	
Question	Response Percent	Response Count	Response Percent	Response Count	Response Percent	Response Count	Response Percent	Response Count
Prior to the December 2010 repeal, I faithfully executed my duty to enforce DADT when confronted with knowledge of a DADT violation.	30.0%	21	57.1%	40	67.5%	106	17.2%	27
DADT created situations where I felt I had to either compromise my sense of justice to a fellow service member or my duty to comply with the law.	52.9%	47	41.4%	29	15.2%	24	73.3%	105
Answered Question	70				157			
Skipped Question	87				9			

In combination, between 13.9 percent[48] and 19.1 percent[49] of all Marine respondents believed DADT placed them in an integrity-compromising position. Between 27.4 percent and 30.4 percent of non-Marine respondents indicated they were placed in an integrity-compromising position while between 66.2 percent and 71.9 percent of gay respondents indicated DADT placed them in an integrity-compromising position. Thus the burden of DADT was greater the more aware the service member was of his or her surroundings and the greater the prevalence of "hidden" gay service members.

> *Men often hate each other because they fear each other; they fear*
> *each other because they don't know each other; they don't know each*
> *other because they cannot communicate; they cannot communicate*
> *because they are separated.*
>
> —Martin Luther King Jr., "Stride Toward Freedom:
> the Montgomery Story"[50]

Table 5.1 How much do you disagree or agree with the following:

In my opinion and irrespective of the repeal of the DADT law, open homosexuality is incompatible with military service.

Respondents	All Marine		Non-Marine		All Gay	
Answer Options	Response Count	Response Percent	Response Count	Response Percent	Response Count	Response Percent
Strongly Disagree	20	13.2%	11	32.4%	128	87.7%
Disagree	44	28.9%	11	32.4%	15	10.3%
Total Disagree	**64**	**42.1%**	**19**	**64.8%**	**143**	**98.0%**
Agree	34	22.4%	6	17.6%	1	0.7%
Strongly Agree	54	35.5%	6	17.6%	2	1.4%
Total Agree	**88**	**57.9%**	**10**	**35.2%**	**3**	**2.1%**
Answered Question	152		34		146	
Skipped Question	5		2		20	

Analysis of Differences

Marine vs. non-Marine. Analysis of the survey results revealed large differences between Marine and non-Marine respondents about whether they had served with a service member they knew to be homosexual, whether or not they knew gay civilians, and whether or not the respondent believed open homosexuality is incompatible with military service.

Table 5.1 summarizes responses to the question of whether the service member strongly disagrees, disagrees, agrees, or strongly agrees with the statement "open homosexuality is incompatible with military service." Directness and simplicity makes this question the most useful in exploring characteristics of respondents that are correlated to nearly 23 percentage points of greater opposition of Marine respondents to open service of homosexuals as compared to non-Marine respondents.

Table 5.2 demonstrates over a 17 percent difference between Marine and non-Marine respondents regarding whether they had served with a service member they knew to be homosexual. Only 46.2 percent of Marines reported serving with someone they knew to be homosexual while nearly 64 percent of non-Marines reported serving with someone they knew to be homosexual.

A significant difference also resulted when respondents were asked if they knew civilians who were homosexual (Table 5.3). More than 97 percent of non-Marines responded affirmatively while slightly more than 86 percent of Marines responded affirmatively.

In an effort to explain the nearly 23 percent difference between Marine and non-Marine answers to the question "do you believe open homosexuality is incompatible with military service?" (57.9 percent of Marines responded affirmatively while only 35.2 percent of non-Marines responded affirmatively), Marine responses were sorted to separate those who had never served with someone they knew to be gay from those who had. Table 5.4 provides the dramatic change in the respondents' answers.[51] Among the population of Marines who had served with a known homosexual, belief that open homosexuality was incompatible with service dropped over 10 percentage points, to 46.3 percent. When separated from Marines who had served with a known homosexual, the opposition of Marines who had never served with a homosexual registered nearly 10 percentage points above the average for all Marines, at 67.5 percent.

In order to compare apples to apples, the data for non-Marines was also sorted to remove responses of non-Marines who had not served with someone they knew to be homosexual. The percentage who believed open homosexuality was incompatible with military service changed only slightly when these respondents were removed. (This analysis becomes difficult to utilize as the size of the data set becomes limiting, as only 23 non-Marines who had served with a known homosexual were surveyed. The issue was not pursued further due to this data limitation.)

Table 5.2 Have you served with a U.S. service member that you knew to be to homosexual?

Answer Options	All Marine		Non-Marine		All Gay	
	Response Percent	Response Count	Response Percent	Response Count	Response Percent	Response Count
Yes	46.2%	72	63.9%	23	98.1%	159
No	53.8%	84	36.1%	13	1.9%	3
Answered Question		156		36		162
Skipped Question		1		0		4

Table 5.3 Do you know civilians who are homosexual?

Respondents	All Marine		Non-Marine		All Gay	
Answer Options	Response Count	Response Percent	Response Count	Response Percent	Response Count	Response Percent
Yes	131	86.2%	28	97.1%	129	98.6%
No	21	13.8%	1	2.9%	2	1.4%
Answered Question		152		34		146
Skipped Question		5		2		20

The End of Don't Ask, Don't Tell

Table 5.4 How much do you disagree or agree with the following:

In my opinion and irrespective of the repeal of the DADT law, open homosexuality is incompatible with military service.

Respondents	All Marine: Served with known homosexual		All Marine: Never served with known		Non-Marine	
Answer Options	Response Count	Response Percent	Response Count	Response Percent	Response Count	Response Percent
Strongly Disagree	14	20.3%	6	7.2%	11	32.4%
Disagree	23	33.3%	21	25.3%	11	32.4%
Total Disagree	*38*	*30.40%*	*27*	*17.82%*	*22*	*64.8%*
Agree	10	15.9%	23	27.7%	6	17.6%
Strongly Agree	19	30.4%	33	39.8%	6	17.6%
Total Agree	*19*	*46.3%*	*56*	*67.5%*	*12*	*35.2%*
Answered Question	69		83		34	

Male vs. Female Marines. Significant differences exist between the Marine and non-Marine answers to whether homosexuality is incompatible with military service. A possible explanatory factor in the demographics of the two populations is the proportion of female respondents. Female Marines comprised 12.7 percent of Marine respondents while females comprised 25 percent of non-Marine respondents. Examination of female Marines' responses found that 36.9 percent believed open homosexuality was incompatible with military service, much lower than the 60.9 percent of their male counterparts who answered similarly (Table 5.5). Interestingly, 100 percent of female Marine respondents indicated they knew homosexual civilians and 80 percent reported serving with someone they knew to be homosexual, a higher percentage as compared to male Marines (Table 5.6).

Table 5.5 How much do you disagree or agree with the following:

In my opinion and irrespective of the repeal of the DADT law, open homosexuality is incompatible with military service.

Respondents	All Marine		Male Marine		Female Marine	
Answer Options	Response Count	Response Percent	Response Count	Response Percent	Response Count	Response Percent
Strongly Disagree	20	13.2%	12	9.0%	8	42.1%
Disagree	44	28.9%	40	30.1%	4	21.1%
Total Disagree	*64*	*42.1%*	*52*	*39.1%*	*12*	*63.2%*
Agree	34	22.4%	31	23.3%	3	15.8%
Strongly Agree	54	35.5%	50	37.6%	4	21.1%
Total Agree	*88*	*57.9%*	*81*	*60.9%*	*7*	*36.9%*
Answered Question	152		133		19	
Skipped Question	5		4		1	

Table 5.6 Have you served with a U.S. service member that you knew to be homosexual?

	All Marine		Male Marine		Female Marine	
Answer Options	Response Percent	Response Count	Response Percent	Response Count	Response Percent	Response Count
Yes	46.2%	72	41.2%	56	80.0%	16
No	53.8%	84	58.8%	80	20.0%	4
Answered Question		156		136		20
Skipped Question		1		4		0

The End of Don't Ask, Don't Tell

Combat Arms Marines vs. All "Other" Marines. The Pentagon study and conventional wisdom hold that Marines in the combat arms Military Occupational Specialties (MOS) are more opposed to the service of open homosexuals than are noncombat arms MOSs. The data was analyzed to compare responses of these populations.

If conventional wisdom holds, a significantly higher percentage of combat arms Marines would respond with agreement to the statement that "open homosexuality is incompatible with military service." While a difference does exist, Table 5.7 shows the percentage of combat arms Marines who believe homosexuality is incompatible with military service differs by only nine percentage points (8.8 percent) from the total Marine population. The percentage of the remaining Marines (57.9 percent) believing homosexuality is incompatible with military service does not approach the percentage of non-Marines (35.2 percent) with the same opinion. Table 5.8 shows a negligible difference between the percentage of combat arms and noncombat Marines who served with known homosexuals.

Table 5.7 How much do you disagree or agree with the following:

In my opinion and irrespective of the repeal of the DADT law, open homosexuality is incompatible with military service.

Respondents	All Marine		Combat Arms Marine		"Other" Marine (male & female)	
Answer Options	Response Count	Response Percent	Response Count	Response Percent	Response Count	Response Percent
Strongly Disagree	20	13.2%	3	6.3%	17	16.3%
Disagree	44	28.9%	13	27.1%	31	29.8%
Total Disagree	**64**	**42.1%**	**16**	**33.4%**	**48**	**46.1%**
Agree	34	22.4%	14	29.2%	20	19.2%
Strongly Agree	54	35.5%	18	37.5%	36	34.6%
Total Agree	**88**	**57.0%**	**32**	**66.7%**	**56**	**53.8%**
Answered Question	152		48		104	
Skipped Question	5		1		4	

Table 5.8 Have you served with a U.S. service member that you knew to be to be homosexual?

Answer Options	All Marine		Combat Arms Marine		"Other" Marine (male & female)	
	Response Percent	Response Count	Response Percent	Response Count	Response Percent	Response Count
Yes	46.2%	72	46.9%	23	45.8%	49
No	53.8%	84	53.1%	26	54.2%	58
Answered Question		156		49		107
Skipped Question		1		0		1

Male Combat Arms Marines vs. Male Noncombat Arms Marines. From the earlier comparison of female and male Marines, a 24-percentage-point difference in responses to the question of whether open homosexuality is incompatible with military service resulted. A final demographic difference will be investigated to determine whether a significant culture difference exists between male combat arms Marines and male noncombat arms Marines. The Pentagon study and conventional wisdom indicate existence of this difference.

To make this comparison, the survey responses of all male Marine respondents were divided between those in the combat arms and noncombat arms MOSs (Table 5.9). While a difference exists, it was less than 10 percentage points. Table 5.9 shows that of all Marine respondents, 66.7 percent of combat arms Marines believed open homosexuality is incompatible with military service while 57.6 percent of male noncombat arms Marines believe open homosexuality is incompatible with military service.

In previous comparisons of Marine and non-Marine respondents' experience with known homosexuals, it was suggested that service with known homosexuals was negatively correlated to belief that open homosexuality is incompatible with

The End of Don't Ask, Don't Tell

military service. In contrast to this trend, Table 5.10 illustrates that fewer non-combat arms Marines (37.9 percent) indicated they had served with a known homosexual while 46.3 percent of combat arms Marines had served with a known homosexual. This would suggest that a difference in culture does exist between the combat arms and noncombat arms communities. Even though combat arms Marines have been more aware of service with homosexuals, they are also more negatively disposed to their service. On the whole, however, opposition to open service of homosexuals is consistent across all male Marines.

Table 5.9 How much do you disagree or agree with the following:

In my opinion and irrespective of the repeal of the DADT law, open homosexuality is incompatible with military service.

Respondents	All Marine		Combat Arms Marine		"Other" Marine (male only)	
Answer Options	Response Count	Response Percent	Response Count	Response Percent	Response Count	Response Percent
Strongly Disagree	20	13.2%	3	6.3%	9	10.6%
Disagree	44	28.9%	13	27.1%	27	31.8%
Total Disagree	*64*	*42.1%*	*16*	*33.4%*	*36*	*42.4%*
Agree	34	22.4%	14	29.2%	17	20.0%
Strongly Agree	54	35.5%	18	37.5%	32	37.6%
Total Agree	*88*	*57.9%*	*32*	*66.7%*	*49*	*57.6%*
Answered Question	152		48		85	
Skipped Question	5		1		3	

Table 5.10 Have you served with a U.S. service member that you knew to be to be homosexual?

Answer Options	All Marine		Combat Arms Marine		"Other" Marine (male only)	
	Response Percent	Response Count	Response Percent	Response Count	Response Percent	Response Count
Yes	46.2%	72	46.9%	23	37.9%	33
No	53.8%	84	53.1%	26	62.1%	54
Answered Question	156		49		87	
Skipped Question	1		0		1	

Opposition to Open Service of Homosexuals Explained. Respondents who answered the question "open homosexuality is incompatible with military service" affirmatively were then asked to explain their opposition by selecting explanations from a list of responses. Table 5.11 indicates Marine and non-Marine respondents provided largely consistent reasons to explain their belief that open homosexuality was incompatible with military service. Moral and religious beliefs and the perception that homosexuals would degrade unit cohesion and mission accomplishment were the predominant explanations. Significant differences between Marine and non-Marine responses again occurred when Marines noted open homosexuals would degrade unit cohesion and impede mission accomplishment nearly twice as often as did non-Marines (51.3 percent versus 32.4 percent and 31.6 percent versus 14.7 percent, respectively). Similar percentages of Marines and non-Marines explained their opposition to open service was due to "moral and religious beliefs" (35.5 percent versus 29.4 percent, respectively). Responses of gay service members were most disparate from other respondents in answering this question. Nearly 100 percent (98.5 percent) of gay respondents disagreed with the statement that open homosexuality was incompatible with military service.

Table 5.11 I believe open homosexuality is incompatible with military service because: (Check all that apply.)

Answer Options	All Marine		Non-Marine		All Gay	
	Response Percent	Response Count	Response Percent	Response Count	Response Percent	Response Count
Of my moral or religious beliefs	35.5%	54	29.4%	10	0.0%	0
Homosexuals are untrustworthy	0.01%	1	0.0%	0	0.0%	0
Homosexuals are physically weak and unable to support/defend fellow service members in combat	0.0%	0	2.9%	1	0.0%	0
Homosexuals are anathema to the warrior ethos	9.2%	14	8.8%	3	0.0%	0
Open homosexuals will degrade unit cohesion	51.3%	78	32.4%	11	0.0%	0
Open homosexuals will impede mission accomplishment	31.6%	37	14.7%	5	0.0%	0

Part of what we need to do is address a number of assertions that have been made for which we have no basis in fact.
—Secretary of Defense Robert Gates, 2 February 2010[52]

Implementation Recommendations

On 2 March 2011 Secretary Gates appointed General Carter Ham and DOD General Counsel Jeh Charles Johnson to complete a review of DADT's repeal.[53] Secretary Gates also directed that "a plan of action to support the implementation of a repeal of the law" accompany this report.[54]

Respondents were asked if they agreed or disagreed with six primary themes or issues from the report and were given an opportunity to provide open-ended comments. *The complete results of the survey are available online at http://www.mcu.usmc.mil/pages/dadt.aspx and at the Gray Marine Corps Research Center in Quantico, Virginia.*

Responses to the first four questions of this section of the survey were consistent across all three groups. Gay respondents expressed greater support for four of the six aspects of the proposed implementation plan than either Marines or non-Marines. One of the remaining two aspects recommended sexual orientation not be included in the Military Equal Opportunity (MEP) program. One explained that no change could be made to benefits regarding "committed relationships" so long as the current federal law defining marriage remained in effect. Gay service members expressed the least support for these recommendations while Marines expressed the greatest support.

Table 6.1 illustrates that the weighted average of all surveyed populations fall nearly midway between agree to strongly agree that leadership will be the key to implementation of the repeal.

Table 6.1 The Support Plan for Implementation repeatedly states that the "most critical predictor of successful implementation" of the repeal of DADT will be effective leadership at all levels of the chain of command.

Question: In my opinion, leadership will be critical to successful implementation.

Answer Options (Rating value)	Strongly Disagree (1)	Disagree (2)	Agree (3)	Strongly Agree (4)	Rating Average	Response Count
All Marine	5	11	45	86	3.44	147
Non-Marine	3	1	8	21	3.42	33
All Gay	2	4	31	95	3.66	132

The weighted average responses of all surveyed populations agree that "leadership-professionalism-respect" is a sound message to guide implementation. Per Table 6.2, a weighted average of 3.53 indicates gay service members are split between agree and strongly agree, while a 2.97 indicates Marines collectively only agree with the message.

Table 6.2 The Support Plan for Implementation recommends that the key message of implementation of the DADT repeal be "leadership-professionalism-respect." More specifically, 1) "Leadership matters most." Leaders at all levels will set the example and demonstrate full commitment to DOD policy; 2) "Focus on professionalism." Service members will be expected to execute their professional obligations and adhere to their oath to support and defend the Constitution; and 3) "Promote strength through respect." All service members will be treated with respect; harassment and discrimination will not be tolerated.

Question: In my opinion, this is a solid foundation for an implementation plan.

Answer Options (Rating value)	Strongly Disagree (1)	Disagree (2)	Agree (3)	Strongly Agree (4)	Rating Average	Response Count
All Marine	10	19	83	35	2.97	147
Non-Marine	0	5	16	12	3.21	33
All Gay	2	1	54	75	3.53	132

Consistent with the trends established in the previous two questions, Table 6.3 illustrates that gay service members again expressed the greatest confidence in the Pentagon's implementation plan. The weighted average of gay responses fell between agree and strongly agree while the weighted responses of Marines and non-Marines fell in neutral territory between disagree and agree.

Table 6.3 The Support Plan for Implementation recommends that emphasis should focus on "behaviors not attitudes." In other words, implementation "should emphasize that no service member is being asked to change his or her personal beliefs" on DADT or homosexuality but that disrespect, harassment, or discrimination will not be tolerated.

Question: In my opinion, this approach will address the moral or religious concerns regarding homosexuality held by some service members.

Answer Options (Rating value)	Strongly Disagree (1)	Disagree (2)	Agree (3)	Strongly Agree (4)	Rating Average	Response Count
All Marine	27	35	61	24	2.56	147
Non-Marine	4	15	8	6	2.48	33
All Gay	4	15	63	50	3.20	132

The End of Don't Ask, Don't Tell

Table 6.4 illustrates that the recommendation that sexual orientation not be made an eligible class for MEP garnered the least support among gay service members with a weighted average of 2.36, on the "disagree" side of "neutral." The weighted average of Marine and non-Marine respondents, at 2.87 and 2.79 respectively, nearly reached the "agree" category. This grouping of collective responses is consistent with responses discussed in the "Opinion Regarding DADT" section that showed Marines to be least likely of any respondent group to agree that DADT was discriminatory. (Table 2.2 illustrated a wide difference in perspective, as 13.4 percent of Marine respondents versus 88 percent of gay service members indicated DADT was discriminatory and was appropriately repealed. Table 2.3 illustrated that Marine respondents collectively believe that DADT had neutral/no impact on justice while gay service members indicated that DADT had a negative to strongly negative impact on justice.)

Table 6.4 The Support Plan for Implementation recommends that sexual orientation NOT be specified as a class eligible for a Military Equal Opportunity program complaint as are the federally protected classes of race, color, religion, sex, and national origin. Rather, implementation should emphasize that evaluations be based on "only individual merit, fitness, and capability" and that "harassment or abuse based on sexual orientation is unacceptable."

Question: In my opinion, NOT considering sexual orientation to be a federally protected class is a workable approach.

Answer Options (Rating value)	Strongly Disagree (1)	Disagree (2)	Agree (3)	Strongly Agree (4)	Rating Average	Response Count
All Marine	16	30	58	43	2.87	147
Non-Marine	6	6	10	11	2.79	33
All Gay	37	31	50	14	2.31	132

Table 6.5 illustrates that billeting and living arrangements following repeal is of primary concern, with the lowest weighted average (or least agreement) of Marine responses to any aspect of the proposed implementation plan. The weighted average of the responses of gay service members (2.92) indicates their agreement with the proposed approach to billeting and a weighted average of 2.64 for non-Marines illustrates their basic agreement also. The weighted average of Marine responses (2.20) is the most negative for any aspect of the implementation plan.

In recognition of federal law, the "Support Plan for Implementation" (SPI) proposes that no changes be made to marriage-related benefits. Regardless of the opinion of Obama administration officials, the DOD is not able to provide marriage-related benefits to same-gender couples due to the federal Defense of Marriage Act (DOMA).[55] This law limits federal recognition of marriage to heterosexual unions and limits marriage-related federal benefits to only federally recognized marriages.

Table 6.5 The Support Plan for Implementation recommends that basing berthing or billeting assignments on sexual orientation be prohibited and that any segregation based on sexual orientation be prohibited. However, the plan also recommends that commanders be given discretion to address privacy concerns on a case-by-case basis.

Question: Prohibiting use of sexual orientation as a basis for berthing or billeting assignments but allowing commanders limited discretion is a workable approach.

Answer Options (Rating value)	Strongly Disagree (1)	Disagree (2)	Agree (3)	Strongly Agree (4)	Rating Average	Response Count
All Marine	42	35	55	15	2.29	147
Non-Marine	7	5	14	7	2.64	33
All Gay	11	14	81	26	2.92	132

This question was included in the survey for the sake of completeness and to diffuse the impact of this topic on repeal discussions since additional action by Congress or the courts is necessary to make changes to the law. While this is the aspect of the implementation plan with which Marines most strongly agree, with a weighted average of 3.21 (the "strongly agree" side of "agree"), it is also the only aspect of the implementation plan with which gay service members collectively disagree, with a weighted average response of 1.95—the "strongly disagree" side of "disagree" (Table 6.6). The weighted average of non-Marines falls just on the "agree" side of "neutral" at 2.82. Of all aspects of the proposed plan, Marines most strongly concur with the aspect of the plan that represents the status quo while gay service members most strongly disagree with that aspect.

Table 6.6 The Support Plan for Implementation recommends that a new status of "committed relationship" NOT be created at this time so NO changes are recommended to be made to marriage-related benefit eligibility. In short, due to the restrictions of marriage to heterosexual couples by federal law, any service member not in a federally recognized marriage will continue to be considered a "single" service member for benefit eligibility.

Question: I agree that no changes should be made to benefits associated with marital status at this time.

Answer Options (Rating value)	Strongly Disagree (1)	Disagree (2)	Agree (3)	Strongly Agree (4)	Rating Average	Response Count
All Marine	14	12	50	71	3.21	147
Non-Marine	5	5	14	9	2.82	33
All Gay	54	38	33	7	1.95	132

The final two questions were included to prompt respondents to consider how or whether repeal would challenge their leadership ability or professionalism if they were the supervisor of, or were supervised by, an openly gay service member. Table 6.7 follows the trend that Marine respondents find open homosexuality more challenging than members of other services, with 10.9 percent of Marines and 6.1 percent of non-Marines stating they would seek a transfer if they had an openly gay commander. More than 12 percent fewer Marine (60.5 percent) than non-Marine (75 percent) respondents indicated that the sexual orientation of their supervisor would not impact their career decisions or attitude. Not surprisingly, 54.5 percent of gay service members would welcome the opportunity to support an openly homosexual supervisor or commander, while only 3.4 percent and 6.1 percent of Marine and non-Marine respondents respectively would be similarly disposed.

Table 6.7 Once the repeal of DADT is implemented, and if my supervisor/commander were openly homosexual, I would:

Answer Options	All Marine		Non-Marine		All Gay	
	Response Percent	Response Count	Response Percent	Response Count	Response Percent	Response Count
Seek a transfer.	10.9%	16	6.1%	2	0.0%	0
Seek to separate from my service.	2.0%	3	3.0%	1	0.0%	0
Seek advice or counseling to adapt to this situation.	7.5%	11	6.1%	2	0.0%	0
None of the above. The sexual orientation of my supervisor would not impact my career decisions or attitude.	60.5%	89	72.7%	24	44.7%	59
Welcome the opportunity to support a professional and openly homosexual supervisor/commander.	3.4%	5	6.1%	2	54.5%	72
Other (please specify).	15.6%	23	6.1%	2	0.8%	1
Answered Question		147		33		132
Skipped Question		10		3		34

The End of Don't Ask, Don't Tell

Table 6.8 indicates that Marine respondents would have less difficulty in supervising an openly gay service member than reporting to or being supervised by an openly gay service member. This attitude is reminiscent of desegregation. In 1941, Admiral Chester W. Nimitz stated that "the policy (of limiting black sailors to the messman's branch) was instituted in the interest of harmony and efficiency aboard ship after many years of experience." Along the same lines, General Henry H. "Hap" Arnold in 1940 said, "Negro pilots cannot be used in our present Air Force since this would result in having Negro officers serving over white enlisted men. This would create an impossible social problem."[56]

Never wanting to be outdone, Marine Commandant General Thomas Holcomb made some of the most egregious comments at the time, stating that "it would be 'absolutely tragic' if blacks were integrated into the services."[57] In comments to the Navy's General Board in 1941, General Holcomb stated, "Negroes did not have the 'right' to demand a place in the corps. . . . If it were a question of having a Marine Corps of 5,000 whites or 250,000 Negroes, I would rather have the whites." He said, "it is essential that in no case shall there be colored noncommissioned officers senior to white men in the same unit."[58] "In seeking to maintain segregation, the Navy argued that its 'personnel had to live and work under close conditions affording minimal privacy.'"[59]

Since survey questions indicated a belief by 50 percent of Marine respondents that open homosexuality would degrade unit cohesion and harm mission accomplishment and warfighting capability, it is logical that working for or being supervised by the source of such negative consequences would be opposed, too. The more positive approach to openly homosexual subordinates, shown in Table 6.8, implies that respect for a leader is more important to Marines than is respect for those who are led. This difference could also reflect confidence in the respondent that their leadership can mitigate any flaws to moral character caused by homosexuality in those they lead.

A sharp difference in enthusiasm for leading openly homosexual subordinates between Marine and non-Marine respondents is the most significant result in Table 6.8. More than 14 percent of Marine respondents indicated they would welcome the opportunity to lead openly gay subordinates while more than 30 percent of non-

Marine respondents and 74.2 percent of gay service members indicated they would do so. It is also of note that between 70 and 78 percent of all three groups indicated the sexual orientation of their subordinates would have no impact on their ability to lead or mentor. Developers of training materials should note that 16.3 percent of Marine respondents and 12.1 percent of non-Marines indicated they would need training or support to understand how to lead and mentor openly homosexual subordinates.

> It is difficult to get a man to understand something when his salary
> depends on his not understanding it.
> —Upton Sinclair, *I, Candidate for Governor: And How I Got Licked*

Table 6.8 Once the repeal of DADT is implemented, I would: (Check all that apply.)

Answer Options	All Marine		Non-Marine		All Gay	
	Response Percent	Response Count	Response Percent	Response Count	Response Percent	Response Count
Lead/mentor openly homosexual subordinates with difficulty.	12.9%	19	15.2%	5	6.8%	9
Have a moral objection to leading or supervising openly homosexual subordinates.	10.2%	15	3.0%	1	3.8%	5
Need training or support to understand how to mentor or lead openly homosexual subordinates.	16.3%	24	12.1%	4	3.0%	4
None of the above. The sexual orientation of my subordinates would have no impact on my ability to lead or mentor them.	70.1%	103	75.8%	25	78.0%	103
Welcome the opportunity to lead or mentor openly homosexual service members.	14.3%	21	30.3%	10	74.2%	98
Other (please specify).	14.3%	21	9.1%	3	6.1%	8
Answered Question		147		33		132
Skipped Question		10		3		34

Prior-Service Students vs. Midshipmen

At the request of a Marine Officer Instructor (MOI) assigned to an East Coast university, the students in his Reserve Officer Training Corps (ROTC) unit were surveyed. By coincidence, the unit is composed of a nearly equal number of students that had enrolled directly from civilian life and students that had been selected for the Marine Enlisted Commissioning Education Program (MECEP) after serving as an enlisted Marine and earning a rank between sergeant and gunnery sergeant.

The MECEP and enlisted Marine group totaled 22 respondents—10 MECEP students and 12 enlisted Marines under the age of 38. Although the findings from a small sample size imply areas for future research rather than provide definitive conclusions, there is a striking difference between the "civilian" students and a combination of the students with prior Corps service and enlisted Marine respondents of similar rank and age.

Table 7.1 In my opinion, the DADT law: (Check all that apply.)

Answer Options	All Marine		MECEP/E6 & Below		Midshipmen	
	Response Percent	Response Count	Response Percent	Response Count	Response Percent	Response Count
Served a valuable purpose and should have been retained	52.2%	82	77.3%	17	10.0%	2
Protected unit cohesion and furthered mission accomplishment	47.1%	74	50.0%	11	50.0%	10
Neither supported nor harmed unit cohesion and mission accomplishment	23.6%	37	9.1%	2	25.0%	5
Wasted resources and was appropriately repealed	8.3%	13	4.5%	1	20.0%	4
Was discriminatory and was appropriately repealed	13.4%	21	0.0%	0	30.0%	6
Answered Question		157		22		20
Skipped Question		0		0		0

Seventy-seven percent of MECEP students and enlisted Marines believed DADT served a valuable purpose and should have been retained versus only 10 percent of ROTC students with no previous Corps experience. No MECEP students or enlisted Marines believed DADT was discriminatory and appropriately repealed while 30 percent of the ROTC students did. Less than 5 percent (one respondent) of MECEP students and enlisted Marines stated DADT wasted resources and was appropriately repealed while 20 percent (four respondents) of the ROTC students did. Table 7.1 shows the data.

Table 7.2 shows greater disparity between MECEP students and enlisted Marines and regular ROTC Students. The absolute difference between MECEP and enlisted Marines and regular ROTC students is greater than a factor of three, with 18.2 percent of the MECEP and enlisted students disagreeing with the statement "open homosexuality is incompatible with military service," while 63.2 percent of

Table 7.2 How much do you disagree or agree with the following:

In my opinion and irrespective of the repeal of the DADT law, open homosexuality is incompatible with military service.

Respondents	All Marine		MECEP/E6 & Below		Midshipmen	
Answer Options	Response Count	Response Percent	Response Count	Response Percent	Response Count	Response Percent
Strongly Disagree	20	13.2%	1	4.5%	3	15.8%
Disagree	44	28.9%	3	13.6%	9	47.4%
Total Disagree	*64*	*42.1%*	*4*	*18.2%*	*12*	*63.2%*
Agree	34	22.4%	6	27.0%	5	26.3%
Strongly Agree	54	35.5%	12	54.5%	2	10.5%
Total Agree	*88*	*57.9%*	*18*	*81.8%*	*7*	*36.8%*
Answered Question	152		22		19	
Skipped Question	5		0		1	

regular ROTC students disagreeing. The position of MECEP students and enlisted Marines was even at strong variance with all Marine respondents, of whom 42.1 percent, or over two times more than the MECEP students and enlisted Marines (18.2 percent), disagreed with the statement "open homosexuality is incompatible with military service."

To repeat, the small sample of midshipmen makes definitive comparisons problematic. However, the significance of the difference is of note and warrants further investigation. Due to the stark difference of the MECEP and enlisted Marine populations compared to the general ROTC population that more nearly resembles that of non-Marine respondents, it could be important to know whether Corps culture is enforcing harmful "group think" among its most junior members. If independent thought is being stifled to the degree indicated by this unrepresentative sample, the gap being between civilian and Corps mind-set that is being inculcated into young Marines potentially does not bode well for DADT implementation.

> So this morning, I am proud to sign a law that will bring an end to "Don't Ask, Don' Tell." (Applause.) It is a law—this law I'm about to sign will strengthen our national security and uphold the ideals that our fighting men and women risk their lives to defend.
>
> No longer will our country be denied the service of thousands of patriotic Americans who were forced to leave the military—regardless of their skills, no matter their bravery or their zeal, no matter their years of exemplary performance—because they happen to be gay. No longer will tens of thousands of Americans in uniform be asked to live a lie, or look over their shoulder, in order to serve the country that they love. (Applause.)
>
> As Admiral Mike Mullen has said, "Our people sacrifice a lot for their country, including their lives. None of them should have to sacrifice their integrity as well." (Applause.)
>
> That's why I believe this is the right thing to do for our military. That's why I believe it is the right thing to do, period.
>
> —President Barack Obama, 22 December 2010[60]

The Way Forward

Gay service members unequivocally believe that DADT has had a deleterious effect on integrity and civil rights. While the outright recognition of this harmful effect and the intensity of recognition varied across the surveyed populations, integrity and justice were the most recognized casualties of DADT across all populations. Although the weighted average of Marine responses indicated a collective Marine belief that DADT's effect on integrity was neutral and that DADT did not compromise the civil rights of gay service members, 28.6 percent of Marine respondents indicated DADT had a negative or very negative impact on integrity and nearly 36.9 percent of Marine respondents agreed or strongly agreed that DADT compromised gay service members' civil rights.

As the late Senator Kennedy noted, "Even if one accepts that there is no constitutional right to serve in the military, that does not end the constitutional inquiry."[61] Senator Kennedy explains the relevant constitutional question—not considered by Congress in its 1993 or 2010 debate—is whether the government has a valid reason (a compelling military interest) to exclude gay people from service. This report has shown that all studies since 1957 indicate sexual orientation is not detrimental to military service and is not a rational basis for exclusion. If effective and just integration of gay people into the armed services is to be achieved, these studies' conclusions—that there is no rational basis for the exclusion of gay people—should be part of repeal implementation training. In addition to addressing the injustice of discriminatory exclusion policies, such an honest exposition could begin to reverse the impact of decades of negative stereotypes that insidiously preclude gay service members from contributing the full measure of their potential to the armed services and their country.

As DOD's review found—from a review of transformational experiences such as the integration of African Americans and women—"the general lesson we take . . . is that in matters of personnel change within the military, predictions and surveys tend to overestimate negative consequences and underestimate the U.S. military's ability to adapt and incorporate within its ranks the diversity that is reflective of American society at large."[62] Acknowledging this finding, and the review's summary of the positive experiences of allies in integrating homosexuals, repeal implementation training could help put anxieties in perspective and facilitate expectations of success.

Gay service members will not be effectively integrated unless and until accession, evaluation, retention, and promotion are based on performance and not sexual orientation. It must be understood that the civil rights of gay service members are as valid as are those of straight service members. In one of the most significant disparities between Marine and gay respondents, Marines collectively disagreed with the statement that "DADT compromised the civil rights of homosexual service members" while gay service members strongly agreed. If the majority of heterosexual service members do not believe gay service members have an inherent right *not* to be discriminated against, it will be difficult to ensure that gay service members and their evaluations, promotions, and assignments will be handled with justice and impartiality.

Another major finding is that DADT was an emotional or moral burden for a significant segment of straight service members as well as for gay service members. Between 13.9 percent and 19 percent of Marine respondents and between 27.4 percent and 30.4 percent of non-Marine respondents indicated DADT created a moral dilemma for them as they were forced to chose between an obligation to comply with all laws or regulations and loyalty to a gay service member or their personal commitment to justice for all service members. Non-Marines experienced a greater moral dilemma; nearly 20 percent more non-Marines served with someone they knew to be gay than did Marines. In addition to the simple integrity-compromising dilemma of hiding their sexuality, between 67.5 percent and 73.3 percent of gay service members also stated they experienced the moral dilemma between an obligation to comply with regulations and their own presence in the services.

The cost of this moral dilemma in terms of degraded communication and honesty between service members and their chain of command, and attendant harm to unit cohesion and mission accomplishment, has never been measured in the U.S. reviews of the Australian and Canadian armed forces, following their removal of bans on open homosexuals identified positive benefits to mission accomplishment and unit cohesion of open service. When open and honest communication was allowed between gay and straight service members, benefits to mission accomplishment and unit cohesion accumulated.[63] Including the positive experience of allies' armed services in repeal training would facilitate the full integration of gay service members and create an expectation of benefits and help mitigate angst over fear of change.

A third finding is that the lower the awareness of homosexual service members, the more significant the belief that DADT protected characteristics such as unit cohesion, mission accomplishment, combat effectiveness, and warfighting capability. Correspondingly, the lower the awareness of homosexual service members, the greater the concern that DADT's repeal would cause negative consequences on these same characteristics. In contrast, the greater the awareness of homosexuality, the less significant the belief that DADT protected things such as unit cohesion and combat effectiveness and the greater the recognition that DADT had a negative impact on integrity and justice.

This correlation indicates ignorance, fear, and associated prejudice are a significant foundation of opposition to open service of homosexuals. Studies completed by DOD, GAO, and civilian organizations have repeatedly demonstrated there is no factual basis for the "findings" in the DADT law. Including this information in transition training would facilitate integration of gay service members and mitigate possible situations in which extraneous opinions, prejudice, or factors other than performance are utilized in recruiting, retention, and evaluation decisions. Augmenting repeal training with an honest discussion of the positive scientific evidence in integrating homosexuals including findings regarding homosexual service, homosexuals and security clearances, our allies' experiences in integrating homosexuals, the experience of the CIA and FBI in integrating gay agents, as well as the experiences of police and fire departments in integrating gay members, would create an expectation of success and illuminate the positive benefits of repeal. Also, a positive approach would demonstrate the commitment of DOD's senior military leadership to a successful repeal process and maximize the benefit to the armed services of an environment of increased honesty and integrity.

Fourth, Marine respondents see more benefit in DADT and are far more opposed to its repeal than other service members. While the survey did not directly explore this factor, Marine opposition and rationale closely follows that of three of the most senior and most respected leaders in the Marine Corps, General Peter Pace (Ret.), General Conway, and Commandant Amos.[64] In General Amos's testimony before the Senate Armed Services Committee on 3 December 2010, he cited (from DOD's review) alarming statistics provided by combat arms Marines who were not deployed and did not relate the positive results provided by Marines who served with a leader whom they believed to be gay, or the less-alarming results from deployed combat arms Marines.[65] Despite citing no empirical or anecdotal evidence that the presence of openly gay service members would harm mission accomplishment or unit cohesion, he recommended that DADT not be repealed.

In contrast, Admiral Mullen has clearly stated that DADT compromises the integrity and values of the DOD. The Chief of Naval Operations, Admiral Gary Roughead, also debunked fears of repeal, stating that "seventy-six percent of sailors believe the impact on these force characteristics (effectiveness, readiness, unit cohesion, and morale) will be neutral or positive." In recommending repeal of 10 U.S. Code 654, Admiral Roughead said, "I have the ultimate confidence in the men and women of the United States Navy and in their character, in their discipline, and in their decency. Navy leaders will continue to set a positive tone, create an inclusive and respected work environment."[66]

It is only possible to speculate whether a positive message from Generals Pace, Conway, and Amos—as exemplified by Admirals Mullen and Roughead—would have had a mitigating impact on the negative opinions of gay service members demonstrated by the Marine Corps' rank and file. The danger in their approach however, is highlighted by General Shalikashvili as well as Dr. Tammy Schultz of the Marine Corps War College, who have warned that this type of opposition could become a self-fulfilling prophecy, complicating implementation and compromising the respect for and dignity of honorably serving gay service members.

While the sample size in this survey was not large enough to be statistically significant, the MECEP vs. midshipman section highlights possible negative consequences of 17 years of openly expressed prejudice against gay service members on the culture of the Corps. Research for this report and the statements of Generals Shalikashvili and Amos acknowledge that there is no empirical or scientific evidence to support the gay exclusion. Pejorative comments regarding gay service members, left unchallenged in the echo chamber of DADT, inspired ignorance and paranoia that prevented gay people from defending themselves and has had a significant impact on Corps culture. With a caveat that additional research is required, the pervasive effect of prejudice embodied in Corps culture upon young Marines (as shown by the survey results) is startling.

An active approach by Corps leaders will be required to overcome cultural bias against gay service members and to execute Congress' and the president's intent to create a more just armed service culture that fully respects the contributions of all service members, regardless of sexual orientation. Ample evidence exists for all leaders to utilize an active approach to disassemble the legacy of ignorance that grew unchallenged during DADT.

To ensure the Corps will "step out smartly,"[67] as Amos has directed, implementation training should not only relate the positive experiences of allied militaries and federal agencies in integrating gay service members but should also emphasize that all Marines are worthy of respect, and that the dignity and civil rights of all Marines will be respected regardless of sexual orientation. All Marines swear the same oath and have earned the "title" the same way, regardless of sexual orientation. Corps leadership must clearly state that as a result, all honorably serving Marines deserve the same respect and consideration. Recognizing and utilizing the honorable examples of gay Marines such as Staff Sergeant Eric Alva, the first Marine casualty of Operation Iraqi Freedom—whose combat injury required the amputation of his right leg—could alleviate fear and ensure gay Marines are accorded the respect due to any combat veteran.

Finally, the comments made during World War II on desegregation by military leaders such as Admiral Nimitz, General Arnold, and General Holcomb are instructive to today's military personnel. Their comments illustrate an important lesson of U.S. history and demonstrate the inexorable trend of more fully applying the rights and privileges of the Constitution to increasing segments of the U.S. population over time. Today's military leaders would do well to recognize this lesson, lest future generations cringe at the ignorance and prejudice on display in 2011, as today's military personnel cringe at that on display in 1941.

Appendix A: Demographics

DADT LEADERSHIP SURVEY—Surveyed Population Demographics

What is your gender?

Answer Options	All Marine		Non-Marine		All Gay Service Members	
	Response Percent	Response Count	Response Percent	Response Count	Response Percent	Response Count
Male	87.3	137	75.0%	27	62.0%	103
Female	12.7%	20	25.0%	9	38.0%	63
Answered Question		157		36		166
Skipped Question		0		0		0

DADT LEADERSHIP SURVEY (continued)

What is your rank?

Answer Options	All Marine		Non-Marine		All Gay Service Members	
	Response Percent	Response Count	Response Percent	Response Count	Response Percent	Response Count
O1-O2	1.2%	2	2.8%	1	9.6%	16
O3	47.8%	75	30.6%	11	9.0%	15
O4	27.4%	43	61.1%	22	5.4%	9
O5	0.6%	1	2.8%	1	4.2%	7
O6 or higher	0.0%	0	0.0%	0	0.6%	1
E1-E3	0.0%	0	0.0%	0	15.7%	26
E4-E5	8.9%	14	0.0%	0	39.2%	65
E6-E7	9.6%	15	0.0%	0	12.0%	20
E8-E9	2.5%	4	0.0%	0	0.6%	1
CWO-CWO2	0.0%	0	0.0%	0	1.8%	3
CWO3-CWO4	1.3%	2	0.0%	0	0.0%	0
CWO5	0.6%	1	0.0%	0	0.0%	0
Other	0.0%	0	2.8%	1	1.8%	3
Answered Question		157		36		166
Skipped Question		0		0		0

DADT LEADERSHIP SURVEY (continued)

What is your duty status?

Answer Options	All Marine		Non-Marine		All Gay Service Members	
	Response Percent	Response Count	Response Percent	Response Count	Response Percent	Response Count
Active Duty	98.7%	155	91.7%	33	79.5%	132
Reservist	1.3%	2	8.3%	3	13.9%	23
Retired	0.0%	0	0.0%	0	1.8%	3
Discharged/ Separated	0.0%	0	0.0%	0	4.2%	7
Other	0.0%	0	0.0%	0	0.6%	1
Civilian	0.0%	0	0.0%	0	0.0%	0
Answered Question		157		36		166
Skipped Question		0		0		0

DADT LEADERSHIP SURVEY (continued)

What is your age?

Answer Options	All Marine		Non-Marine		All Gay Service Members	
	Response Percent	Response Count	Response Percent	Response Count	Response Percent	Response Count
18-24	3.8%	6	2.8%	1	41.0%	68
25-31	35.0%	55	25.0%	9	37.3%	62
32-38	43.9%	69	55.6%	20	13.3%	22
39-45	14.0%	22	13.9%	5	6.0%	10
46-52	3.2%	5	2.8%	1	1.8%	3
53-59	0.0%	0	0.0%	0	0.6%	1
60 or older	0.0%	0	0.0%	0	0.0%	0
Answered Question		157		36		166
Skipped Question		0		0		0

The End of Don't Ask, Don't Tell

DADT LEADERSHIP SURVEY (continued)

What is your service component?

Answer Options	All Marine		Non-Marine		All Gay Service Members	
	Response Percent	Response Count	Response Percent	Response Count	Response Percent	Response Count
USMC	100.0%	157	0.0%	0	21.1%	35
U.S. Army	0.0%	0	41.7%	15	20.5%	34
U.S. Air Force	0.0%	0	16.7%	6	37.3%	62
U.S. Navy	0.0%	0	25.0%	9	19.9%	33
U.S. Coast Guard	0.0%	0	16.7%	6	1.2%	2
U.S. Civilian	0.0%	0	0.0%	0	0.0%	0
Answered Question		157		36		166
Skipped Question		0		0		0

DADT LEADERSHIP SURVEY (continued)

What is your military occupational specialty (MOS) area?

Answer Options	All Marine		Non-Marine		All Gay Service Members	
	Response Percent	Response Count	Response Percent	Response Count	Response Percent	Response Count
Combat Arms	31.2%	49	25.0%	9	12.7%	21
Combat Service Support	38.9%	61	22.2%	8	28.3%	47
Air	18.5%	29	8.3%	3	16.3%	27
Other	11.5%	18	36.1%	13	41.0%	68
Not Applicable	0.0%	0	8.3%	3	1.8%	3
Answered Question		157		36		166
Skipped Question		0		0		0

DADT LEADERSHIP SURVEY (continued)

What is your military occupational specialty (MOS) area?

Answer Options	All Marine		Non-Marine		All Gay Service Members	
	Response Percent	Response Count	Response Percent	Response Count	Response Percent	Response Count
Combat Arms	31.2%	49	25.0%	9	12.7%	21
Combat Service Support	38.9%	61	22.2%	8	28.3%	47
Air	18.5%	29	8.3%	3	16.3%	27
Other	11.5%	18	36.1%	13	41.0%	68
Not Applicable	0.0%	0	8.3%	3	1.8%	3
Answered Question	157		36		166	
Skipped Question	0		0		0	

Notes

1 John Bartlett, *Bartlett's Familiar Quotations*, 17th ed. (New York: Little, Brown and Company, 2002), 704.

2 Text of HR 2965, signed on 22 December 2010 by President Barack Obama to become Public Law 111-321.

3 United States Marine Corps, "Repeal of Don't Ask, Don't Tell Policy", ALMAR 047/10, 23 December 2010, http://www.usmc.mil/news/messages/Pages/ALMAR047-10.aspx. United States Marine Corps, "Execution Guidance For Repeal of Don't Ask, Don't Tell," MARADMIN 108/11, 16 February 2010, http://www.marines.mil/news/messages/ Pages/MARADMIN08-11.aspx/; and

"Reporting Instructions for Repeal of Don't Ask Don't Tell," MARADMIN 143/11, 03 March 2011, http://www.usmc.mil/ news/messages/Pages/MARAD-MIN143-11.aspx.

4 National Defense Research Institute, *Sexual Orientation and U.S. Military Personnel Policy: Options and Assessment* (Santa Monica, CA: RAND, 1993).

5 Office of the Press Secretary, "Remarks by the President in State of the Union Address," transcript, 27 January 2010, http://www.whitehouse.gov/the-press-office/remarks-president-state-union-address.

6 U.S. Department of Defense, *Report of the Comprehensive Review of the Issues Associated with a Repeal of "Don't Ask, Don't Tell": Support Plan for Implementation.* (Arlington, VA: Department of Defense, 2010), 1, 3, www.defense.gov/home/features/2010/0610_dadt/DADTReport_FINAL_201011 30(secure-hires).pdf.

7 In its *Lawrence v. Texas* ruling in 2003, the Supreme Court overturned *Bowers v. Hardwick*, finding that criminalization of homosexual sodomy between consenting adults was unconstitutional. This subsequently prompted lower courts to require a heightened level of scrutiny in DADT cases.

8 DOD, *Report of the Comprehensive Review*, 27.

9 Johnny L. Barnes, "'Don't Ask, Don't Tell' A Costly and Wasteful Choice" (master's thesis, Naval Postgraduate School, 2004), 14–16. The original report has not been declassified.

10 On 2 March 2011, Gates directed a comprehensive review of the impact of DADT repeal be completed. He also directed that this report include a proposed implementation plan.

11 Elizabeth Knowles, ed. *The Oxford Dictionary of Phrases, Sayings and Quotation* (NY: Oxford University Press, 1997), 28.

12 National Defense Research Institute, *Sexual Orientation*, 3.

13 Nathaniel Frank, *Unfriendly Fire* (New York: Thomas Dunne, 2009), 2–3.

14 Jack Drescher, "Queer Diagnoses: Parallels and Contrasts in the History of Homosexuality, Gender Variance, and the 'Diagnostic and Statistical Manual,'" *Archives of Sexual Behavior* 39 (2009): 435.

15 APA Task Force on Appropriate Therapeutic Responses to Sexual Orientation, *Report of the Task Force on Appropriate Therapeutic Responses to Sexual Orientation* (Washington, DC: American Psychological Association, 2009), 11, www.apa.org/pi/lgbt/resources/therapeutic-response.pdf.

16 American Psychiatric Association, *Homosexuality and Civil Rights Position Statement*, December 1973, www.psych.org/share/OMNA/positionstatements.aspx

17 APA Task Force, *Report of the Task Force, 11.*

18 Frank, *Unfriendly Fire*, 810.

19 Ibid., 10; National Defense Research Institute, *Sexual Orientation*, 7, 10.

20 Senator Edward M. Kennedy of Massachusetts, "Additional Views of Mr. Kennedy," Excerpted from the Senate debate regarding the National Defense Authorization Act for Fiscal Year 1994, *Congressional Record* 139 (9 September 1993), S11194 , http://dont.stanford.edu/hearings/hearings.htm.

21 DOD, Report of the *Comprehensive Review*, 21.

22 DOD, DoD 1332.14, *Enlisted Administrative Separations*, 21 December 1993.

23 Public Law 103-160 § 546, 107 Stat. 1670 (1993) (codified at U.S. Code, title 10, subtitle A, section 654), accessed March 4, 2011, http://www.law.georgetown.edu/solomon/background.html.

24 Theodore R. Sarbin and Kenneth E. Karols, *Non-Conforming Sexual Orientations and Military Suitability,* Defense Personnel Security Research and Education Center, PERS-TR-89-002, 1988; and Theodore R. Sarbin, *Homosexuality and Personnel Security* (Monterey: CA, Defense Personnel Security Research and Education Center [PERSEREC], 1991).

25 General Accounting Office, *Defense Force Management: Statistics Related to*

DOD's Policy on Homosexuality, GAO/NSIAD-92-98S (Washington, DC: GAO, 1992), archive.gao.gov/d33t10/146980.pdf; and *Homosexuals in the Military: Policies and Practices of Foreign Countries*, GAO/NSIAD-93-215, (Washington, DC: GAO, 1993), www.gao.gov/products/NSIAD-93-215.

26 Kennedy, "Additional Views of Mr. Kennedy," S11194.

27 Frank, *Unfriendly Fire*, 115–16.

28 Om Prakash, "The Efficacy of "Don't Ask, Don't Tell," *Joint Forces Quarterly* 55 (2009): 89.

29 Aaron Belkin, "'Don't Ask, Don't Tell': Is the Gay Ban Based on Military Necessity?" *Parameters* (2003): 117.

30 Prakash, "The Efficacy of "Don't Ask, Don't Tell," 89.

31 National Defense Research Institute, *Sexual Orientation*, 29; Prakash, "The Efficacy of "Don't Ask, Don't Tell," 90–91; Lawrence J. Korb, Sean Duggan, and Laura Conley, *Why Repeal "Don't Ask, Don't Tell*, PublicSquare.net, 22 November 2010, http://publicsquare.net/repeal-dont-ask-dont-tell.

32 Frank, *Unfriendly Fire*, 113–15.

33 Kennedy, "Additional Views of Mr. Kennedy," S11196–S11198.

34 Belkin, "Is the Gay Ban Based on Military Necessity?," 117.

35 National Defense Research Institute, *Sexual Orientation*, 338–41.

36 DOD, *Report of the Comprehensive Review*, 26–27.

37 Carl Mundy, "Maintain Military Gay Ban," *Washington Times*, 12 January 2010, http://www.washingtontimes.com/news/2010/jan/12/maintain-military-gay-ban/print/.

38 Center for Military Readiness, "Open Letter to Congress and the President on Behalf of Over 1,100 Retired Flag and General Officers in Support of Section 654, Title 10, U.S.C.," 9 April 2009, http://cmrlink.org/HMilitary.asp?docID=350; Flag & General Officers for the Military, 31 March 2009, www.FlagandGeneralOfficersfortheMilitary.com.

39 John M. Shalikashvili, "Gays in the Military: Let the Evidence Speak," *Washington Post*, 19 June 2009, http://www.washingtonpost.com/wp-dyn/content/article/2009/06/18/AR2009061803497.html. Others also echo this claim. See Tammy S. Schultz, "Why are the Marines the Military's Biggest Backers of 'Don't Ask, Don't Tell?'" *Washington Post*, 22 November 2010.

40 Kevin Baron, "Marine Commandant Concluded DADT Repeal May Risk Lives," *Stars and Stripes*, 14 December 2010, http://www.freerepublic.com/focus/f-news/2642976/posts.

41 Lawrence J. Korb, Sean Duggan, and Laura Conley, *"Don't Ask, Don't Tell": Support for Repeal from Conservatives*, PublicSquare.net, 22 November 2010, http://publicsquare.net/dont-ask-dont-tell-support-for-repeal-from-conservatives.

42 Belkin, "Is the Gay Ban Based on Military Necessity?," 118.

43 Martin Luther King Jr., "Letter from Birmingham City Jail," in *A Testament of Hope: The Essential Writings of Martin Luther King, Jr.*, James M. Washington, ed., (San Francisco, CA: HarperCollins, 1986), 293.

44 Martin Luther King Jr., "Stride Toward Freedom: The Montgomery Story," *A Testament of Hope*, 429.

45 In most cases, responses to the questions of Table 3.1 below should paint the same picture as the questions from Table 2.1. Ten of the characteristics examined in Table 2.1 are repeated in Table 3.1. Marine responses were consistent with those detailed in Table 2.1 as the weighted average of all Marine responses regarding DADT's repeal fell between "2" (negative) and "3" (neutral/no effect).

46 Senate Committee on Armed Services, *Department of Defense Authorization for Appropriations for Fiscal Year 2011 and to Receive Testimony Relating to the "Don't Ask, Don't Tell" Policy: Hearing Before the Committee on Armed Services*, 111th Congress, 2nd sess., 2 February 2010, 64.

47 *The Comprehensive Review*, released by the DOD on 30 November 2010 asked only if they served with someone they "believed" to be gay or lesbian.

The End of Don't Ask, Don't Tell

48 Forty-six point two percent of Marines who served with known homosexuals multiplied by 30 percent of whom failed to faithfully execute their duty to enforce DADT.

49 Forty-six point two percent of Marines who served with known homosexuals multiplied by 41.4 percent of whom indicated DADT created situations where they had to compromise their sense of justice to a fellow service member or their duty to comply with the law. Remaining percentages in this paragraph were computed in the same manner.

50 King, "Stride Toward Freedom: The Montgomery Story."

51 *The Comprehensive Review* conducted by DOD found similar phenomena, to include in front line combat units. See DOD, *Report of the Comprehensive Review*, 4–7.

52 Senate Committee on Armed Services, *Department of Defense Authorization for Appropriations for Fiscal Year 2011*, 2 February 2010, 69.

53 DOD, *Report of the Comprehensive Review*, 1.

54 Ibid.

55 For more on how DOMA affects implementation, see the report in this book by LtCol Thomas Dolan, USMC, and Cdr Randall J. Biggs, USN.

56 DOD, Report of the *Comprehensive Review*, 81–82.

57 Randy Shilts, *Conduct Unbecoming: Gays and Lesbians in the U.S. Military* (New York: St. Martins Press, 2005), 187–89.

58 Morris J. MacGregor Jr., *Integration of the Armed Forces, 1940–1965* (Washington, DC: Defense Historical Studies Committee, 1979), http://www.gutenberg.org/files/20587/20587-h/20587-h.htm#page099.

59 Shilts, *Conduct Unbecoming*, 188.

60 President Barack Obama and Vice President Joseph Biden, "Remarks by the President and Vice President at Signing of the Don't Ask, Don't Tell Repeal Act of

2010" www.whitehouse.gov, 22 December 2010, http://www.whitehouse.gov/
the-press-office/2010/12/22/remarks-president-and-vice-president-signing-
dont-ask-dont-tell-repeal-a.

61 Kennedy, "Additional Views of Mr. Kennedy," S11194.

62 DOD, *Report of the Comprehensive Review*, 8.

63 Columbia Law School, *Sexuality & Gender law Clinic, Open Service and Our
Allies: A Report on the Inclusion of Openly Gay and Lesbian Servicemembers in
U.S. Allies' Armed Forces* (New York: Columbia Law School, 2010), 8–10, 12–14.

64 Tammy S. Schultz, "The Few, The Proud, The Problem. Can the Corps' Warrior Ethos Accept Openly Gay Marines?" *Washington Post*, 21 November 2010.

65 DOD, *Report of the Comprehensive Review*, 181–96.

66 Senate Committee on Armed Services, *Hearing to Continue to Receive Testimony on the Report of the Department of Defense Working Group that Conducted
a Comprehensive Review of the Issues Associated with a Repeal of Section 654 of
Title 10, United States Code, "Policy Concerning Homosexuality in the Armed
Forces,"* 111th Congress, 2nd sess., 3 December 2010, 9.

67 General James Amos, *Statement on the Repeal of Title 10, U.S. Code 654 "Policy
Concerning Homosexuality in the United States Armed Forces" (Don't Ask Don't
Tell),* (Arlington, VA: Headquarters Marine Corps, 2010).

It's Time to Redefine the Marine Warrior
by Maj Alasdair B. G. Mackay, USMC

The "Don't Ask, Don't Tell" (DADT) repeal implementation has the potential to disrupt unit cohesion and impact the perception of combat readiness of the U.S. Marine Corps, particularly within the combat arms, unless the Commandant initiates cultural change focused on a shift in the concept of a Marine warrior that is all-inclusive of gender, race, age, religion, and sexual orientation.

The Corps' lack of attention to its own cultural perceptions during the DADT repeal implementation process is likely to increase the propensity for known gay active duty Marines to experience the ostracism, harassment, abuse, and/or violence experienced by women in the Corps. This will lead to an increase in disruption of unit cohesion and affect the perception of combat readiness beyond what is felt with the service of female Marines.

Introduction
In the Words of the Commandant
The Marine Corps prides itself as being a service that demands discipline, exemplifies professional ethos, defines cohesion and esprit de corps, and is exuberant with customs and tradition. On 22 December 2010, President Barack H. Obama signed into law the Don't Ask, Don't Tell Repeal Act, which allows gay men, lesbians, and bisexuals to serve openly in the Department of Defense. This action could result in the largest cultural paradigm shift in the 235 years of the Marine Corps: how Marines self-identify as Marine warriors. On 28 January 2011, the 35th Commandant of the Corps, General James F. Amos, aided by the Marine Corps Sergeant Major Carlton W. Kent, released a video statement to Marines that expressed General Amos' intent for implementation within the service. In his address, Amos said,

It is important that we value the diversity of background, culture, and skills that all Marines bring to the service of our nation. As we implement repeal, I want leaders at all levels to reemphasize the importance of maintaining dignity and respect for one another throughout our force. We are Marines. We care for one another and respect the rights of all who wear this uniform. We will continue to demonstrate to the American people that discipline and fidelity, which have been the hallmarks of the United States Marine Corps for more than 235 years, will continue well in to the future.[1]

The Commandant's vision for implementation is clear and fully supportive of the recommendation that accompanied *The Report of the Comprehensive Review of the Issues Associated with a Repeal of "Don't Ask, Don't Tell"* that distilled the keys to successful implementation down to "leadership-professionalism-respect."[2] However, Corps culture portends a less than ideal implementation process for the law that allows gay and bisexual Marines to serve openly.

As with the rest of the U.S. military, Corps culture traditionally has been homophobic. Gary Mucciaroni says that "the military has been among the most homophobic and repressive institutions in American society."[3] The perception of many Marines is that openly gay and bisexual Marines will display overt behavior or act effeminately.[4] Within this report it is assumed that the Corps' institutional foundation is that of the "Marine warrior," which the Corps sees as the ideal image and behavior of a Marine.

Based on this premise this report offers the theorem that, although the concept of the Marine warrior may be used to refer to all Marines, those Marines who are not included in this paradigm, such as women, are considered cultural outsiders. If gay Marines, potentially excluding lesbian and bisexual Marines who feasibly portray a different and smaller cultural dynamic, decide to serve openly, it is more than likely they will become excluded as an ideal Marine warrior. (They no longer fit the "Marine Warrior Paradigm" [MWP] or cultural image.) As an organizational consequence, there is potentially a higher propensity for ostracism, harassment, abuse, or violence against openly gay Marines (see chart).

The End of Don't Ask, Don't Tell

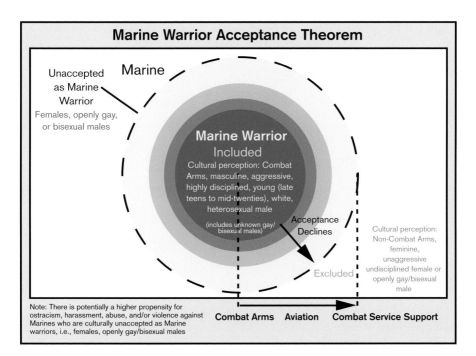

Marine Warrior Acceptance Theorem

Unaccepted as Marine Warrior
Females, openly gay, or bisexual males

Marine

Marine Warrior
Included
Cultural perception: Combat Arms, masculine, aggressive, highly disciplined, young (late teens to mid-twenties), white, heterosexual male
(includes unknown gay/bisexual males)

Acceptance Declines

Excluded

Cultural perception: Non-Combat Arms, feminine, unaggressive undisciplined female or openly gay/bisexual male

Note: There is potentially a higher propensity for ostracism, harassment, abuse, and/or violence against Marines who are culturally unaccepted as Marine warriors, i.e., females, openly gay/bisexual males

Combat Arms   Aviation   Combat Service Support

As a consequence, the DADT repeal implementation has the potential to disrupt unit cohesion and affect the perception of combat readiness in the Corps, particularly within the combat arms, unless the Commandant initiates a cultural change establishing a Marine warrior concept that is inclusive of gender, race, age, religion, and sexual orientation.

To formulate an understanding and need for the Commandant to initiate what many would consider a radical cultural change, this report centers on the Marine warrior concept in a cultural sense. Also, this report provides background to the DADT repeal act and the DADT report, and presents the concerns as expressed by the Corps. This author tries to give readers an understanding of the culture and subcultures of the Corps through the study of history, traditions, customs, values, and social models, including how MWP exists, adapts, and has changed.

This chapter also presents two case studies. One examines how female Marines fit into the current MWP from a historical and cultural perspective and how this relates to gay Marines serving openly. The second looks at how the warrior paradigm was purposely changed to better support the needs of the Corps in its acceptance of maneuver warfare, and how this deliberate change in organizational culture provides the way forward in adapting how the Marine Corps currently views the Marine warrior.

The DADT Repeal Act

The DADT Repeal Act of 2010 rescinded the DADT policy (U.S. Code, title 10, section 654), which, since 1993, prevented openly gay and bisexual people from serving in the U.S. Armed Forces. The Corps, as with all services within the DOD, was required to prepare policies and regulations to ensure implementation was consistent with the standards of readiness and effectiveness, unit cohesion, and recruiting and retention.

On 30 November 2010, the DOD released the DADT repeal report, which focuses on two areas: "assess the impact of the repeal of DADT on military readiness, military effectiveness, unit cohesion, recruiting, retention, and family readiness; and recommend appropriate changes, if necessary, to existing regulations, policies, and guidelines in the event of repeal."[5] The report determined that when coupled with prompt implementation, the risk of repeal of DADT to "overall military effectiveness would be low."[6] The report says that "while a repeal of 'Don't Ask, Don't Tell' will likely, in the short term, bring about some limited and isolated disruption to unit cohesion and retention, we do not believe this disruption will be widespread or long lasting."[7] The most significant recommendations in the report state that the "successful implementation of the repeal of DADT will depend upon strong leadership, a clear message, and proactive education."[8] Except for addressing long-term commitment "to core values of leadership, professionalism, and respect for all," the report makes little mention about culture or the need for cultural change.[9] In particular, it fails to address the issue of how openly gay and bisexual service members will be culturally perceived within their respective services. For instance, the report recommends that services focus on fostering command climates of trust, although no mention is given to fostering command climates that perpetuate inclusiveness. The idea of perpetuating inclusiveness requires more than trust; it also includes cultural understanding and awareness.

The End of Don't Ask, Don't Tell

The Corps' Concerns

On 14 December 2010, General Amos told the press, "I don't want to lose any Marines to the distraction. I don't want to have any Marines that I'm visiting at Bethesda [National Naval Medical Center in Maryland] with no legs be the result of any type of distraction."[10] On the same day, at an Office of the Commandant of the Marine Corps media round table, General Amos further expressed his concerns with the repeal of DADT:

> This is what I call the real deal. And the forces that wear this uniform that are in the middle of what I call the real deal, came back and told their Commandant of the Marine Corps they had concerns. That's all I need. I don't need a staff study. I don't need to hire three PhDs to tell me what it—what to interpret it. I've got—I've got Marines that came back to me as their Commandant and said, we are—we have concerns. So if they have concerns, I do too. That's as simple as that.[11]

It is clear from these comments that there are deep-seated reservations from the Corps' senior officer, and thus the Corps as an institution, in allowing gay and bisexual Marines to serve openly. The Commandant's concerns are echoed in the DADT repeal report that highlights the Corps in several areas, including combat arms, as being opposed to repealing DADT.[12] Similarly, the responses of Marines and combat arms personnel were more negative in comparison to the other services in response to questions about unit cohesion.[13] The DADT report says, "While slightly under 30 percent of service members as a whole predicted repeal would have a negative impact, that number was 43 percent among the Marine Corps . . . and 58 percent among Marine combat arms."[14] The report says "nearly 60 percent of respondents in the Marine Corps . . . said they believed there would be a negative impact on their unit's effectiveness in this context; among Marine combat arms the number was 67 percent."[15] Although cultural influence can stem from personal opinion and bias, it is conceivable that many of these concerns are products of cultural influence. This report is concerned with how Corps culture influences Marines' perceptions and opinions, and how a deliberate change in organizational culture would affect these perceptions and opinions.

The Corps: A Warrior Culture

The MWP is very much a part of the image of the Corps and of what it is to be a Marine. Based upon historical narrative, recruitment campaigns, demographics, and cultural perception, this paper proposes that the Marine warrior image is typified by a masculine, aggressive, highly disciplined, young (late teens to mid-20s), white, heterosexual, male lance corporal. Using this as a foundation, and in order to establish the MWP, it is necessary to develop an understanding from definitional, doctrinal, demographical, historical, and cultural perspectives. It is also essential to comprehend the process by which the paradigm is learned, reinforced, and often fractured within the organization through these perspectives. (Fracturing, for instance, results in areas of the paradigm in which both heterosexual women and gay males fall outside the paradigm due to a stereotype perception of a lack of masculinity, aggressiveness, and discipline.)

Definition and Doctrine

The *Merriam-Webster's Collegiate Dictionary* defines a "warrior" as "a man engaged or experienced in warfare" or more broadly, "a person engaged in some struggle or conflict."[16] From a doctrinal perspective, Fleet Marine Force Manual (FMFM) 1-0, *Leading Marines*, says, "The primary goal of Marine Corps leadership is to instill in all Marines the fact that we are warriors first."[17] *Leading Marines* describes the bond among warriors as "the steel cable that binds every Marine, one to another, and all Marines to the Corps . . . every Marine a warrior and a leader is more than a capability: *it is an attitude and a standard of excellence.*"[18] It is uncertain when the concept of the warrior became part of Corps vernacular; however, Corps doctrine sees it as an important part of its heritage and leadership. General Anthony C. Zinni, USMC (ret.), enhanced the concept of the Marine warrior with his observation that "[Marines] carry a sense of responsibility for those who went before us, which ends up meaning a lot to Marines in combat. We don't want to let our predecessors down or taint our magnificent heritage."[19] Such doctrine both reinforces and perpetuates the demographics of the Corps.

Demographics

The Marine warrior image stereotype is to a degree reflected by the gender and racial distribution in the Corps. According to Corps data for fiscal year 2009, males

The End of Don't Ask, Don't Tell

make up 94.2 percent of active duty officers and 93.6 percent of active duty enlisted Marines. In terms of race, white males make up 82.6 percent of active duty officers (77.8 percent of overall officers) and white males make up 71 percent of active duty enlisted Marines (and 66.4 percent of the overall enlisted population).[20] In age distribution in the active duty Marine forces, only 34.9 percent of the Marine officer corps is between 18 and 25, but 72.3 percent of the enlisted ranks are in this distribution.[21] Importantly, enlisted infantry occupational distribution makes up more than 20 percent of the enlisted active duty force.[22] Active duty male lance corporals make up a quarter of the overall active duty enlisted distribution; female lance corporals make up 0.01 percent of the active duty enlisted force.[23] Putting aside intelligence, physical fitness, and other less tangible characteristics, Corps demographics seem to support the Marine warrior cultural stereotype, which is also perceptually reinforced at the top of the organization. Except for Commandant Amos, who is a naval aviator, all Commandants have been white infantry males.

Historical Narrative

Although the study of the MWP from doctrinal and demographical perspectives is useful in providing an understanding of the characteristics of a warrior and demonstrating the importance of this idiom to the Corps, this analysis falls short of exposing the in-depth background behind the current cultural norms and behaviors of what would be considered today's Marine warrior. Terry Terriff, says that "[t]he narratives that constitute cultural identity . . . are not always composed exclusively from moments in history . . . [instead] they mix historical fact with the apocryphal and the mythical."[24] The Corps' self-identity, for instance, is ingrained in the stories that the Corps tells itself and that each Marine tells the next.[25] "The character of the narratives or stories is such that individual historical figures often become the subject of organizational folklore," Terriff claims, "emerging as larger-than-life figures, which are constituted as much by legend as they are of facts."[26] Perhaps one of the Corps' larger-than-life figures "indelibly etched" in the heart of every Marine warrior is the icon Marine Lieutenant General Lewis B. "Chesty" Puller.[27] Terriff points out that "such organizational 'icons', and even 'mythological' heroes, serve as archetypes to be emulated, and hence their deeds and words persuasively inform what it means to be, in this case, a Marine and for what constitutes appropriate behavior."[28]

The self-identity of the Marine warrior also derives from the past activities or behavior of Marine units, groups, and individuals and is often related to battles. The raising of the U.S. flag at the top of Mount Suribachi on Iwo Jima on 23 January 1945 has not only become imbued with multiple meanings for the identity of the Corps but also what it means to be a Marine warrior.[29] Narrative and symbolism support Corps customs, traditions, and values, and "fashion a mutually constitutive understanding of what it means to be a Marine (or what is the Marine Corps) and how they should behave."[30] Terriff also notes that "such narratives about behavior, whether that of individuals or groups, not only serve initially to constitute identity, they serve in the constant telling and retelling at both the organizational and individual levels to propagate and validate what it means to be a Marine, and in turn shape what is perceived as acceptable and not acceptable."[31] The words supposedly uttered twice by Medal of Honor recipient Gunnery Sergeant Daniel J. Daily during the Battle of Belleau Woods in June 1918 offer one narrative example that pertains to the Marine warrior: "Daily in the midst of this battle is reported to have yelled to a Marine platoon, which had lost its leader and was under intense German fire, 'Come on, you sons of bitches, do you want to live forever' to rally those still able to follow in an assault toward the enemy lines."[32] Narratives such as this are known within all ranks of the Corps and can be considered living history. Such narrative also transcends into many of the comments on military values collected in the surveys for the DADT report.

As pointed out by the Westat analysis to the report,[33] the following quotation exemplifies the idea held by some in the Corps that homosexuality undermines military values: "Belief systems are hardened in the Marines—I re-enlisted because I was afraid to be a civilian—there are things you might accept in the civilian world that you won't accept in the Marines."[34] The quotation is evidence of the narrator's perception of values tied to the Corps experience.

Theoretical Concept

Narratives may also be reinforced by theoretical concepts. For instance, the concepts established by Air Force Lieutenant Colonel Karen O. Dunivin, in her study of military culture, partially supports the MWP and in particular the cultural archetype that characterizes the Marine warrior as a masculine male. Dunivin establishes a "combat masculine warrior paradigm" in her depiction of military culture.[35] She states that "since the primary role of the military is preparation for and conduct of war, the image of the military is synonymous with the image of combat."[36] Dunivin also says that "the second element of the military's cultural paradigm is the 'masculine warrior image.'"[37] She suggests that a "cult of masculinity" has been engrained in military culture throughout history expressing "masculine norm, values, and associated lifestyles."[38] The MWP theorem is directly linked to Dunivin's discussion of the cult of masculinity. Also emphasizing the masculine image, Ray B. Zimmerman states that "the preservation of one's masculinity, in this epistemological system, is dependent on one's renunciation of the feminine and one's acceptance of the violent masculine ethos of the Corps."[39] The "masculine ethos" is clearly linked to the MWP.

Process, Reinforcement, and Fracture

In order to provide a fuller comprehension of the MWP and its elite image, the Corps needs to examine the processes that initiate and perpetuate this culture. This includes the study of recruiting, where the MWP is first initiated; basic training, where the paradigm is enhanced; occupational schools, where MWP starts to become distorted; and the subcultures of the Corps, where the concept of the Marine warrior often becomes intensified, diluted, or challenged.

The sharing of Corps culture begins prior to entry into the service through exposure to the media, movies, and friends and family members who served in the Corps. Zimmerman explains that films such as Stanley Kubrick's *Full Metal Jacket* emphasize "the Marine Corps' 'misogynistic mythology' to basic training and the pervasiveness of its terms to the rhetoric of Marines in the combat zone."[40] Cultural indoctrination is enhanced and accelerated at boot camp for enlisted recruits and at Officer Candidate School (OCS). The image and physical behavior of the Marine warrior begins on the first day with an introduction to their drill instructors, primarily staff noncommissioned officers who can be considered as the primary keepers of Corps culture. Carol Burke, says the Marine Corps is "implacably committed to making men in the mold of the warrior ethos . . . and . . . has set the standard for basic training."[41] This role is passed on from drill instructor to drill instructor with little change in the recruit message.

It could be argued that the reinforcement of the paradigm for female Marines begins on their first day in the Corps. Boot camp and OCS are segregated by gender, and women have women drill instructors and officers. Although this is perhaps lessened by the teaching of Corps history, values, and traditions, it is only strengthened when women recruits become aware of the differing standards for women such as physical fitness, cosmetics and hair, or uniforms.

Either way, the MWP in its purest form is indoctrinated into all new Marines and provides an ingrained foundation for the remainder of their service. Included within the foundation is the simple concept that being inside the MWP is acceptable and being outside the paradigm is unacceptable. Such a concept is not so different from tribal cultures throughout history in which male warriors are put through their paces to be accepted as adults and part of the tribe. Rick Johnson explains that the male initiation ritual within the Zulu tribe of South Africa includes a process of "circumcision . . . seclusion (especially from women), humiliation, and being taught discipline and respect for their culture."[42] Ultimately, the tolerance of acceptability will vary from Marine to Marine; however, invariably much will depend on his or her respective military occupational specialty (MOS) and subculture assignment. The Center for Strategic and International Studies' report, *American Military Culture in the Twenty-First Century*, says that such subcultures play a role in distinguishing and supporting the unique roles different elements play in combat, which includes the cultural perception of outside subcultures.[43] The role subcultures play in reinforcing the MWP is clear, especially for infantry Marines.

The cultural perception of the Marine warrior, particularly for enlisted Marines, is either reinforced or diluted upon graduation from recruit training or OCS. Those Marines assigned to the infantry, arguably the personification of the Marine warrior, attend Infantry Training Battalion (ITB) at the School of Infantry. All other Marines (including women) assigned noninfantry specialties attend Marine Combat Training Battalion (MCT) at the same school. The MWP is reinforced for Marines assigned to ITB to include reinforcement of discipline, esprit de corps, camaraderie, and the elite image. Unlike MCT, all Marines at ITB are male and have male infantry instructors.

For those Marines attending MCT, the cultural reinforcement of the Marine warrior image is less strong. Besides having noninfantry instructors who perhaps are less centered on the paradigm, male Marine students are exposed to female instructors and female students. Although these women perhaps fit the description of "Marine," they do not necessarily fall inside what male Marines consider to be Marine warriors. For noninfantry Marines, the process of dilution continues into MOS school and beyond, into communities or subcultures. A Marine's perception—or tolerance level—of what is acceptable as a Marine warrior generally becomes codified within their various subcultures such as combat arms, aviation, and combat service support.

The path for Marine officers (OCS, The Basic School or TBS, and MOS school) generally mirrors that of their enlisted counterparts, although all officers attend TBS prior to their respective MOS schools. The only variation to this plan is the small percentage of Marine officers who attend the U.S. Naval Academy instead of OCS. However, they attend TBS and MOS schools and are shaped in Marine culture. The bottom line is that by the time enlisted Marines and officers who are assigned to the combat arms, particularly infantry jobs, have completed the training pipeline and have spent a year in the Fleet Marine Force, their cultural indoctrination is significantly more ingrained than their noncombat arms counterparts.

The existence and perpetuation of the MWP and its allied cultural image is apparent from definitional, doctrinal, demographical, historical, and cultural perspectives. Although most Marines do, some do not fall inside the cultural acceptance limits of what a Marine warrior is. By studying these unaccepted warriors, this report asserts that gay Marines who intend to serve openly will become unaccepted warriors even if they were culturally considered a Marine warrior before.

Female Marines: The Unaccepted Warrior

With the passage of the Women's Armed Service Integration Act in 1948, female Marines became a permanent part of the regular Corps.[44] The Marine Corps History Division says that "today, women account for 4.3 percent of all Marine officers and women make up 5.1 percent of the active duty enlisted force in the Marine

Corps . . . Ninety-three percent of all occupational fields and 60 percent of all positions are open to women."[45] But after more than 70 years of active duty service, women are still not included in the MWP. There are multiple reasons why women are not fully accepted as equals in the Corps. This study examines specific areas in which women and gay males have similarities that fall outside the MWP. Lesbians are excluded from examination for two reasons. First, because women make up only a small percentage of the Corps, the number of lesbian Marines on active duty is marginal in terms of this study. Also, lesbians do not necessarily fit the same cultural profile perception or stereotype as gay men. In terms of masculinity and aggressiveness, it is conceivable that some lesbian Marines may be perceived as more acceptable as a Marine warrior than some of their gay male counterparts.

Cultural Masculinity

The perceptual importance of masculinity in the MWP should not be underestimated. General Amos emphasizes the need for "macho warriors" in his response at the media round table on 14 December 2010:

> We recruit on what is historically been—what I would call, and I don't have any other way to say this—but a warrior ethos. We have. And I don't think anybody that has either been around us—and this is not a—I'm not trying to be a macho thing here, I'm just saying this is why—this is—this is what, you know, the nation hires—we're the smallest service. The nation hires its Marines to be that—to be that crisis-response force.[46]

Much of the Marine Corps' iconic culture wraps itself in this warrior ethos to which Amos referred.

In her explanation of masculinity, Melissa S. Herbert goes beyond the simplistic cultural perception that men are masculine and women are feminine with the latter not aligning with what both society and the military consider to be a warrior. She suggests that "when a given role is defined as masculine, many automatically challenge women's ability or suitability to assume that role."[47] Herbert continues, "In a society where we either fail to acknowledge traits in women that seem masculine or censure them, women who seek to enter a work role that is defined as masculine are faced with a number of barriers to their participation."[48] She says, "women may be seen as deviant, and they may find that they have to work at creating an image that allows them to balance their sex-defined gender role with the gendered occupation."[49] In the case of the MWP, this gender-role identity conundrum is perceived as not meeting the masculine cultural norm, particularly when the behavior is seen as deviant. This conundrum is also compounded by women successfully occupying traditional male roles which, as Michael Rustad points out, can generate concerns about the changing nature of the military.[50]

Aggressive Confusion

Aggressiveness is another trait of the Marine warrior that is perceived to be lacking in female Marines and offers a similar conundrum, as does the perception of femininity. The Merriam-Webster's dictionary defines aggression as "a forceful action or procedure (as an unprovoked attack) especially when intended to dominate or master."[51] Theodore Nadelson states "the view that aggressiveness is 'natural' for men and 'unnatural' for women derives more from cultural expectation than from innate female attributes . . . because of the relative limitations imposed on women's aggression in our culture, even defiance is made unnatural for women."[52] The cultural expectation, and indeed the image on which the Corps recruits, is that all Marines need to be aggressive.

The expectation for female Marines at boot camp is for them to display aggressiveness in the same fashion as males. After Marines leave this segregated environment and both sexes begin training alongside each other (except for infantry Marines), the aggressiveness expected of females begins to work against them. Their male counterparts by "virtue of the sex-gender connection" find such behavior abnormal compared to their understanding of societal norms.[53] Herbert says women who are seen as too aggressive (i.e., too much focus on aggressive or violent activities) are not seen as normal or trustworthy.[54] Herbert also says women who are seen as too aggressive or as violating gender norms often become perceived as being gay. In a Catch-22-type dilemma, however, males also penalize women who are considered to be lacking in aggression for not falling inside the culture norm of the Marine warrior. Women in the Corps then often find themselves in a no-win situation when they are compelled to strike a balance of aggression to meet the demands of both their sex role and work role.

Perception of Discipline

Another key trait of the MWP is discipline. As applied in a military sense, the definition of discipline includes "orderly or prescribed conduct or pattern of behavior," "control gained by enforcing obedience or order," and "training that corrects, molds, or prefects the mental faculties or moral character."[55] The lack of discipline that is perceived of women in the military, and which is very much contrary to the MWP, partly comes from their supposed deviant or culturally nonstandard behavior. Frank J. Barrett validates this idea in his study on hegemonic masculinity in the U.S. Navy. He says, "women [in the military] are often depicted as 'innately unsuited,' lacking aggression, discipline, and commitment."[56] Barrett says that "discipline, obedience, compliance, and exacting detail, ideals that are depicted as 'tough' and masculine, depend upon contrasting images of the feminized 'other'—being undisciplined, scattered, emotional, unreliable."[57] The perception of deviancy is generated by women's behavior and actions that require their projecting a balance of masculinity-femininity and aggressiveness-nonaggressiveness. Herbert also says that "while, in general, masculinity is more valued than femininity, being perceived as masculine may have negative repercussions for women."[58] She says, "women who are perceived as having masculine traits [i.e., aggressiveness, tough discipline, directness] may be called names like 'castrating bitch,' but still are generally respected and get the job done."[59] It is therefore feasible that female Marines who are very feminine are further outside the MWP than women who exhibit traits of masculinity that allow them to sit on the peripheral boundary.

Effeminacy: A Warrior Character Flaw

How then, do these perceived Marine warrior character flaws, which place female Marines outside the paradigm and make them unacceptable warriors, also apply to gay Marines who decide to serve openly? "Because homosexuality is read as effeminate," says Elizabeth Kier, "the presence of openly homosexual men shatters the homosocial unity . . . needed to successfully carry out aggression against the enemy conceived as less than a man, that is, a woman."[60] It is this perceived need for masculine unity that underlies the view that women and gay men are a threat to the capabilities of the force. In the more conservative Corps there exists a "culturally embedded view that homosexuality represents a feminization of men."[61]

This perception of a threat is based on stereotyping and has no basis in rational thought. Joshua S. Goldstein believes that "in modern Western wars . . . the intense love that men feel for their comrades creates a sentimental bond associated with femininity in modern thought. . . . This bond easily shades into sexuality."[62] This supposed threat to masculinity has been a recurring theme of concern. According to Magnus Hirschfield, in World War I "homosexuality in military forces was a recurrent concern of commanders, but the actual extent of such activity was quite limited."[63]

The perception of effeminate behavior as a source trait in gay men puts gay males in a cultural inclusion with women in the military. Marine warriors then may assume that if gay Marines are effeminate, they also lack aggressiveness and discipline, and a perception of homosexual deviancy may reinforce a lack of apparent discipline among gay Marines. Therefore, gay Marines who decide to serve openly are perceived as being effeminate, risk being viewed in the same light as women and as a threat to masculine cohesion. This places them outside the MWP and perpetuates the need for culture awareness and change.

Propensity for Ostracism

Another similarity between women and gay service members is a higher propensity for ostracism, harassment, abuse, or violence. Much of the negative behavior, language, and attitudes that are common toward women in the military also exist against gay service members. According to the RAND Corporation report *Sexual Orientation and U.S. Military Policy*, "Interpersonal relations between men and women in the military remain strained, and issues of sexual harassment remain prevalent almost 70 years after the formal integration of women into the military."[64] The report says that "while there is some concern that gay men and lesbians will be harassed or assaulted if they are allowed to serve without restrictions, our discussions with personnel from foreign militaries indicate that the same processes that combat harassment and physical violence against service women can also be used to combat harassment and violence against gay men and lesbians."[65] If the findings of the *Armed Forces 2002 Sexual Harassment Survey* that point to the frequent unprofessional behavior and sexual harassment against female Marines are combined with how gay Marines are perceived against the MWP, it is conceivable to suggest that those gay Marines who serve openly will more than likely experience, at minimum, ostracism and harassment, and perhaps abuse or violence.[66]

Based on their gender, female Marines do not fit the MWP. Although women have been serving in combat alongside infantry Marines in Iraq and Afghanistan, they are culturally unaccepted as Marine warriors. Similarly, although gay Marines have never officially been integrated, they have served in combat throughout the history of the Corps.

Maneuver Warfare and Redefining the Warrior
Changing Culture in the Corps

In 235 years, Marine Corps culture has changed; indeed, there are occasions when the Corps has endured a significant cultural shift. In addition to the integration of black service members in 1948, as well as women later, the Corps experienced a successful introduction of maneuver warfare as its warfighting concept during the tenure of General Alfred M. Gray Jr., the 29th Commandant. Studying maneuver warfare and the associated cultural change required for its implementation provides an opportunity to understand the effort necessary to undertake a cultural paradigm shift within the Corps.

Maneuver warfare as a "warfighting concept was officially introduced as the Marine Corps' overarching doctrine with the promulgation of FMFM-1, *Warfighting*, in 1989."[67] MCDP-1, *Warfighting*, defines maneuver warfare as "a warfighting philosophy that seeks to shatter the enemy's cohesion through a variety of rapid, focused, and unexpected actions which create a turbulent and rapidly deteriorating situation with which the enemy cannot cope."[68] Prior to this, Corps doctrine called for methodical battle, which was a "set piece, closely orchestrated" form of warfare.[69] As Terriff says, "This single event, however, was preceded by a long intra-organizational debate about the potential adoption of maneuver warfare as the Marine Corps' approach to warfighting that stretched back at least to late 1979."[70]

Often referred to as the "attritionists" versus "maneuverists" contest, the foremost part of the early intra-organizational debate began in late 1979 and tailed off toward the end of 1984.[71] Furthermore, "Gray's appointment as the Commandant of the Marine Corps and his promulgation of FMFM-1 was accompanied by a reemergence of this particular debate that persisted until after his retirement in

1991, such that it was not until 1993 that it was argued that the Marine Corps had finally fully 'accepted' maneuver warfare as their concept for warfighting."[72] Maneuver warfare had been successfully tried and tested by the Corps during Operation Desert Storm in 1991.

Selling a New Concept

The implementation of maneuver warfare into the Corps as a new warfighting concept can be equated to selling a new product line. Terriff notes that "the length of the debate preceding the official introduction of maneuver warfare as the Marine Corps warfighting approach, and the time it took after its introduction before it could be contended with confidence that it had been accepted within the Corps, is indicative of how difficult it was to effect this particular innovation."[73]

There were many reasons for the organizational resistance to a new way of war. One of the most important explanations was that the new approach to warfare posed a significant challenge to the Corps' self-identity as "warriors," or more particularly as Terriff states, "how being a 'warrior' (i.e., being a Marine) was interpreted with respect to how they fought."[74] The perception that being a warrior means to "find, close with, and destroy the enemy" stems in no small part from the Marine Corps' role in World War II as "amphibious assault infantry."[75] The change in warfighting was perceived as a distinctive threat to the traditional concept of fighting. "Maneuver warfare as an approach to the conduct of battle with its emphasis on fighting smart thus stood in distinct contrast to fighting tough and tenaciously up close in order to kill the enemy, and hence posed a distinct challenge to a prevailing interpretation of what it meant to be a warrior," Terriff says. The change in tactics was perceived to threaten the constructed identity of Marines as warfighters. "Many Marines at the time perceived that employing maneuver warfare meant that 'there need be no real fighting, no killing'" according to Terriff.[76] A cultural force with which to be reckoned, the concept of maneuver warfare directly challenged the self-identity of Marines, particularly officers.

The New Warrior

In July 1987 General Gray became Commandant—intent on reinvigorating the Corps as a warfighting force and reinstilling a warrior spirit. He understood that doing so would entail wide and deep change in all aspects and practices of the organization. As part of his effort to introduce the new philosophy, Gray attempted to redefine an aspect of the self-identity of the Corps. He saw the characteristics of being a warrior as a hindrance in the acceptance of this change. According to Terriff, "The introduction of maneuver warfare proved successful in large part as various initiatives worked in different ways to overcome this obstacle that had been posed by the Marine Corps' self-identity as 'warriors.'"[77]

General Gray focused on two areas: the redefinition of Marines' self-identities as being warriors and initiatives to change behavior. In the redefinition of Marines' self-identity, Gray consistently articulated that the Corps needed to learn to fight smartly, or execute warfare with intelligence, which altered the definition of the warrior over time. Through the use of terms such as "intelligent warrior" and "fighting smart," Gray reinforced the idea that in order to be warriors, Marines could no longer simply fight "tough." They needed to be able to fight "smart" as well.[78] Terriff says, "Gray's consistent contention that Marines now needed to fight smart as well as tough was given extra weight by the fact that he himself was at the forefront in delivering the message."[79] This message is part of the Corps today.

Initiating Change

Gray also initiated reforms that altered Marine behavior in a manner that was consistent with his interpretation of a warrior and the shift to maneuver warfare. Reforms included overhauling the Corps' education system and creating the Marine Corps University, issuing "The Commandant's Reading List," and replacing scripted, rehearsal-like field exercises with field exercises based on free play and creative intelligence.[80] These reforms opened up Marines, particularly officers, to new ideas and developed their critical thinking. "Even more compelling than Marines learning the benefits of maneuver warfare piecemeal through their personal experiences in the revamped military exercises," Terriff says, "was the successful application of the mind-set of maneuver warfare by the U.S.-led Coalition during Desert Storm in 1991."[81] This reinforces the point that positive experience within the organization over time will significantly codify initiatives put into place to purposely change culture.

Undertaking a Corps cultural paradigm shift, which not only changes the way the organization functions but also changes cultural self-identity, is a feasible endeavor owing to strong leadership that understands the organizational culture and the benefits of change. Gray's approach to culture change, to include shifting the Corps' understanding of what it was to be a warrior, is pertinent today. In order for the Corps to better support the spectrum of military operations, it must consider redefining the Marine warrior identity to be more inclusive. "Changing a persistent cultural characteristic cannot be accomplished quickly," Terriff says, and "managing the problem will take careful thought, sustained effort, and considerable patience if the change desired is to be accomplished successfully."[82] Although Gray's approach to changing Marines' self-identity of what it meant to be a warrior was subtle, it was holistic and came from the top of the hierarchy.

The Future

The lessons learned from General Gray's leadership in changing the Corps' identity are applicable here. Leadership is vital to cultural change. Without proactive, aggressive leadership, the cultural change needed for the MWP to evolve to include gay and female Marines is not possible. The existing MWP has the potential to disrupt unit cohesion and impact the perception of combat readiness in the Corps, particularly within the combat arms fields that are the center of the paradigm. As gay Marines become open about their sexual orientation and are forced outside the paradigm as a result, the nature and level of disruption is most likely to be comparable to units that have women. For units such as combat arms, in which the MWP is most prevalent, it is likely that disruption to unit cohesion will be the greatest and have a perceived impact on combat readiness.

Studies argue that a lack of unit cohesion has a perceived impact on combat readiness. "Cohesion's value stems from its presumed and demonstrated relation to individual and group performance in social psychology," James Griffith says, "and in relation to combat effectiveness and performance in the military."[83] Unless the MWP changes, disruption to unit cohesion and the resulting perception of decline in combat readiness will only marginalize those who are different even further, perpetuating a continuing cycle.

The Corps' future does not necessarily rest on whether the MWP shifts toward being all-inclusive. However, as a military institution that represents a diverse nation, the Corps should consider how it projects its self-identity and supports equality. The culture of the Corps, and associated perceptions and opinions, will have to adjust if openly gay Marines, as well as female Marines, are to be included as more than nominal warriors. Gray proved that Corps culture and identity could transform to include what Marines understood to be a Marine warrior. He demonstrated that undertaking a radical cultural paradigm shift is achievable.

Undertaking such a change is not easy and requires effort and resources on the part of the leadership, particularly the Commandant. Gray understood that alteration had to be seen as coming from the top. Just as Gray sold the benefits of the maneuver warfare and the more intelligent Marine warrior, the current Commandant needs to sell the benefits of a new Marine warrior that draws on the experiences, talents, and diversity of all its members, and which better suits the operational needs of the Corps. In establishing a new Marine warrior initiative, the Corps must also determine if the future operational requirements will satisfactorily be met by a force structure and cultural environment that has a by-product of harassment, abuse, and violence against a small percentage of the organization, or if future operational commitments would be better met by a Corps that is structurally diverse, culturally inclusive, and without diversion to unit cohesion or perceived combat readiness.

The Marine Corps has a history and foundation in customs, traditions, and values. Its culture and subcultures are complex to comprehend and a strong force to reckon with when attempting to incorporate an unpopular cultural change. Although the current MWP is strong on the battlefield, its divisive nature only harms the elite image it seeks to perpetuate.

Notes

1 Palm Center, "Marine Commandant Sends Strong Signal of Inclusion of Gays and Lesbians," 30 January 2011, http://www.palmcenter.org/press/dadt/releases/marines_commandant_sends_strong_signal_inclusion_gays_and_lesbians.

2 U.S. Department of Defense, *Report of the Comprehensive Review of the Issues Associated with the Repeal of "Don't Ask, Don't Tell": Support Plan for Implementa-*

tion (Arlington, VA: Department of Defense, 2010), 2, http://www.defense.gov/home/features/2010/0610_dadt/.

3 Gary Mucciaroni, *Same Sex, Different Politics* (Chicago: University of Chicago Press, 2008), 177.

4 Westat, *Support to the DoD Comprehensive Review Working Group Analyzing the Impact of Repealing "Don't Ask, Don't Tell," Volume 1: Finding as from the Qualitative Research Task* (Rockville, MD: Westat, 2010), 34, http://www.defense.gov/home/features/2010/0610_dadt/.

5 U.S. Department of Defense, *Report of the Comprehensive Review of the Issues Associated with a Repeal of "Don't Ask, Don't Tell* (Arlington, VA: Department of Defense, 2010), 1, http://www.defense.gov/home/features/2010/0610_dadt/.

6 Ibid., 3.

7 Ibid.

8 Ibid., 10.

9 Ibid., 3.

10 Palm Center, "Amos under Fire For DADT Comments," 30 January 2011, http://www.palmcenter.org/press/dadt/in_print/amos_under_fire_dadt_comments.

11 General James F. Amos, *Officer of the Commandant of the Marine Corps Media Round Table* (Washington, DC: Federal News Service, 2010), http://www.usmc.mil/unit/hqmc/cmc/Documents/Media%20Round%20Table%20101214.pdf.

12 Department of Defense, *Report of the Comprehensive Review*, 4.

13 Ibid., 74.

14 Ibid.

15 Ibid.; U.S. Marine Corps respondent demographics for this survey were 10,740 active duty and 5,869 reserves. Westat, *Support to the DoD Comprehensive*

Review Working Group Analyzing the Impact of Repealing "Don't Ask, Don't Tell," Volume 2: Findings as from the Qualitative Research Task (Rockville, MD: Westat, 2010), 25, http://www.defense.gov/home/features/2010/0610_dadt/.

16 *Merriam-Webster's Collegiate Dictionary*, 11th ed., s.v. "warrior."

17 Headquarters U.S. Marine Corps, *Leading Marines*, FMFM 1-0 (Washington, DC: U.S. Marine Corps, 1995), 93.

18 Ibid., 33.

19 Tom Clancy, Tony Zinni, and Tony Koltz, *Battle Ready* (New York: Putnam, 2005), 142.

20 Statistics derived from Headquarters U.S. Marine Corps, *USMC Concepts & Programs*, 2010 (Washington, DC: Headquarters, U.S. Marine Corps, 2009), 226–75.

21 Ibid.

22 Ibid., 273.

23 Ibid., 274.

24 Terry Terriff, "Warriors and Innovators: Military Change and Organizational Culture in the U.S. Marine Corps," *Defense Studies* 6 (2006): 217.

25 Ibid.

26 Ibid.

27 Ibid.

28 Ibid., 218.

29 Ibid.

30 Ibid.

31 Ibid.

32 Ibid., 221.

33 Westat, a corporation that provides research services, surveyed half-a-million

active duty and reserve military members and spouses for their views on the impact of possible DADT repeal.

34 Westat, *Support to the DoD Comprehensive Review Working Group*, 31–32.

35 Karen O. Dunivin, "Military Culture: Change and Continuity," *Armed Forces and Society* 20 (1994): 533.

36 Ibid.

37 Ibid.

38 Ibid., 534.

39 Ray B. Zimmerman, "Gruntspeak: Masculinity, Monstrosity and Discourse in Hasford's The Short-Timers," *American Studies* 40 (1999): 69.

40 Ibid., 65.

41 Carol Burke, *Camp All-American Hanoi Jane, and The High-and-Tight: Gender, Folklore, and Changing Military Culture* (Boston: Beacon Press, 2004), 45.

42 Rick Johnson, *The Power of a Man: Using Your Influence as a Man of Character* (Grand Rapids, MI: Revell, 2009), 107.

43 Center for Strategic and International Studies (CSIS), *American Military Culture in the Twenty-First Century* (Washington, DC: CSIS Press, 2000), 4.

44 U.S. Marine Corps History Division Online, "Women in the Marine Corps," July 2006, http://www.tecom.usmc.mil/HD/Frequently_Requested/Women.htm.

45 Ibid.

46 General James F. Amos, *Office of the Commandant of the Marine Corps: Media Round Table*, 14 December 2010, http://www.marines.mil/unit/hqmc/cmc/Documents/Media%20Round%20Table%2020101214.pdf

47 Melissa S. Herbert, *Camouflage Isn't Only for Combat: Gender, Sexuality, and Women in the Military* (New York: NYU Press, 1998), 31.

48 Ibid.

49 Ibid., 31–32.

50 Michael Rustad, *Women in Khaki: The American Enlisted Women* (New York: Praeger, 1982), 191.

51 *Merriam-Webster's Collegiate Dictionary*, 11th ed., s.v. "aggression."

52 Theodore Nadelson, *Trained to Kill* (Baltimore: The Johns Hopkins University Press, 2005), 157.

53 Herbert, *Camouflage Isn't Only for Combat*, 46.

54 Ibid., 75.

55 *Merriam-Webster's Collegiate Dictionary*, 11th ed., s.v. "discipline."

56 Frank J. Barrett, "The Organizational Construction of Hegemonic Masculinity: The Case of the U.S. Navy," *The Masculinities Reader*, eds. Stephen M. Whitehead and Frank J. Barrett (Malden, MA: Polity Press, 2001), 96.

57 Ibid.

58 Herbert, *Camouflage Isn't Only for Combat*, 33.

59 Ibid.

60 Joshua S. Goldstein, *War and Gender: How Gender Shapes the War System and Vice Versa* (Cambridge: Cambridge University Press, 2001), 374.

61 Ibid., 375.

62 Ibid.

63 Ibid., 376.

64 National Defense Research Institute, *Sexual Orientation and U.S. Military Personal Policy* (Santa Monica, CA: RAND Corporation, 2010), 400, http://www.rand.org/pubs/monograph_reports/MR323.html

65 Ibid.

66 Rachel N. Lipari and Anita R. Lancaster, *Armed Forces 2002 Sexual Harass-*

ment Survey (Arlington, VA: Defense Manpower Data Center, 2002), http://www.defense.gov/news/Feb2004/d20040227shs1.pdf.

67 Terriff, "Warriors and Innovators," 220.

68 Headquarters U.S. Marine Corps, *Warfighting*, MCDP-1 (Washington, DC: U.S. Marine Corps, 1997), 73.

69 Richard D. Hooker, *Maneuver Warfare: An Anthology* (Novato, CA: Presidio Press, 1993), 248.

71 Ibid., 221.

72 Ibid.

73 Ibid., 220.

74 Ibid.

75 Ibid., 222.

76 Ibid.

77 Ibid., 223.

78 Ibid.

79 Ibid.

80 Ibid., 224.

81 Ibid., 226.

82 Ibid., 239.

83 James Griffith, "Multilevel Analysis of Cohesion's Relation to Stress, Well-Being, Identification, Disintegration, and Perceived Combat Readiness," *Military Psychology* 14 (July 2002): 217.

Part Two
The Essays

Introduction to the Essays

by J. Ford Huffman

Each compelling essay you are about to read is signed.

Why did this anthology insist on attaching a name to each article? Why not permit active duty, gay service members to write anonymously?

Because anonymity lacks credibility, adds mystery, and breeds distrust in many readers' minds. None of that seems appropriate in a collection about the impact of the repeal of a law that required some service members to remain anonymous or be discharged.

The decision to use bylines did limit the number of submissions. One soldier wanted to write but to do so would mean outing himself before 20 September: "For me to participate in this very important and timely submission," the officer e-mailed from Iraq, "I would have to engage PAO [public affairs office] prior to the full repeal—and that has its own inherent pitfalls."

One Marine predicted few on-base parades and few on-the-record essayists: "Most active duty Marines I know do not intend to come screaming out of the closet on 20 Sept," wrote the gay officer, an Iraq veteran. "Most only intend to tell a select few of their colleagues, if anyone. Even those who are secure in their orientation may not be ready to have their feelings about such a personal subject published with their name attached."

Some did. In this book, three active duty Marine officers publicly identify as gay for the first time. Another Marine officer-essayist, Major Darrel L. Choat, publicly came out last September when he mentioned this anthology in a commentary he wrote for the *Washington Post* and in an NPR interview.*

---

* Darrel Choat, "When Will Marine Leadership Stand Up for Gay Service Members?" *Washington Post*, 20 September 2011, www.washingtonpost.com/opinions/when-will-marine-leadership-stand-up-for-gay-service-members/2011/09/16/gIQARLXfhK_story.html; Rachel Martin, "'Don't Ask, Don't Tell' Is Done; What Now?" *Morning Edition*, NPR, 20 September 2011, www.npr.org/2011/09/20/140615384/dont-ask-dont-tell-is-done-what-now.

Requests for essays were sent to 121 active duty service members and veterans—straight and gay, female and male, officer and enlisted—plus a dozen civilians with military expertise. What was the reward for agreeing to write a maximum 1,500 words without pay? Being considered for publication, being edited, and receiving a copy of this book.

The result? "Good gouge," as Marines say. There are essays from 25 diverse voices, each with individual insight: 14 are Marine, 5 are Army, 4 are Navy, and 2 are Air Force. Eighteen essayists are male and seven are female. What is the gay-straight breakdown? Readers may compile their own tallies. Two essayists' research studies are in the book, also.

The editors sought diversity in race, age, and viewpoint. Examples of this diversity are apparent throughout the essays. In addition, the editors heard these perspectives:

- Colonel Anne M. M. Weinberg, USMC, whose sense of humor allows her to identify as an "openly straight and dedicated heterosexual woman," responded that the DADT policy "always struck me as antithetical to the warrior ethos I was attracted to when I chose to make the military my career." Weinberg wrote, "The DADT policy was akin to an ostrich's sticking its head into the ground. The policy lacked the integrity Marines espouse daily in every clime and place. Rather than confronting this issue, the Corps chose to force patriotic, loyal, and dedicated men and women to deny a part of their existence. Cowering from a challenge is not a part of our learned or taught Marine culture."

- Writing from a war zone, Staff Sergeant Carlos J. Guitron, USMC, responded with a handful of questions after 10 years in the Corps, including this one: "I'm deployed to Afghanistan. Marines and sailors die here, and I wonder how many of these brave men and women who gave their lives are gay. I wonder if their loved ones are not being officially notified about their deaths. Must their partners learn about the deaths through the news media or some other unofficial way—because of a stupid policy?"

- A career military member presumed an antirepeal essay would not be considered. On the contrary—we encouraged the service member to explain how "the military up until now has provided a wholesome 1950s-style environment for raising a family with traditional American values" and how the repeal might affect that traditional atmosphere. The service member chose not to take the opportunity to be a part of this anthology.

Others accepted the invitation, and here are their words. The first essay is by former Marine Corps War College director, retired Colonel Michael F. Belcher, and the others are in the following thematic order.

Serving while openly gay: An enlisted Marine and a Navy officer continued to serve during the lengthy legal processes that resulted from their discharges.

Women at war: Three women write about the pressures of being female and gay in a combat zone traditionally considered to be a straight man's world.

Return to duty: Four essayists express their hopes for resuming their service to their county despite the anguish of being humiliated by their discharges.

One of my best friends: A former sailor and a former Marine officer write about fellow service members—their friends—who happened to be gay.

At ease with myself: Six men and two women describe the arduous path toward self-acceptance in an organization that by law could not accept them.

Marching forward: Five writers look at the past to see a future when the "knife is out of (gay service members') backs."

To Think Critically and Creatively, to Dare to Know
by Col Michael F. Belcher, USMC (Ret.)

Malaise:
> *1. A vague feeling of physical discomfort or uneasiness, as early in an illness.*
> *2. A vague awareness of moral or social decline.*[*]

Admit it. It's no big deal. Really. You're not alone. You're not different, unusual, or strange. Many people share similar thoughts and feelings. It's only natural. Be honest. Admit that you feel uneasy reading this anthology.

Stop pretending that you did not feel the slightest twinge of anxiety in opening this book. Accept the queasiness that has crept into the pit of your stomach. Acknowledge the apprehension that gnaws at the back of your brain. Notice how since picking up this book you've glanced around furtively to observe who is observing you. Note how you've devised a ready quip to discount the text and thereby deflect interest away from your interest in the topic. Armed with this new consciousness, have the mental clarity and moral courage to accept the discomfort brought on by contemplating the repeal of the Department of Defense's "Don't Ask, Don't Tell" (DADT) policy.

Whether you are unabashedly homophobic, unashamedly homosexual, or somewhere safely in between, talk of sexuality is always disquieting. Even in private, such discussions are intensely intimate and frighteningly revealing. They require the participants to examine bedrock beliefs (theological, biological, sociological, and philosophical) as well as personal passions. So then, how much more disconcerting is a public debate regarding the effects of admitting openly homosexual and bisexual individuals into the ranks of the U.S. military? Exponentially so. Such discourse calls into question not only the beliefs, biases, and behaviors of individuals,

---

[*] *Webster's New World Collegiate Dictionary*, 11th ed., s.v. "malaise."

but also those of the institutions they serve. Such discussion exposes to public scrutiny the organization's most sacred artifacts—its history, values, norms,* and narratives—the institutional infrastructure that provides its members with unity and identity. Open debate opens the doors for insiders and outsiders to explore the closed and close confines of military society. Whether armed with scholarly intent or social agendas, these critics and champions project harsh light into the dark corners of the military's organizational and psychological terrain. The light cast can be illuminating or distorting, depending on its angle and intensity. It can reveal stark truths, even as it casts false and frightening shadows. Either way, these intellectual expeditions are not for the faint of heart because they invariably raise more questions about the future than they resolve about the past.

As scholars, sociologists, and students of the military shed light on what is behind us, they project looming shadows on what is ahead. They give shape, if not substance, to our phantom fears about such issues as gay marriage, benefits, entitlements, billeting, and housing. In the shifting images, we discern male Marines dancing cheek-to-cheek at the Marine Corps Ball, displays of affection between military partners at the mall, and awkward glances in the shower stalls. Alternatively, we foresee hurtful berating and horrific beatings of gay service members who happen to demonstrate the courage or candor to reveal their sexual orientation. We question whether enduring leadership principles can sustain "good order and discipline" in the more socially permissive environment ahead. Never officially having had admitted gay personnel, the U.S. military does not know or understand its gay members. Never having served in an accepting military environment, gay members do not know or trust the U.S. military. Yet, both sides are united in their fear of the unknown future and the changes—major or minor—that will result. Consequently, no matter what your orientation or outlook on the repeal, your discomfort is defendable; your uneasiness is understandable. More importantly, it is critical to coming to terms with this modern military malaise.

---

* *Cultural norms* are defined as "the rules that a group uses for appropriate and inappropriate values, beliefs, attitudes, and behaviors. These rules may be explicit or implicit. They have also been described as the "customary rules of behavior that coordinate our interactions with others." Robert Axelrod, *The Evolution of Cooperation* (New York: Basic Books, 1984).

The End of Don't Ask, Don't Tell

By acknowledging our shared anxiety, we have highlighted the fact that this is an issue that must be addressed openly, honestly, intelligently, and unemotionally. As a mentor once advised me, "if you are reluctant to ask a hard question of your subordinates or yourself because you fear the response or consequences, you must ask it! Don't take counsel of your fears, but take the clue, then take action." He noted that because of their responsibility to the nation and those with whom they serve, military leaders do not have the luxury of avoiding uncomfortable situations or turning a blind eye to complex, confusing, or contentious problems. Instead, he stressed that leaders must seek them out and confront them at each and every opportunity. To paraphrase his guidance, good leaders see the world in black and white, right or wrong, go or no-go. Great leaders see the gray areas and operate accordingly, amidst the uncertainty and ambiguity, making the hard decisions others can't or won't.

Another former commander talked about how his "spidey senses [sic]"[*] alerted him to situations requiring his immediate and rapt attention. Given the common apprehension regarding the repeal of DADT, I detect our communal "spidey sense" is tingling, notifying us that our attention is required.

In a 2010 blog entry, Admiral James G. Stavridis, Commander, U.S. European Command, and Supreme Allied Commander, Europe, highlighted the value of both fear and professional authorship and provided the way ahead for addressing our DADT angst:

> The enormous irony of the military profession is that we are huge risk takers in what we do operationally—flying airplanes on and off a carrier, driving a ship through a sea state five typhoon, walking point with your platoon in southern Afghanistan—but publishing an article, posting a blog, or speaking to the media can scare us badly. We are happy to take personal risk or operational risk, but too many of us won't take career risk.[**]

---

[*] Reference to the Marvel Comics superhero Spider-Man, aka Peter Parker, created by writer-editor Stan Lee and writer-artist Steve Ditko in 1962. His creators gave Spider-Man the ability to react to danger quickly with his "spider-sense."

[**] Admiral James Stavridis, *EUCOMversations Blog*, "From the Bridge: Whispers on A Wall," *EUCOMversations Blog*, 25 October, 2010, http://useucom.wordpress.com/2010/10/25/whispers-on-a-wall/.

Implicit in his comment is the recognition that—individually and collectively— we in the military are operationally successful because we embrace fear. We accept the anxiety that comes when putting ourselves in harm's way. We recognize fear as the natural by-product of the uncertainty, volatility, and hazard inherent in our work. Fueled by this awareness, we plan, prepare, and proceed accordingly, conscientiously assessing the risks then meticulously mitigating their negative effects. Explicit in Admiral Stavridis' comment is a call for service members to think and write. He chides us to broadcast our thoughts on critical issues regarding the nation and its armed forces and to do so without fear of personal rebuke or professional retribution. Absent from his comment is any restriction regarding what issues to address. Instead, he challenges service authors to be outspoken on issues that could jeopardize their careers. In doing so, he champions diverse, divergent thought like the views expressed in this anthology.

Whether military or civilian, straight or gay, liberal or conservative, we feel trepidation as we contemplate the DADT repeal. For some, repeal means aligning their personal ideology with organizational policy. For others, it means aligning personal authenticity and cultural identity. For all, it means adapting and accepting: adapting to new social models and accepting those with different beliefs, biases, and behaviors; adapting to change and accepting the fear that comes from it. Our shared anxiety is our alarm, a wake-up call to think critically and creatively about the post-DADT military.

I encourage you to recognize your mental discomfort, revel in your emotional duress, and attentively read on. The personal essays and scholarly studies in this anthology can fascinate and can infuriate. Some will alter your outlook and others will affirm your opinion. But taken in full measure, these works are the right medication for treating the vague uneasiness—the mental, moral, and social malaise— we all suffer waiting for the unknown to become known.

Coming Out in 1993 and Serving as a Gay Marine
by Justin Crockett Elzie

After spending nearly 10 years in the closet in the Marine Corps, I decided in January 1993 to stand up and come out.

Why? If I had not said something about the discrimination against gay people in the military, I would have been a coward. I love the Corps and thought my coming out could change the Corps for the better and make a difference for gay Marines. At the time I trusted that President Clinton would lift the ban on gay men and women in the military, but later I found out that would not happen.

In March 1993, a discharge board hearing acknowledged that I was an exemplary Marine but that my statement that I was gay was sufficient to discharge me.

I had thought my record would be enough to change minds. I was idealistic and didn't realize I was trying to use a logical argument for an issue that involved a lot of emotion for most Marines, including me. I thought that if a Marine was good, the Corps would be hard-pressed to discharge him. As soon as President Clinton announced DADT, the Marine Corps moved quickly and I became the first Marine discharged under DADT.

After my discharge, I was reinstated by the courts until my case was completed. I thought that if I worked really hard during reinstatement I might be able to stay a Marine and be promoted to staff sergeant. I wanted to see how far I could go in breaking the glass ceiling for an openly gay Marine.

The troops and fellow noncommissioned officers were comfortable around me. In April 1994 I got a fitness report from the major I worked for, and he rated me "outstanding" in all areas: handling enlisted personnel, training personnel, personal appearance, military presence, attention to duty, initiative, judgment, cooperation, force, economy of management, leadership, loyalty, and growth potential. I was "excellent" in administrative duties and qualified for promotion. He wrote:

Sergeant Elzie is a personable NCO, amiable and likeable. Honest, sincere, with the highest integrity, he is meticulously thorough in his work. A rapid and intense worker, he produces accurate and timely results. He possesses a high degree of initiative and requires a minimum of supervision, and choice of methods of accomplishing desired results are exceptionally good. Likeable, with an excellent sense of humor, and an ingrained respect for his fellow Marine, he secures a high degree of loyalty and cooperation from his subordinates in whom he instills a great sense of personal responsibility for the quality of their work. His subordinates respect him and honor his judgment, as he is always willing to and does accept their suggestions when they have merit.

When my report went up the chain of command, the colonel added these comments:

I do not disagree with the Reporting Senior's evaluation of Sergeant Elzie's technical competence and his work ethic. Nor do I disagree that the results of Sergeant Elzie's efforts are not generally well above the norm, considering his time in grade and time in service and in this supporting establishment environment of Base Logistics. I have directly and indirectly observed these things myself.

However, given his professed sexual preferences and Department of Defense policy regarding homosexual conduct, Sergeant Elzie cannot be considered qualified for retention. Thus, he cannot be considered qualified for promotion.

When I saw the colonel's response, I realized that some in the Corps were not going to let me move up the ladder, even if my supervisors recommended my promotion. I began to understand that I might not be able to stay in the Corps, even if I won in the courts.

At the rifle range in September 1994, I qualified as expert, with 237 points out of a possible 250 points, and was the high shooter in my detail that week. I liked shooting weapons and was a qualified rifle and pistol expert.

Later that month a story about my second year of serving openly in the Marines was published in *Navy Times* (*Marine Corps Times* was not introduced until 1999).

The article mentioned my shooting score, my fitness report, and the colonel's rebuttal. The story created a firestorm and was a watershed in how I was looked at by many Marines.

Navy Times received a deluge of responses. On-base, my interactions with other Marines were overwhelmingly positive, as though I had broken through a ceiling. Attitudes changed from contempt to respect. But Marines who didn't want me in the Corps were livid. In the local newspaper, a couple of sergeants wrote that I had dishonored the Corps. Obviously they had problems seeing that a gay Marine could do well, and my record went against their prejudices. Many other Marines said they had read the article, didn't realize I was still in, and said that I ought to "hang in there."

I was outside the chow hall a couple of days after the *Times* article and a Humvee pulled up and stopped in front of me. A staff sergeant jumped out, came to me, reached out his hand, thanked me, and told me to "hang in there." I was surprised and overwhelmed and didn't know what to say except "thanks."

In November 1996 I attended my last Marine Corps Ball. I felt a little detached because I had changed and matured while serving as openly gay for three years. I loved the Corps but had outgrown it.

In February 1997 a court settlement said I could be discharged honorably. I was happy to move on—I was burnt out—but sad because I was ending a 14-year career. I had made a difference, but I hadn't changed the Corps in the way I had wanted.

I proved that a Marine who happens to be gay can serve as well as a Marine who happens to be straight, with no detriment to morale or impact to mission operation. But my victory was hollow because DADT was still there. The ban on gay service members had a profound effect on my life.

However, I had earned the title of Marine and was able to leave the Corps with my dignity and self-worth. Once a Marine, always a Marine, and nobody could take that away from me.

An Openly Gay Navy Officer for Four Years

by R. Dirk Selland

It was my father's naval service and his civilian career that followed that helped inspire me to join the Navy. I wanted to be a part of a tradition that took young men and women and prepared them to be leaders. I wanted to be a contributing member of an organization that fought for the protection of this country's rights. So when the Navy offered me a Reserve Officer Training Corps (ROTC) scholarship at North Carolina State University, I signed acceptance to the program.

My four years as a midshipman, including being editor of the ROTC newsletter and being in charge of the color guard, were challenging but inspiring. There were also the hot summers steaming off the coast of Liberia on the USS *Saipan* (LHA 2), as well as tackling the Marine obstacle course at the amphibious base in Norfolk. And after graduation I was thrilled to be 1 of the 14 officers aboard the 123-member crew fast-attack nuclear submarine USS *Hammerhead* (SSN 663). I'll never forget or regret these years.

I accepted the possibility that pursuing a military career meant I might one day be called to war. But I never thought the battle I'd have to fight would be against the Navy. In the past several years, I had to make some of the toughest decisions I would ever have to make, decisions that would set my career and my life's dream on a crash course with the U.S. armed services.

The social environment within the wardroom changed once a new commanding officer (CO) took command the summer of 1992, and Bill Clinton promised during his campaign that he would lift the ban on homosexuals serving in the military. As time went on, crude and disgusting jokes about gay men and lesbians dominated the mealtime conversation. These insensitive remarks were gnawing at me inside but in no way affected my performance. When the president was sworn in, I felt it was my duty to talk to the CO about exercising good judgment in helping change the tone of the wardroom.

As the news media began focusing on President Clinton's vow to sign an executive order lifting the ban, I made decision number one. With the squadron chaplain by my side, I confided to my CO—the day after Clinton was sworn in—what had been common knowledge to most shipmates for several months: I was gay, a perception that was generated in great part by the fact that I did not talk about women or bring a date to officer socials.

Rather than keep this information in confidence, the CO called the commodore with the news and then told me to gather my belongings and leave the ship. I was surprised by his actions and told him that I couldn't fathom the idea that this would be the last time I would ever sit in his stateroom. I couldn't believe that I would not have the chance to say goodbye to my fellow officers or the guys who worked for me. I told the captain that I didn't have a bag to pack my clothes, and without hesitation he offered me his gym bag. It was a lonely walk down the end of the pier to my car, and on my drive home in the middle of the night, I was thinking, "What have I just done?" I have not been back on the submarine since that night.

Although there had been the perception that I was gay, I had been able to integrate myself fully into ship operations and to command the respect of my superiors, peers, and subordinates. I had a strong working relationship with everyone. I can state emphatically that there was no adverse effect whatsoever on order, discipline, or morale, and that we were able to function as a cohesive unit.

After I was assigned to shore duty, I made decision number two: to challenge a powerful institution and its discriminatory policy. Through the help of my lawyers, I was able to serve an additional four years, which was considered (at the time) to be the longest period anyone had served as an openly gay Navy officer.

We won an injunction in federal court under the pre-DADT policy to keep me in the Navy, though on shore duty. As one of the few active duty members litigating the pre-DADT policy, I was invited to be one of two officers to testify at the Senate Armed Services Committee hearing, a dramatic event held in Norfolk on the world's largest naval base before a nationally televised audience—all for the purpose of allowing Congress to deliberate Clinton's proposed policy.

I told the senators and the world that

> I am here for one simple reason—because I love my country and I want to

be able to continue in its service. And I do not believe that I, and other men and women like myself, should be denied this opportunity merely because of our sexual orientation. I have worked hard at my profession and, I believe, have served my country with distinction. Now I am being separated not because of any misconduct on my part, nor because of a lack of competence or commitment, but because I have acknowledged that I am gay. A characteristic that I am born with, not a choice as some would lead you to believe. Sir, one would not choose a lifestyle that is the subject of hatred and discrimination.

Thus I ask: what is the crime in wanting to serve my country? Sure, some people should be exempt from serving based on their inability to perform their duties. All other prescriptions against doing a certain job are based on the individual's own shortcomings, i.e., lacking the proper vision to fly a jet, which happened to me. The policy barring gays from serving is based on other people's shortcomings—their fears, their insecurities, their inabilities to deal with differences in society.

As a party in the first case decided under the DADT policy (in 1994), I saw firsthand how the unjust policy was enforced. However, as I continued to litigate the case to the Supreme Court, I was able to continue to serve openly and saw firsthand how the presence of "open" homosexuals was not going to be a detriment to the service. Many gay men and women have given honorably and unselfishly, and with courage and strong leadership, this nation is finally implementing a more tolerant system in which gay individuals will be able to serve without fear of retaliation.

After the Navy I attended law school, graduated cum laude, resumed public service by working for the Social Security Administration in Baltimore, and this year I was selected to be chief judge for the Atlanta North office. My success would not have been possible without the support of my family, and in particular, my spouse and child. My immediate family had taken a new shape when I fell in love with Henry, one of four children of an El Salvadoran father and Virginian mother. Faith was important to us, and we received a warm welcome as a couple at Christ Lutheran Church in Baltimore.

We wanted our relationship to be blessed before God at Christ Lutheran. However, the congregation council decided the church could not host a same-gender wedding ceremony. Although the institution said no, many parishioners and our pastor said yes, and 200 people joined us in our ceremony on the top deck of a ship in the Baltimore harbor.

Henry and I had built a relationship that we believed would be a great environment for a child. Through prayers, patience, and fortitude, we were matched with a teenager who had the courage to give her child up for adoption. We were at the hospital for the birth of our daughter, Cameron, in 2008. Holding Cameron is a soothing joy, a glimpse of grace, and we are in the process of enlarging our family by having a second child.

Despite being discharged as a gay man and branded with the words "homosexual admission" on my DD-214 discharge papers, I do not regret my decision to come out or my decision to challenge the policy. The military instilled in me characteristics that helped me succeed in civilian life, success that I had hoped to achieve by serving my country in the military.

I Represent the People Whose Voices Aren't Heard

by Vernice Armour

I was a woman. I was black. I was gay.

"Don't ask, don't tell."

I was invisible.

Since the age of four, my dream was to be a mounted-patrol police officer. When I finally made it to college, student loans and the Federal Pell Grant Program covered my room and board, tuition, and books. I didn't have extra money for hanging out. One afternoon in the hall of the student union I saw a flyer advertising "Free Trip to Mardi Gras!" To go, all I had to do was join the Reserve Officer Training Corps (ROTC) rifle team. The rifle team was not a part of the dream but "free" fit my budget, so I joined.

A few months later I found myself marching and twirling a rifle through the streets of New Orleans during Mardi Gras. The irony is that I discovered something that could help me prepare for my passion. I was 18 and couldn't be a cop until I was 21. Discipline, camaraderie, physical fitness—the military encompassed everything I felt could help me get accepted to the police academy, excel in training, and maybe even save myself when I got out on the streets.

In August 1992 I entered the Delayed Entry Program of the U.S. Army Reserve (USAR). While at the Military Entrance Processing Station, I was asked if I were a homosexual. I was extremely nervous, but serving was something I really wanted to do. "No," I replied. I took a semester off and enlisted in the USAR.

The summer after completing my training, I came back to school as a private in the Reserve and successfully made up the classes I should have taken during the spring semester of my sophomore year. Then I realized the military had given me a strategic advantage that I wanted to leverage. So I took the next step and joined the ROTC program as a cadet.

One particular day I remember being really upset. I can't remember why, but

The End of Don't Ask, Don't Tell

I was so upset that I told the command sergeant major that I was gay and the Army didn't want me anyway!

I'll never forget his response.

"Now, now, that's not true," he said.

I stared at him in disbelief, thinking, I just came out to this man and told him I was gay. Surely I would be thrown out. But he was standing there telling me it didn't matter that I was gay. I just needed to be the best soldier I could be.

What happened the next summer changed my life. It was career day of Army Leadership Advance Camp in 1994 at Fort Bragg.

After a little over half the day had passed, my battle buddy—who was on an aviation contract—wanted to go to the aviation tent. I reluctantly walked past all of the static displays showcasing exciting Military Occupational Specialties such as Delta Force and sniper platoon and went to the aviation tent, the whole time thinking, black people don't even fly, right?

Let me make this quick insertion. Life is about access and exposure. Of course there were black pilots—the Tuskegee Airmen, Bessie Colman, and Willa Brown, to name a few—but aviation wasn't something I had access or exposure to while growing up. I had no interest in it.

Then I walked into the tent. I saw a black woman in a flight suit. "Wow!" was all I could initially say to myself. I had never in my wildest dreams imagined that I would see someone that looked like me inside that tent.

I introduced myself and we spoke for five minutes. In that moment I experienced the tangibility of the possibility. I could see her, touch her, talk to her, and ask her questions. Not reality TV, but my reality. Seeing the image of a black woman in a flight suit planted a strong seed. I know the only reason I can share the story now—the story of my being a pilot—is because I saw a woman in the flight suit on a hot summer day in 1994.

My intentions immediately shifted and I knew I wanted to fly. I also knew if I went active duty, I wanted to be a Marine. My grandfather was a Montford Point Marine who completed boot camp at Camp Johnson when the Corps still had segregated training for black Marines, from 1942–48. My stepdad was also a Marine and crew chief on a CH-46 transport helicopter and served three tours in Vietnam.

I, too, wanted to serve my country as a Marine.

I applied twice to Marine Officer Candidates School (OCS). The first time was in 1995 and I didn't get accepted. Meanwhile, I was accepted into the police academy and became a police officer in June 1996 for the Nashville police department. After a few months in the department I applied again to OCS . . . and again I was not accepted. Although I felt like a kid in a candy store as a police officer riding a "steel horse" (also known as a Harley Davidson Road King) downtown, living my childhood dream, I couldn't forget about that woman in the flight suit. In 1998 I applied for the third time and was accepted.

So many words run through my head: Honor. Duty. Commitment. Courage. Integrity. Then there are the phrases: Marines don't leave Marines behind. *Semper fidelis*. Once a Marine, always a Marine.

By the time I became a Marine, DADT was in place. The historic accomplishments of my becoming the Corps' first black female aviator and America's first African American female combat pilot, or my honorable service would not have been my experience had the Corps known that I was gay. Had I perished in battle, my mom would have been notified but my partner could potentially have found out by watching the TV news. The lives I saved as part of my attack helicopter division would have been saved by someone else. Or not.

The issue for me all these years hasn't been about pay or benefits for a partner, even though those things matter. The issue has been about potentially giving the ultimate sacrifice for my country with the desire to live in full integrity as the woman I am. The men and women I served with knew I was gay, which didn't impact mission readiness or unit morale and cohesion.

I slept in the tents with the guys while on alert in the middle of Iraq and awoke to the same alarm when troops were in harm's way, being attacked by enemy forces. As a tightly knit crew, we would jump up, get dressed, and strap into our attack helicopters to provide close air support for the troops on the ground in the middle of combat.

Ironically, I served my last tour as a diversity officer and liaison to the Pentagon for Headquarters, Marine Corps. Diversity and inclusion for our military services encompassed almost everyone—except the LGBT (lesbian, gay, bisexual, and transgender) service members.

Don't ask, don't tell.

I always said I would serve honorably, and when I got out I would help pave the way for others to serve our country without having to hide.

I resigned my commission in August 2007 and started my company but the stigma of DADT still weighed heavily in my life. Even though I was out of the military, there was another reason for me not to be out: it was too risky for business, or so I felt.

As I write this essay, I have had four successful years running my company, traveling the globe, speaking on leadership and creating breakthroughs, and I have written my first book, *Zero to Breakthrough: The 7-Step Battle-Tested Method To Accomplishing Goals That Matter.* Yet, there is one major breakthrough I haven't created for myself: going from zero to breakthrough and living openly as the woman I am.

I show people how to create "flight plans" for life, how to go from where they are to where they want to be. And perhaps most helpful, how to preflight goals and dreams, and how to mitigate risks. Yet, here I am, years after becoming a civilian, living under the veil of DADT. Not mitigating my own risks. I finally got it.

Since leaving the military and starting my company, if someone were to ask if I were gay, I have had no problem answering them honestly. But proactively, talking about it didn't happen. The issue is, I also didn't talk about it without being asked. It was my "private life."

I had been asking my Corps to do something I wasn't willing to do: making its "private" life public.

Let me be clear in this moment. Some might call this coming out publicly. I call it leading from the front. For years, I rationalized my actions by saying that I wasn't hiding the fact that I am a lesbian; I just wasn't announcing it from the mountaintops.

---

* Vernice Armour, *Zero to Breakthrough: The 7-Step Battle-Tested Method To Accomplishing Goals That Matter* (New York: Gotham, 2011).

Today I choose not to live by the phrase "don't ask, don't tell." Instead, I choose to live as a positive role model for the people I represent, the people whose voices aren't heard.

Change and transition can be difficult, and there will be casualties along the way. If sharing my story helps someone in the military whether they are gay or not, it will have been worth it. If it helps the leadership make different decisions that include and help everyone with the transition of the repeal of DADT, it will have been worth it. If sharing my story prevents one gay teen suicide, it was worth sharing.

I am not invisible.

I am a woman. I am black. I am gay.

A High Five Instead of a Kiss

by Kristen Kavanaugh

I never thought that I would say this, but the DADT policy was a blessing and a curse for me.

Despite the negative emotional and psychological impact that the policy had on my life, serving under DADT as a lesbian taught me invaluable life lessons.

- I learned the importance of resiliency.
- I embraced the need to stand up and fight for others and myself when we are hesitant or unable to stand up for ourselves.
- I learned to accept my sexuality and to embrace my experiences. All of this has afforded me the opportunity to help thousands of other service members and veterans who may have had a similar experience serving under DADT.

My career began at the U.S. Naval Academy, where I was introduced to the Navy's core values of honor, courage, and commitment. I embraced them and strived to live my life by them. However, I was 18, and like many other teenagers, I had yet to explore my sexuality thoroughly. As I became aware of my sexuality, I found it increasingly difficult to live by the Navy's core values. My sexual orientation was in conflict with DADT. By law I was required to lie to others and hide in shame in order to honor my commitment to my country.

While at the academy, I hid in plain sight and attempted to live by the values. Despite success in leadership positions and in athletics, I struggled with many personal demons. I was ashamed and embarrassed about being different. I harbored immense guilt and looked to place blame on someone else. I lived in fear of being outed and subsequently discharged from the service.

For my own protection and sanity, I isolated myself from my classmates and my family. The few relationships that I maintained were superficial. I didn't want anyone to get to know me well enough to discover my secret. I constantly envisioned my family's disappointment if they were to find out that their only daughter was a lesbian.

I was drawn to the Marine Corps' values from the beginning. I knew that Marines held themselves to the highest standard in all aspects of their lives. Becoming a Marine officer meant that I would have to challenge myself to meet those standards, and I accepted that challenge. When I was commissioned as a second lieutenant, I vowed to be true to those values and to live my life to the Marines' higher standard despite DADT.

As I began to mature and to accept myself as gay, I found that I was torn between my personal values and those of the Corps. I believed in integrity, yet I was forced to lie to protect my career. I believed in leading from the front, yet I felt that I could not be an effective leader because my Marines did not know the true me. I believed in honor, courage, and commitment, but I didn't have the courage to stand up for my personal honor.

In 2003, I was selected to play on the All-Marine basketball team and was recognized by the Corps as the Female Athlete of the Year. Although I was honored to win the award, secretly, I was ashamed to receive it. I felt like I did not deserve it and I would be judged if anyone found out I was a lesbian. The stress instilled in me such deep-seated shame and guilt that I could not see past it enough to accept my contribution to the team or the honor.

I faced one fear head-on early in my career. Prior to deploying to Iraq, I felt compelled to come out to my parents. I wanted them to know the truth about me in case it was the last time I saw them. I finally worked up the courage to tell them during Christmas leave. To my surprise, they were not disappointed in me. My mother told me that they loved me unconditionally, and she meant it. Although I did not feel comfortable enough to talk about relationships with them, I found comfort in knowing that they finally knew the truth about me.

My deployment to Iraq in support of Operation Iraqi Freedom was the first strain that DADT imposed on my partner. My partner accompanied me to the departure point on base, and we watched other families seal their goodbyes with kisses and tears. Our parting was sealed with a solid high five. I could not help but think that cold and unemotional moment could be our last together.

The End of Don't Ask, Don't Tell

I carried that fear with me throughout my deployment. E-mail and phone conversations with my partner were superficial in case either was being monitored. I could hear the pain in her voice when we had to say goodbye without saying "I love you." I felt helpless and hopeless. These feelings intensified after the first time our base came under intense rocket fire. For the first time, I recognized my mortality, and I thought of her. If something were to happen to me, she would have no way of being contacted because no one in the Corps knew she existed. This weighed heavily on my soul.

After five years in the Corps, the stress of living two separate lives became unbearable. I felt selfish for giving in to my desire to live my life by my rules and standards but, ultimately, I left the Corps because I respected myself too much to continue a life of lies. I valued my personal honor and integrity too much to ever be untrue to anyone—including myself—again.

Although I missed leading Marines, for the first time in my life I enjoyed my emotional freedom. I felt as though a weight had been lifted off my shoulders. I had the opportunity to be open and honest on my terms. Unfortunately, this took time. I thought DADT was behind me, but sadly, I carried with me the residual fears.

Indeed, there were people who judged me but that would have been true regardless of my sexual orientation. There were also people who were intrigued by my experience. I began to speak about serving under DADT, and people became receptive to listening. They were able to grasp the emotional and psychological impact of DADT on service members. It was in these discussions that I found my voice and my calling.

In 2010 I was accepted into graduate school at the University of Southern California, whose School of Social Work offers one of the few military social work programs in the nation. I was drawn to the helping nature of the social work profession, and I felt that as a social worker I could help service members in a profound way. I chose to focus my studies on gay and bisexual service members and vowed to assist those who continued to serve under DADT. Little did I know the extent to which I would be helping my brothers and sisters in arms.

As part of a policy project I cofounded the Military Acceptance Project (MAP) with the intention of supporting gay service members throughout the repeal of DADT. From experience, I understood the emotional and psychological effects the policy could have on individuals' lives without appropriate support. From education, I understood the positive impact that support organizations could have on reducing these long-term effects. Thus, the mission of MAP was born: to promote acceptance of gay service members within the military by providing education, support, and an avenue for connecting with each other during and after the repeal. The heavy lifting for the organization began after the repeal process. It is our goal to assist service members in learning how to accept themselves, each other, and differing viewpoints in the context of their service.

My personal mission with the organization is to help people put a name and face on the trauma of serving under DADT and engage in discussions that help to normalize the experience. I want gay service members and veterans to understand that they are not alone in their struggles and that they do not have to live with the guilt and the shame. From the repeal of DADT forward, we are all recognized as equally qualified to serve our nation with honor.

Since the national launch of the MAP, I have been contacted by many military colleagues, some I had not spoken to since graduation. Surprisingly, the people I thought would judge me harshly are the people who have given me the most support. I view this as a testament to the military's ability to forge competent leaders as well as compassionate human beings.

The lessons that I learned by serving under DADT made me the person that I am and gave me the tools to help others like me. My experience reinforces the importance of being true to the values that I hold, and the knowledge that my honor and integrity are not worth compromising.

Courage is having the confidence to stand up for others and for myself in the face of adversity. And commitment does not have to be to my detriment.

In a Combat Zone I Was Worried That I Would Be Found Out

by Julianne H. Sohn

"Be careful what you wish for . . ."

Those words haunted me the entire time I was in the Marine Corps. Before I applied to Officer Candidate School (OCS), I was an intern at the City of West Hollywood, one of the most liberal and gay-friendly places in the country. I was a senior at UCLA and I asked one of the city council deputies to write a letter of recommendation for my OCS application.

Fran, the deputy for an openly gay councilman, called me into her office. She uttered the words that followed me through Quantico, Virginia, to the dust of Fallujah, to the moment I received a phone call from a colonel who read to me my Article 31 rights for violating the DADT policy.

"Be careful what you wish for . . ."

Before I got off the bus and stepped onto the hallowed ground of OCS, I thought I knew what I was getting myself into. It was 1999, six years after DADT became federal law. The Corps wouldn't ask and as long as I kept my mouth shut, I was good to go.

But life didn't turn out that way.

The Marines has the fewest number of women compared to the other military branches. When I found myself on the parade deck of Marine OCS, women made up 6 percent of the Corps. Add to that the fact that I am Korean-American and know that my being a minority made it hard for me to hide, despite being only five feet tall.

My motivation for being a Marine was simple. I wanted to serve my country and give back to a nation that gave my family so much. My parents, who survived the Korean War, had moved to the United States to pursue their graduate education and give their children more opportunities. I knew that I wanted to be a Marine and lead Marines. The fact that I was gay was an afterthought.

I found myself in a Corps still trying to get rid of the term "Women Marines" (WMs) and live up to "all Marines are riflemen." And a Marine was a Marine, regardless of rank, Military Occupational Specialty, gender, and everything else.

My wake-up call came while I was in Charlie Company, First Platoon, and our sergeant instructor ordered us into the squad bay. Her face was turning scarlet and she bellowed, "You candidates are so nasty and pathetic!" She taped up the test scores of the entire OCS company, lowered her voice and told us to "look for the female with the highest average." We had to go down a few pages to see a female name. "You have to be better because the guys are judging you. This isn't good enough." She kept those scores posted so that we would remember that each of us represented not only ourselves but all women in the Marines.

It's true some of our women could run faster than the male candidates, but in order to earn the respect of male Marines, we had to do better. We were the only female platoon in our company. When we stood in the daily 0515 formation, my platoon mates and I would yell, "First to fight!" A male in another platoon would yell, "Last to fall in!" (First platoon took a little longer to get ready in the morning and often we were one of the last platoons to get into formation.)

So I ran faster and trained harder. When my Marines were having problems with pull-ups when I was stationed in Okinawa in 2000, I learned how to do pull-ups so I could motivate them to do more.

At Camp Foster on Okinawa I realized what DADT and the Marines really meant to me. I was a second lieutenant learning how to be a public affairs officer. I spent most of my work schedule with my Marines and the press chief. After hours, I would meet fellow lieutenants at the Bachelor Officers Quarters and would find myself holding back. I didn't date while I was on Okinawa. I had recently broken up with a girlfriend and I didn't have anyone to talk to besides my younger brother, an enlisted Marine at Camp Hansen.

I couldn't share anything with my friends, at least not until I learned their opinions about civil rights and women's rights. When I felt comfortable, I came out to them. It wasn't easy. Most of my friends were junior officers tasked with being the front line of enforcing polices such as DADT. What I found was that most didn't care that I was gay. They viewed me as a friend and knew that I did a good job and took care of my Marines. Telling about myself gave me a chance to be closer to the people I cared about. DADT drove a wedge between people and units because it asked people to lie about who they were and who they loved.

Some Marines didn't see the policy that way. A few retired generals defended DADT on moral or religious grounds. Some still argue that unit cohesion is undermined in the presence of queer service members. But during a time of war, most Marines care only that you can do your job and help get everyone home.

The stress of living under DADT took a toll on me while I was stationed at Parris Island. This was ground zero for the lesbian witch hunts in the early 1980s, and the stigma attached to 4th Battalion, the female recruit training battalion, remained. My physical examination in 2003 showed that my blood pressure was abnormally high. I was having problems sleeping. It didn't help that my friend, who also happened to be our legal officer, came into my office one day and almost gave me a heart attack.

"Jules," he said, "I have a question for you that I can't really ask and you can't really answer."

I was a deer in the headlights. "Look," he said, "I want you to know as a friend that some of the Marines were saying stuff about you and I wanted to either dispel the rumors or at least discredit them." He and a few other friends did their best to cover for me.

I left active duty in 2003 and went to graduate school. In March 2005 I deployed to Iraq as a Reserve captain with a provisional Marine Corps civil affairs group. On Father's Day, I was working late in one of the command posts on Camp Blue Diamond in Ramadi. An officer who I knew well turned to me and asked whether I had called home during my seven-month deployment.

"No. I haven't had a chance to," I said.

The captain handed me a satellite phone and said, "Call whomever you want, but just know that sometimes they monitor the lines."

"Thank you." I said. At that moment I was reminded that despite the homophobia and sexism that exists in military environments, there are Marines who do the right thing and take care of their own despite their gender, race, religion, and sexual orientation.

So I took the phone and walked outside into the night. After staring at the phone for a while, I called my dad. I really wanted to call my girlfriend but I did not, even though my friend had indicated it was all right with him if called her. But I was worried—in the middle of a combat zone—that I would be found out.

I never told anyone I didn't trust about being gay while I was on active duty. I loved the Marines too much to jeopardize myself, but when I returned from my deployment from Iraq I realized that silence doesn't change policy or minds. It is the act of telling that can change policy and make things right.

The End of Don't Ask, Don't Tell

Gay Troops Will Continue to Conduct Themselves with Honor

by Antonio G. Agnone

When I was invited to write this essay, I labored over structure. As a result I have chosen a chronology that highlights a theme I see when talking to other gay men and lesbians affected by DADT.

We are patriotic, we come from different backgrounds, and we joined out of our desire to serve the greater good. In telling my story chronologically, I paint my entire picture rather than focusing only on when DADT became a critical problem for my military career. This is my story.

I finished my undergraduate degree at the Ohio State University only because I wanted my Marine Corps commission. Born in the late 1970s, my childhood was idealistic. Similarly, my early adulthood in the late 1990s might have been too easy. Like many of my generation, I think that watching news reports about the attack on the United States in 2001 woke me up.

My feelings must have mirrored those of my grandfather, an Italian immigrant, when the Japanese struck Pearl Harbor in 1941. And, like my grandfather, when I chose to serve my country in uniform, the only choice was the Marine Corps.

I graduated in June 2003 and accepted my commission the same day. I was truly a green lieutenant who put his eagle, globe, and anchor insignia on wrong the first time—a big no-no that a sergeant quickly corrected me on. I spent the next three months before shipping off to The Basic School (TBS), the second stage of officer training that all Corps officers attend, working toward my perfect 300 score on the physical fitness test.

I had never had a serious relationship nor had I come out to myself. I remember signing the DADT clauses of my commission paperwork believing that I could uphold the standard. I realized that I was not straight but that realization is different from admitting you are gay. At the time, I figured that I could simply concentrate on work, physical fitness, and drinking with my friends. That plan worked—for a while.

My experience at TBS started out well and I made friends quickly. An extrovert at heart, I love being around people. However, I was walking a fine line because if I let people get too close, they might discover the secret that I was even trying to keep from myself. I got excellent grades and was assigned as a 1302, Combat Engineer Officer, a huge honor because it is considered combat arms. I thought, "Shit, I should have taken physics."

My career progressed and I received accolades well above those normal for my rank. I was promoted quickly to first lieutenant and later to captain. But I had no personal life and that began to take a toll. Plus, my TBS fear of letting people get too close to my secret proved well-founded because people did start to figure things out. I reacted by overcompensating—thereby ruining several friendships. Until this point, I had not yet admitted the truth to myself. I was 25. Admitting that I was gay meant admitting that a part of me could cause me to lose a job I loved and, worse, be shunned by all those who I respected.

My life changed in 2005, ironically, at President George W. Bush's second inauguration. President Bush had just run, largely, on a promise to amend the U.S. Constitution to define marriage as being between one man and one woman. I was stationed at the 2d Combat Engineer Battalion in Camp Lejeune, North Carolina, and had just been selected to command the engineer detachment to the 22nd Marine Expeditionary Unit (MEU)—a great honor. My parents invited me to accompany them to the inauguration ceremonies in Washington, DC.

During the weekend I encountered some of the most vitriolic, anti-gay rhetoric of my life that made me angry—not as a gay man but as a human. I decided to check out this "gay thing" and promptly reported to the Duplex Diner, a popular gay restaurant and bar in Washington, after the three days of ceremonies ended. It was there, somewhere between talking to the head chef of the White House and realizing that there were gay men and lesbians in every profession, that I met Brandon.

He changed my life. Meeting Brandon made me realize that, as fulfilled as I was with my career, personal connections and relationships are so important. So is honesty. Brandon had just gotten out of the Air Force. Our relationship quickly progressed. He ended up moving from Washington to North Carolina so we could live together. At the time, I was preparing to deploy with the 22nd MEU for a year. In

The End of Don't Ask, Don't Tell

this respect, we were no different than a newly married couple, only without the legal status. While my married friends were spending time with their wives, Brandon and I were on road trips to Raleigh on the weekends to find lawyers who could provide us a "marriage-lite" through a series of contracts, in case I were to die while deployed.

My deployment forced me to come out to my family. Realizing that the Corps would never, ever, notify my same-sex "roommate" if I were injured or dead, I had to introduce Brandon to my parents. It was then that I came out to friends and family.

While deployed, I got to know my Marines better than I knew myself. They remain some of the best men I have ever known. We shared a successful deployment. Upon our return, our families met us. Met everyone but me. Brandon had to wait until all others had gone, and then I walked to a neutral location so I would not be seen by anyone when he picked me up.

Along with the successes of our deployment came the tragedies after. One of my Marines killed himself. Another was in a car accident, while drinking, that left him disabled. Several continue to struggle with alcohol addiction. Some struggle to hold jobs. I still feel responsible for every single one and would drop everything to help them if they asked me. I am thankful for the support services that are available, services that were not there when we returned.

However, those services were not, under DADT, available to gay men and lesbians (for fear of outing themselves) or their spouses.

Dealing with the additional stresses imposed by DADT made me realize that I should use my experiences to speak out. I accepted an internship at the Human Rights Campaign in Washington. I began speaking honestly and directly about the effects of DADT on me personally and overall readiness. I caught the attention of some officers for whom I had worked while on active duty. One, a major, outed me to the Corps. I was in the Inactive Ready Reserve (IRR), but thought that because I had finished my active duty, there would be no problems with my speaking out. I was wrong. I was discharged in 2008 "honorably under homosexual conditions." Being kicked out was bruising. I had spoken out about DADT repeal because I wanted to remain in the Corps.

But I realized that the underlying expectation of DADT was unsustainable. Given the stresses of combat, one cannot be expected to survive without deep personal connections. DADT made connecting on personal levels all but impossible.

On a personal level, I am so proud to be able to speak for and with gay service members who have stood with me. I serve as a political officer for the Foreign Service, and I am starting Urdu studies before being reassigned to Islamabad, Pakistan. I am happy that Brandon and I are still together—six years and counting. In addition, I volunteer with the affinity organization Gays and Lesbians in Foreign Affairs Agencies (GLIFAA) to help gay people and their spouses when serving overseas. With GLIFAA, I look forward to the full integration of military members and their spouses in U.S. foreign missions abroad.

As we move forward as a military community, I am eager to reintegrate into the Marine Corps Reserve and return to the legacy of my grandfather. I know that all of the gay service members at home and abroad will continue conducting themselves with honor, especially those in the Corps—because there is no greater organization than the U.S. Marines.

I Hope to Resume My Career as an Officer and Leader

by Michael D. Almy

I joined the military in the summer of 1993 as a distinguished graduate of the Air Force Reserve Officer Training Corps from Wright State University, where I had earned a full scholarship. I came on active duty during the height of the debate over gay service members, when Congress was holding hearings and would soon pass the law that came to be known as DADT. As a brand new second lieutenant, I followed the headlines with little more than passing interest. I didn't identify myself as a gay man at the time, nor did I think the military was ready for gay people serving openly.

I was focused on learning as much as I could, eager to reach my potential and excited to begin my military career. I grew up in a family with a rich history of military service. My father graduated from West Point, flew helicopters in Vietnam, taught at the Air Force Academy and retired as a senior Air Force officer. One of my uncles retired from the Army, with service in Korea. Another uncle retired as a master gunnery sergeant in the Marine Corps, with service in World War II, Korea, and Vietnam. A third uncle was a career police officer. I always knew I would follow in the footsteps of these men in my family, whom I idolized, and join the military. I never envisioned anything else for my life and as a child I never really understood what civilians did.

As my military career progressed and I started to identify as a gay man, I became acutely aware of the heavy toll DADT had placed upon my career and my life. I also realized that as long as I was silent about my personal life, my career would be fine. That was the promise of DADT. Shortly after joining I realized I would make a career as an Air Force officer, as my father before me had done. As I gained seniority, I became aware I likely would never have a significant personal relationship while serving, because of DADT. I accepted this as the sacrifice I had to make to serve my country.

During my fourth deployment to the Middle East, I served as the chief of maintenance in an air control squadron, leading a team of 180 men and women. My unit controlled the air space over most of Iraq, notably when the Marines liberated Fallujah. Most of my career had been spent in tactical communications so I was thrilled to deploy with such a fine team as one of their leaders. Shortly before my unit left Iraq, I received an award designating me as the top Air Force communications officer in Europe and was likely on my way to a command assignment.

Six weeks after my unit left Iraq, my commander called me into his office for what I thought was a routine meeting. He opened the meeting by reading to me the military's policy on homosexuality. Next, he handed me several personal e-mails I had written in Iraq to a few close friends and someone I had dated, another Air Force officer. I was speechless and dumbfounded. My worst nightmare was coming true. A 50-pound weight pressed me down in my chair as the room started spinning. I could see my career shatter before me, like shards of glass on the floor.

Later I learned someone in Iraq had inadvertently discovered my personal e-mails that I thought I had deleted. During the height of the insurgency, the commander of the unit that replaced mine ordered a search of hundreds of my e-mails to find whatever evidence there might be that I had violated DADT. He forwarded about a dozen e-mails to my commander back in Germany, where I was stationed.

My commander demanded I explain the e-mails to him but I refused. I simply begged him not to pursue the matter, still in disbelief at the inquisition that was unfolding before me. After several tense minutes, as his demands grew more belligerent, he relieved me of my duties. My legal and administrative hell was just beginning. I somehow found the strength to drive myself home, where I took off my uniform and curled up on the bathroom floor. I sobbed for several hours until I had no more tears. I sought any relief I could find to end my pain but I found none.

This process would drag on excruciatingly for 16 months until I was finally discharged. As I awaited determination of my fate, the Air Force recommended I be promoted to lieutenant colonel, ahead of my peers. Instead, my security clearance was suspended, part of my pay was terminated and on my final day of active duty, I was given a police escort from the base. My reward for putting myself in harm's way was to be thrown out and treated like a common criminal or a threat to national security. My discharge paperwork listed "homosexual admission" as the reason for discharge. I refused to sign the document because I had never admitted anything to the military.

After 13 years as an officer, my career was over. The Air Force asked and I never told, yet I was still thrown out. I returned home to stay with my parents for a few months until I found a job. I was not out to my family or any of my friends, who struggled to determine the reason why I suddenly left a career that I loved. The ripple effect of DADT was that I had to continue to lie about my personal life even after I left the military.

On 2 February 2010, Secretary of Defense Robert M. Gates and Admiral Mike G. Mullen testified before the Senate Armed Services Committee about DADT and advocated for repeal. Early the next morning, I received an e-mail from an NPR producer, who asked if I would do an interview. I nervously agreed to my first public interview because I wanted to play an active role in repeal so that no one would have to endure what I had gone through.

The following morning, I asked my brother to play a recording of my NPR interview for my parents. At last my family and friends knew the true reason why I had left the military, and I was blown away by how supportive they were. I would later testify before the Senate Armed Services Committee, where I had a tense exchange with Senator John McCain (R-AZ) about the law. I spoke at press conferences in the House and the Senate when the repeal bill was passed in each chamber. I stood directly behind Speaker of the House Nancy Pelosi (D-CA) as she signed the bill to send to the president. During the ceremony she whispered in my ear and asked if I would say a few impromptu words. I was the only nonmember of Congress who spoke at the ceremony and I told the story of my military career. I concluded by saying that now is the time for gay and lesbian leaders and role models in our military, officer and enlisted alike, to show that we can serve right alongside our straight counterparts. The next day I watched history as President Obama signed the bill into law, emphatically stating, "This is done!" Afterward I was able to shake his hand and say thank you.

I certainly never envisioned that I would become a casualty of DADT. Nor did I ever anticipate that I would play such an active and public role in the repeal of this law. I've received hundreds of e-mails from people I served with as well as complete strangers thanking me for being one of the faces of DADT. Many members of my old unit have said they'd be honored to serve with me again. Soon I hope to resume my career as an officer and leader in the Air Force, without the mandatory silence of DADT and the constant fear that I will be fired. On 20 September 2011, the law was dumped into the trash bin of history. All who are qualified to serve can do so, not just the straight service members. Now our military can judge its men and women on their merit and not their sexual orientation.

A Law That Said I Am Not Good Enough to Serve
by David Hall

I decided to join the Air Force in November 1995 when I went to the recruiting station with my friend Dave, who was also thinking about joining. Our good friend Melanie had already signed up and was scheduled to leave in March. I was the last one to speak to the recruiter but the first one to leave for training.

I enlisted on 6 March 1996, but I wasn't new to the Air Force. My dad and stepdad had retired from the Air Force after serving 20-year enlistments, and I had spent my childhood in Japan and the Philippines.

The thought of DADT never crossed my mind when I joined. I hadn't come out to myself, so I didn't consider myself gay. And I had never heard of DADT, or if I had, I never paid attention.

It wasn't until I arrived at Langley Air Force Base that I started realizing I was gay, and the Internet helped me understand there were other gay military people. While at Langley, I didn't have any gay friends, never went to any gay bars, or dated anyone. I was uncomfortable being gay and afraid of being caught. I was invited to a gay bar in Virginia Beach by one of the people I had chatted with online, and I decided to go. I drove there but never got out of the car; instead I went home.

Then I moved to Elmendorf Air Force Base in Alaska, where I became more social and started meeting more gay people. I also met my first boyfriend.

As I started hanging out with nonwork friends, I started getting questions at work. How was your weekend? Did you go on a date? I gave generic answers and never mentioned who I was hanging out with. I started distancing myself from my coworkers so I wouldn't have to answer questions. I kept my work life separate from my social life.

One of my gay Air Force friends had coworkers who knew he was gay and could not care less. When I would stop at his office they would ask me about my dating life and how things were going.

I never had any problems at work, although one of the guys in my squadron was gay and told me some people made comments about my being gay—a "faggot"—when I wasn't around. I wasn't bothered. I knew they were angry and venting when I went to the flight line to evaluate them on loading missiles and bombs on aircraft.

After I served six years, the Air Force let me out of my enlisted commitment so I could go into a two-year Air Force Reserve Officer Training Corps (AFROTC) program and come back as an officer. On 20 August 2001, I separated and started AFROTC the next day.

Three weeks later was 9/11. I remember seeing the news, waking my roommate, who was active duty Air Force, and telling him he needed to see what was happening. I think everyone in uniform that day realized everything was about to change.

My boyfriend was also in the AFROTC detachment at the University of Alaska in Anchorage. He was already a cadet when I joined, and his good friend, also a cadet, knew we were dating.

In my first year I moved up in leadership, received my pilot slot, was ranked first in my class, and was preparing to attend field training during the summer. One day I was waiting in the lobby at my AFROTC detachment for my semester review from my cadre member. I overheard the commander tell my advisor to call the Judge Advocate General (JAG) office, and that he wanted to talk again with a female friend of mine. I told my boyfriend that I suspected our friend might have told them we were gay.

A few months later I was at field training at Tyndall Air Force Base and called my boyfriend during base liberty. He told me he just met with the JAG and that we were being investigated. I tried to focus on passing field training, which I completed.

The day after I returned from field training I was called into the office. The JAG officer was waiting and had a lot of questions. I offered no comment, and I left not knowing what would happen.

The questioning took place while I was helping the other cadets as part of my assignment. My boyfriend and I were part of the cadet wing staff responsible for coming up with the plan for the fall semester. Before the classes started I got a call from my commander, who asked me to see him. I stopped at his office and he sat me down. He slid a piece of paper across the desk, and he told me he was disenrolling me from AFROTC due to homosexual conduct.

My Air Force career ended just like that. Not because I was horrible at my job or I did something wrong but because I am gay.

I remember walking out of my commander's office. He walked with me while giving me instructions to turn in my uniforms. I remember taking my military ID card from my wallet and handing it to him. The NCO who handled all of our paperwork appeared and I could see the look of shock on her face as I handed over my ID card.

My boyfriend was discharged as well. All of my friends were shocked that I had been discharged, but they were never told the reason why. One of my AFROTC friends told me some of rumors she had heard: cheating, drugs, bad grades, security clearance issues. But to my surprise no one ever mentioned DADT. When I finally started telling people the reason I was discharged, they were shocked.

I called my parents and told them what happened. My stepdad told me he was disappointed with the Air Force but proud of me for everything I had accomplished. They were very supportive.

I was lucky to have an understanding family, great friends, and a boyfriend who knew what I was going through. I can't imagine having to go through this alone, as some people do. The support made it easier for me to refocus and figure out what to do with my life now that my Air Force dreams were over.

I think about the Air Force every day and it still bothers me that I lost a great opportunity because of a law that said I am not good enough for the military because I am gay.

That is the reason I went to work for Servicemembers Legal Defense Network (SLDN). Not only did they provide helpful advice when I was being discharged but they have also helped thousands of others who have gone through the same thing. They were instrumental in getting rid of this law so no one else has to go through the same pain I did.

I plan on going back into the Air Force and have talked to the Air Force Reserve recruiters. I am hopeful that I will again serve my country.

Repeal Is a Testament to the Core Values of the United States

by Joseph Christopher Rocha

It has been seven years since I joined the armed forces, escaping a life of parental abuse, and seven years since I took an oath "that I will support and defend the Constitution of the United States . . . so help me God."

It has been six years since I was a teenager serving overseas, being forced by my superior to get on my knees in uniform and simulate gay sex on video for my fellow explosive-detection, military working-dog handlers. This was just one of countless humiliation tactics used to punish me for not being "straight enough" by refusing to drink, gamble, smoke, and express interest in prostitutes. Mostly, for refusing to say "I am not gay."

It has been five years since I was accepted to the U.S. Naval Academy Preparatory School (NAPS) in pursuit of achieving my life-long dream of becoming a Marine Corps officer. Five years since my military role model and mentor, who had told me the news of my acceptance to NAPS, tragically took her life under the pressure of a command investigation into 93 counts of reported abuse in our canine unit overseas.

But the most crushing moment in my life took place four years ago. It was at NAPS that I turned myself in under the DADT policy.

After over two years of harassment and hazing while serving overseas—for nothing more than refusing to "prove" my straightness—it had become overwhelmingly clear to me that no matter how well a closeted gay woman or man performed in uniform, and no matter how far we went to protect the secret of our sexuality, we would never be safe from abuse, shame, and the disgrace of a discharge. So four years ago I made the toughest decision of my life—to end my career on my own terms, on the merit of my service, and out myself before I was outed. Under DADT it was never a matter of whether you would be kicked out but a matter of when.

On my last day with my peers at NAPS, I made a promise that I could not possibly have known was achievable but one that I refused to give up on: "I will see you in the fleet, brothers and sisters (when we can all serve with job security and basic human dignity)."

Three years later and with the help of countless selfless individuals, I found myself testifying before the Department of Justice and federal Judge Virginia Phillips on how the DADT policy encouraged and allowed the antigay abuse that took place in my unit. My testimony was thoroughly researched by the Justice Department, the district court and the Court of Appeals, and my testimony contributed to Phillips' ruling DADT is unconstitutional and unenforceable.

In a remarkable twist of fate, if I am selected for Marine Officer Candidate School, I will commission around the same time as my peers from NAPS who are now at the Naval Academy and whom I have missed dearly.

Today I stand by what I said nearly two years ago on national television when CNN broke the news of the then-unpunished abuse that had occurred overseas (resulting in the forced retirement of the abuser, with full rank and benefits).

What happened overseas was an isolated incident and not reflective of our armed services as a whole, and I eagerly await serving again in the uniform of the nation that I love. It is the policy that was a disgrace, and its repeal is a testament to America's core values.

Repeal of DADT ensures that each man or woman willing to give his or her life for our nation and our allies is equal under the law. It is a promise that the sacrifices of every woman and man who ever has or ever will wear the uniform of our Armed Forces is valued equally. Most notably, it is a guarantee to young people that they must never again have to fear their military, much less their government, while dedicating their lives to its service.

To activists and allies, straight and gay, I thank you with my continued service. The wounds inflicted on our gay women and men in uniform, dead and alive, begin to heal as our nation grows stronger.

Of 5,936 Floggings, Only 5 for "Homosexual Offenses"

by Mark D. Faram

When I joined the Navy in the late 1970s, sex and sexuality were lurking beneath the surface of military life, particularly at sea. At all-male commands the atmosphere always had an undercurrent of sexual innuendo—gay and straight. And it was in the language company commanders used in boot camp to communicate the things of military life. Even folding clothes was described in sexual terms.

The message given the young sailor was that heterosexual promiscuity was manly and a source of pride while gay sex was jokingly ridiculed. The message bled over to the attitudes of the rank and file, where it was joked about, played with, and teased. Those considered "homos" would be singled out and became the butt of verbal abuse and vicious practical jokes.

The Navy has long had to deal with homosexuals in the ranks and same-sex relationships among ships' crews. But history suggests the Navy and its leadership have either operated under a de facto DADT policy since the Revolutionary War or pretended that homosexuality didn't exist.

The stereotype of the gay sailor has been in the minds of the public, too. After announcing to my friends that I'd enlisted, I'd be greeted with remarks such as, "Well, if you drop your soap in the shower, don't bend over to pick it up. Kneel down if you have to. You don't want to give anyone a target."

Another quip was, "What's the worst part about getting out of the Navy?" Pause. "Oh, it's leaving your buddy's behind."

Even faux gay behavior was common at sailors' parties, where men and women would engage in kissing and French kissing their same sex—and other suggestive actions designed to make others uncomfortable. For many, role-playing was a way to confirm their heterosexual leanings. These types of humor, along with the nearly hazing-like behavior toward those thought to be gay, were a defense mechanism. It masked a fear of homosexuality by promoting the idea that along with homosexuality came predatory behavior—and you could be raped by deviants lurking in the shadows.

Ironically, references to homosexual behavior in the Navy's historical records are scant, showing up so infrequently that some believe this is evidence that homosexuality was nearly nonexistent. Others take a practical view that homosexuality was tolerated as long as it was in the shadows and consensual.

"The extent and nature of homosexual activity in the Old Navy is one of the major question marks in its social history," writes James E. Valle, author of *Rocks and Shoals: Order and Discipline in the Old Navy, 1800–1861.*[*] "Precise evidence in the form of records, documents, and statistics is almost wholly lacking."

Valle says the Navy's first recorded accusation of sodomy occurred onboard the frigate USS *Constitution* during a Mediterranean cruise in 1805. The case was against Marine Private George Crutch, who was attempting to sodomize a seaman named Geregano on the ship's spar deck. Witness Dominico Otesio awoke Marine Sergeant James Mix, who with Sergeant James Reynolds ran up on deck. Despite Reynolds' later testimony that he'd caught Crutch attempting to consummate the offense with "with his Pantaloons down, and shirt above the Navel and on top of Geregano," the offense went unpunished. The officers voted unanimously for acquittal.

Valle's research turned up only four court-martial cases for homosexual behavior in the early nineteenth century, and there are only scant references to homosexuality from most of the century's sailors-turned-authors.

"One of the reasons for this was the subject was repulsive to most sailor authors," says historian Harold D. Langley. "They either ignored such topics completely or gave them brief treatment."[**]

A list of offenses punishable by flogging, included in a Navy report on that disciplinary practice in 1846 and 1847, has no direct reference to homosexuality—only references that lead a reader to assume homosexual activity was involved. For

---

[*] James E. Valle, *Rocks and Shoals: Order and Discipline in the Old Navy, 1800–1861* (Annapolis, MD: Naval Institute Press, 1980).

[**] Harold D. Langley, *Social Reform in the United States Navy, 1798–1862* (Urbana: University of Illinois Press, 1967).

example, "taking indecent liberties with boy in hammock" was punishable by 12 lashes with a cat-o-nine tails.[*]

Langley says during those years, 60 ships administered 5,936 floggings and only 5 of those are for "clearly homosexual offenses: three attempts at sodomy, one case of 'improper conduct, too base to mention,' and one case of 'filthy and unnatural practices.'"

The same phenomenon exists in the early-to-mid-twentieth century. In "Enlisted Men in the United States Navy, 1899–1939," Frederick S. Harrod notes that in his research, references to "crimes involving homosexuality, a possible concern in an all-male organization, were negligible."[**] None of the scholars goes so far as to say that homosexuality didn't exist, either. Deployments of at least a year meant that sailors were left with little or no sexual outlet, save for short periods in port.

When I joined the Navy in 1978, my knowledge of homosexuality was nonexistent. I would eventually discover that homosexuals were onboard ships and adept at finding those whose orientations met their own, while keeping a low profile. Rarely were sexual advances made in an overt manner to anyone outside this nearly secret group, and most of the crew were unwise to a gay presence.

For me, that changed in 1980 during my second Mediterranean cruise onboard the carrier USS *John F. Kennedy* (CV 67), where I faced a reality that shook my naivety and beliefs. In the end, the reality changed my understanding of homosexuality—in the Navy and in society.

I was in charge of the ship's photo supplies and equipment maintenance. Both are full-time jobs and normally assigned to more senior sailors than I. I'd just made third class petty officer—E-4—but the Navy was undermanned, and many junior sailors were in roles normally handled by those of higher ranks.

That was when I met Ray, a petty officer first class who joined us at mid-cruise. Ray had 19 years in the service, one year shy of the 20 years needed to collect a pension and benefits. He was assigned to relieve me of supply duties so that I could concentrate on maintaining the photo lab.

---

[*] House Executive Documents, 31st Cong., 1st sess. (Serial 576), Doc. 26 (1850).

[**] Frederick S. Harrod, "Enlisted Men in the United States Navy, 1899–1939" (PhD dissertation, Northwestern University, 1973).

With three storerooms and thousands of dollars of cameras and supplies to inventory as we turned over duties, Ray and I became friends despite the difference in ranks. Soon we started to go ashore together on liberty. One night in a bar in Spain, we were drinking, laughing, and swapping stories, and he got serious.

"We are really becoming good friends and before we go any further, there's something I need to tell you," he said, looking me straight in the eye. "I'm gay."

It was as if an explosion occurred in my brain. I was dumbfounded. My nearly three years in the Navy's homophobic environment and my religious upbringing wanted me to bolt. But my face didn't move. Ray took my reaction another way.

"That doesn't bother you, does it?"

"No, not at all," I lied.

Ray had taken the weight of the world off his shoulders and I felt it was now on mine. What were his motives? Was he coming on to me? Why would this man—a year away from retirement—risk it all to tell me he was a homosexual?

The next day at work I was uncomfortable, didn't talk much, and kept thinking about what he had said in the bar. Ray didn't seem to notice my change in attitude, so when we were alone I asked him whether he had been making advances toward me or if he thought I was gay, too.

"Oh hell no," he said. "I know you're not. You're hopelessly hetero as far as I can tell; we've become good friends and I just thought you needed to know. You didn't seem like the type to turn someone in."

During the remainder of the cruise and our friendship, which lasted past Ray's retirement when he could come out of the closet, I learned much about the Navy's gay subculture, which went against stereotypes. I learned that many gay people were in loving, monogamous relationships and often happier than some heterosexual couples I knew. I often went to dinner with Ray at the home of a gay couple. One was a career sailor and the other a nurse, and they had managed to stay together while going from base to base during two decades of service.

Though we lost touch and Ray is dead, he has never left my mind. In the 1990s when the military adopted DADT, I recalled my experiences with Ray and how they changed my life positively. I concluded that DADT was a step forward but wasn't the solution. Sex in the Navy is a personal conduct issue. Unwanted sexual advances or harassment, heterosexual or homosexual, should not be tolerated.

My experiences led me to believe that gay men and lesbians were serving and had been serving alongside heterosexuals for longer than I'd been in the service. As a result, I concluded—despite the prevailing culture—that "gay" wasn't a big deal.

Joe's Story Is the One I Tell Most Often
by Seth Moulton

It was the winter of 2007, and a lot of us who were recent veterans were receiving letters from the Pentagon calling us "involuntarily" back to service in our volunteer military. The Iraq surge was beginning and the country needed more troops.

My friend Joe was honorably discharged after four years of service in the Marines, including two long tours in Iraq, and was on his way to Columbia University graduate school when he received that same notice. But he had to make just one phone call and utter only two words, the shortest possible statement of fact, to get out of returning to war: "I'm gay."

To do so made all the sense in the world. Joe came out of the closet when he got out of the Marine Corps, finally able to admit a fundamental truth about himself that he'd come to terms with during his final years in the service. Why not use that fact—hardly an excuse—to allow him to start graduate school as he intended? With two tours under his belt, he had surely done his time.

Joe thought long and hard about the decision. I know, because he called me and we talked about it a lot. I faced returning for another tour rather than starting graduate school as well, but I didn't have a life I would have to keep hidden in order to put on the uniform again.

From the first day of Marine officer training, we are taught that there is nothing more important than integrity, which makes sense when you put your life in the hands of your fellow Marines. I saw a number of officer candidates manage to graduate after failing an occasional test or falling short on a run, but if you ever lied about anything, you were labeled an "integrity violator" and summarily dismissed, never to return.

This is, in my opinion, what made DADT a fundamentally flawed policy. In a place where honesty is valued above all else, it demanded dishonesty of my fellow gay service members. It's hard to think of a more fundamental contradiction in policy in our modern military.

So why was there so much resistance to summarily dismissing DADT? Conservative ideology aside, one reason is that too many people calling for its repeal had no idea what its implications could be for the troops. Most of the high-minded members of the "chattering classes" decrying the policy's questionable legality had no military experience—or no relatives in Iraq or Afghanistan who would be affected by the change.

The problem is that accommodating gay service members might not be as simple as, for example, accommodating women in an all-male workplace. Building a new bathroom or implementing maternity leave does not put any lives at risk. But how would you feel as the Marine platoon commander writing the parents of an 18-year-old in your platoon, explaining how their son was killed digging a separate latrine or switching foxholes late at night in order to meet new rules about accommodating gay Marines? These are not abstract notions. Some generals have fervently declared that gay and straight Marines would not share the same accommodations, yet I've spent nights in the infantry when I slept against the Marine next to me so we didn't freeze to death. When lives are at stake, this is not simply a question of civil rights.

The military, in fact, discriminates on many grounds to increase its effectiveness. We have physical standards that largely exclude the obese from serving, for example. I would not want someone in my platoon who is too overweight to keep up, too lacking in intelligence or initiative to have completed high school, or who violates many of the other standards the Corps maintains.

Personally, I don't think being gay impairs your effectiveness as a Marine. While some contend that gay service members threaten unit cohesion, I have served with plenty of gay troops whose presence never undermined that trust. Meanwhile, hundreds of critical service members, such as Arabic translators, have been discharged—when we've needed them most—simply because of their sexual orientation.

Still, it will be different when gay troops are allowed to serve openly, and there were important questions that needed to be answered, such as what to do about accommodations and what support structures might be needed for gay troops. I'm a young man with plenty of gay friends, so I never thought the answers would be hard to come by, but rushing into these decisions—as would have occurred with a sudden or court-ordered repeal—would have required that they be made hastily by an older generation of military leaders.

Indeed, one of the biggest mistakes the generals could have made is that gay and straight troops not be allowed to share facilities. I believe we need "good order and discipline" not "separate but equal," which could serve more to undermine trust and camaraderie than maintain it. The same military rules that have discouraged and punished inappropriate sexual relationships in the past should be sufficient for the future.

I served with several great gay Marines just like Joe. We used the same showers and foxholes and slept in the same tents and barracks without any trouble. Numerous studies and the experience of many of our allies have shown that gay troops do not, in fact, hurt unit cohesion.

But only with time and careful consideration has this view prevailed. Our military leaders needed to hear the views of troops like myself and understand the reality on the ground, not hear the disconnected proselytizing of those who know little of what putting your life on the line for your country—and your fellow servicemen and women—is all about.

Could the change have happened sooner? Absolutely. Congress should have amended the policy years ago. But the point remains that the change had to happen carefully and deliberately, implemented by people who knew and studied the issues rather than by those who were completely disconnected from the results.

And in no time is this more important than now. Although most of America easily forgets, we are in a time of war.

So what did my friend Joe do? He called the Corps and he said he would go. When millions of Americans who had never served should have been asked to go instead, Joe said he didn't want anyone to serve in his place. So he hid a fundamental part of who he is in order to do another tour in Afghanistan. His officer evaluation from the period states that he "is an example for others to emulate" and "should be promoted to major as soon as possible."

There are thousands of stories I could tell about the dedication and patriotism of our troops, but when my classmates in graduate school ask, Joe's story is the one

I tell most often. America's military should respect and embrace its gay service members, erasing the fundamental contradiction of DADT. But it needs to make these policy changes carefully and deliberately. Protecting the lives—and rights—of all Americans who serve demands nothing less.

The End of Don't Ask, Don't Tell

I Allowed Law to Compromise Honor, Courage, and Commitment

by Maj Darrel L. Choat, USMC

What is honor? Courage? Commitment? What do they mean to you? These are common discussion starters in recruit training, Officer Candidate School (OCS), and hip-pocket classes throughout the Marine Corps. Understanding these terms is critical to the personal and professional development of every Marine.

Despite knowing the textbook definitions to the above questions, my 13 years of service have been full of dilemmas. Something as simple as casual Monday morning conversations became a moral minefield. "How was your weekend? What did you do?" As I sought to craft a truthful answer, answering innocuous questions became internal struggles between maintaining my ability to serve, courage, personal integrity, and—ultimately—honor. Such was the insidiously debilitating nature of the disreputable and discriminatory DADT law on gay service members.

I worked in the U.S. Senate in the early 1990s when Senator Jesse Helms (D-NC) and Representative Bob Dornan (R-CA) often disparaged homosexual people, their "sinful" and "deviant" behaviors, and their "agenda." Both lawmakers deemed gay people an anathema to everything good, right, and honorable. Feeling helpless in the face of their diatribes was infuriating. One day as I rode an empty Senate elevator and Helms stepped in, and I faced a decision about how to address him. I realized no words could be adequate. His hate and ignorance could not be rationally discussed or disproved in a debate. The only effective course would be to disprove him by example, by exemplifying and personifying a proud, honorable, and gay American who—by existing—refuted Helms' lies and demagoguery.

I had completed the process of coming out several years earlier by telling family and letting coworkers become aware of my sexual orientation. Often I made no pronouncements. Engaging in honest discussions about weekend activities or sharing the truth about personal relationships was all that was required and is common discourse that heterosexuals take for granted. My guiding principle was if I was saying something or compromising out of fear or shame because I was gay, I had to stop and take the honorable—and honest—course. If I got fired, I got fired. Another job could be found. I was adamant that a job was not worth the sacrifice of honor and courage.

Ironically, my encounter with Helms prompted reconsideration of an old goal. I had been awarded a four-year Marine Corps Reserve Officer Training Corps (ROTC) scholarship in 1981 that I did not pursue due to shame and a lack of courage. At the time I was aware that I was different and I didn't like being different—I *hated* it. I was self-conscious and paranoid and found it difficult to interact with other midshipmen and Marines. Despite wanting to serve, I felt incapable of embracing a Marine career. Although I had never touched another man intimately, I was aware of my attraction to men. After years of praying daily and begging God to make the feelings stop, they never did. So I left ROTC.

The year was 1997, and DADT didn't preclude my service. It required only that I shut up about being gay. I now possessed the physical strength, courage, and ability to be a Marine and was determined to prove it, most importantly, to myself. The compromise? Minor, I thought. Cavalier assumptions supported my decision. Joining the Corps would have little negative personal impact because I had embraced my sexuality and overcome a lifetime of negative messages and shame.

The first unanticipated compromise occurred before I left the Senate job. Standing before my coworkers on 18 September 1997, to thank them and say farewell, I was compelled to censor my remarks. After signing the papers to join the Corps, a public statement indicating I was gay would violate DADT. The iron curtain of DADT descended, and my internal struggle with the compromise of honor and integrity began again.

The first couple of years of active service were manageable. Focus on training and being a successful Marine allowed compromises to pass. My being single was not at issue because the majority of lieutenants were single. Blending in was possible.

Once assigned to the fleet, queries from girlfriends and wives started. "I've got this great friend—you'd love her." No, I wouldn't. But how to beg off? How to answer without a lie, keep the secret, and preserve the ability to serve? My old habit

The End of Don't Ask, Don't Tell

of crafting comments that cleverly reassured inquisitive heterosexuals I was one of them came back. Were they lies? No. Was I choosing words that allowed them to draw a false conclusion? Yes. Avoiding well-meaning spouses became prudent.

The greater compromise was the daily absorption of insults, put-downs, and homophobia. In DADT, Congress deemed homosexuality incompatible with military service and decreed gay service members dangerous to camaraderie, unit cohesion, and mission accomplishment. This sanctioned an environment in which unprofessional and homophobic comments were acceptable. Critical thinking about the nature of sexuality and justice was subsumed by moralism and prejudice. Real Marines didn't tolerate fags, and regulations required gay Marines be processed out quickly because they were not one of "us."

When confronted by a comment such as "fuckin' fag," tirades against the imaginary "homosexual agenda," insistence that fags were weak and unsatisfactory, threats to beat any fag to death, and assertions that a gay son would never be tolerated, what does a gay Marine do? Being nearly 40, single, and never dating or talking about women, wouldn't my confronting homophobia turn the spotlight on me? Paranoia took over, courage vanished, and ignorance went unchallenged. Feelings of helplessness and cowardice piled up. The paranoia was intense when the perpetrator was a senior officer, one who wrote my fitness report. The daily walk on eggshells was exhausting. The bond that arises from shared challenges and sacrifices of a deployment or service in a combat zone? Not for me. Familiarity was dangerous.

Unit functions? How to avoid small talk, inevitable discussion of personal life and maintain integrity? I withdrew. My personality went flat. Having nothing to talk about meant that lies and compromises to my integrity were not required. Camaraderie, the sense of belonging, and unit cohesion had to be sacrificed. I accepted my cowardice, kept my personal life to myself, and tried not to be angry. I fought depression. Had shame returned? Where could I turn? Confiding in the doctor or chaplain was risky. I'd heard horror stories about these officers going directly to the commanding officer when they found out a Marine was gay. When my relationship with Mr. Perfect fell apart and the motivation to get out of bed barely existed, I sucked it up and made sure no one had any idea. When a friend died from complications of AIDS, I told no one and sneaked off for an afternoon to attend the funeral. If a topic such as gay marriage came up and a Marine expounded that fags had no claim to the civil rights he took for granted, I left the room. I swallowed my pride. I forsook courage and tried to find the strength to continue to serve and to come to work the next day.

As recently as August 2011 I lost my nerve during my first meeting with a new commanding officer. The 9th Circuit Court had suspended DADT and I had made the decision to write this essay. But when my commanding officer asked, "What should I know about you that is not in your service record?" I demurred.

I'm a volunteer. No one forced me to serve. I could have walked away. By the time I seriously questioned my ability to serve under the burden of cowardice and dishonor, I had served nearly 10 years. I was over age 40 with no retirement plan. Survival in the civilian world was possible, but what about the mortgage and car payments, and retirement and health care? I was caught in my own trap.

Does unwavering commitment to serve country, Corps, and fellow Marines justify a daily compromise of honor and an accumulating sense of cowardice? Were living standards and retirement benefits really worth this sacrifice? Can outwardly honorable service mitigate internal dishonor? If I deemed it did, could my mental health be sustained for seven more years? Would growing anger over damaged self-respect manifest itself in unmanageable depression? Could I live again with shame? I'd secretly sought help in the past, but some days the dark clouds were overwhelming. Could I make it to 20 years of service?

I am thankful that answers to these questions are no longer required. On 20 September 2011, as a Marine, I reclaimed the honor and integrity that I had as a civilian in September 1997. I am a patriotic American. I am an officer of Marines who loves country, Corps, and my Marines. I am doing my best to serve proudly and honorably.

And I happen to be gay.

It Is Possible That Someone in the Room Is Gay
by Maj Dirk Diener, USMC

"The people at work don't know I'm gay," the sailor said. "I can really be butch when I want to."

My friend the sailor was a stereotype of effeminacy, and I'm fairly certain that using "butch" to describe yourself is an indicator that you're not fooling anyone.

I'm cognizant of the fact that we don't always view ourselves with honest eyes. But when I say you would never know I was gay, I am telling the truth. How do I know? I've been fooling one of the most fiercely heterosexual organizations in the world throughout my 17-year career.

I was in college when I enlisted in the Army Reserve. In 1988 the recruiters were allowed to ask about sexual orientation, and I lied. I can't say why—it was so long ago—except to say being in the military is something I always wanted to do. I wanted to join after high school but my father's advice was to go to college first. "You can always join the military after college," he said, "but you probably won't do college after the military." I think he knew me better than I did, so I enrolled in college and then enlisted.

Being gay has always been a conflict for me. I have always known I was gay and never—in my mind—denied my sexuality, but as a kid I tried never to let my being gay show. I knew that being interested in girls was normal and I wanted to be normal, to fit in. I didn't want to stand out. Fitting in was not a problem. I was a bigger than the average kid, liked sports and hunting, and made friends easily. I was not always the center of attention but usually I was somewhere close. I honed my skills of engagement with the opposite sex well enough to keep everyone fooled, although that's an area in which I was never comfortable.

Being a "weekend warrior," going to college, and being gay were never a problem; the three were never in conflict. I pretended to be straight while I was in college, including in front of my fraternity brothers. During my Reserve drill weekends

I hung with the rest of the soldiers, drilled, drank beer afterward, and kept up the facade.

After college I left the Reserve so I could enlist in the Marine Corps as a Russian linguist. DADT, the political compromise, was in effect and the recruiter never asked about my sexual orientation. However, to become a Marine is to be cut from the same cloth as other Marines of the past, present, and future. To be perceived as different only gained you the attention of those who were senior and could make your life miserable. I had to continue the lie and pretend I wasn't gay. This wasn't a stretch for me. My family never knew, I had kept it to myself in college, and I've been pretending I wasn't gay my whole life. However, I wasn't "acting straight"; I was being myself.

Unfortunately, while at language school and trying to assimilate into the hyper-hetero, masculine Marine Corps, I almost became a homophobe. This was part of my front, right or wrong. I always had girlfriends or women I pretended to be interested in. I distanced myself away from other Marines and military personnel who showed up on my "gaydar"—which was no guarantee that they were gay—and I made fun of them. However, occasionally I would feel the burden of the facade and drive to a different city, looking for a gay bar in a desperate attempt to make some kind of intangible connection I felt I was missing.

My first duty station after school was in England, where I maintained my front and had a girlfriend. I always wanted children and never believed that as a gay man I would have any. But before I left for Officer Candidate School (OCS), my girlfriend wanted to get pregnant. Without seriously considering how being a father would change my life, I agreed. After beginning OCS and finding out she was pregnant, I asked her to marry me. I wasn't in love. I asked her because I wanted to be a father and not just a sperm donor. I believed that my commitment to the child (and later, another child) would enable me to maintain my marriage.

I was wrong. My marriage was over seven years after the vows. I never cheated or sneaked out to connect with the gay world I was missing, and being intimate with my wife was never a problem. I believe the marriage could have lasted regardless of my sexuality but, unfortunately, we had too many other insurmountable differences.

As an officer of Marines, my career has led me across the globe to places I consider lucky to have been and with people I'm lucky to have met. I've been on exercises throughout the Pacific, deployed in support of Operations Iraqi Freedom and Enduring Freedom, and completed a tour with the United Nations in the Republic of Georgia.

Throughout these adventures, I tried to maintain a professional manner. My sexuality was never a deterrent to how I performed and accomplished the mission. Also, I came out to some members of the military after I had established a level of trust. Why? I wanted to get closer to them so that I could bond and feel accepted. I have never been betrayed by any of those sailors and Marines, and I thank them for seeing me as a person regardless of who I am attracted to.

I love my children, my family, my service to my country, and the Corps. I chose to lie when I enlisted the in the Army Reserve and then later when I put up a front in the Corps. I justified my lie because I wanted to do something with my life and be a part of something bigger than myself. I wanted to make a positive difference not just in my life but in the lives of others. Have I done this? Maybe.

What about the service members and civilians I distanced myself from or publicly belittled because I thought they might be gay? What about all the Marines and the institution of the Corps I've lied to every day for more than 17 years?

The repeal of DADT is amazing to me. I never believed I would serve in the Marine Corps and be able to be myself.

I've thought about staying in the closet after the repeal. My concern is that all my professional relationships might be re-evaluated by other Marines. "Did Major Diener give me a bad fitness report because I said I don't like homosexuals?" "Did Major Diener only want to be my gym partner because he was attracted to me?"

During DADT repeal training in 2011, comments by some of my fellow Marines reinforced those concerns. I was in a class of officers and staff NCOs who discussed the repeal as if it were impossible that someone in the room could be a homosexual.

So I've made the decision to come out. I won't be wearing tiara or boa, and I won't leave a trail of glitter. I am just tired of lying. Although freeing, the repeal and my coming out are a Damocles' sword because the perception of who I am as a Marine and as a person will change for some.

However, I haven't changed. I am who I am:

A Marine . . . and gay.

Coming Out to a Fellow Marine Was No Big Deal
by Brian Fricke

We are U.S. Marines, and for two and a quarter centuries we have defined the standards of courage, esprit, and military prowess.

– Gen James L. Jones, Commandant of the Marine Corps, 2000

The definition of a Marine is absent gender, color, religion, or class. But when I joined the Marines in July 2000, exclusion was in place. DADT dictated that I not tell fellow Marines I was gay.

The DADT policy inferred what a service member was not. DADT implied that we warfighters could not stomach or function if we knowingly served with a gay Marine. It also inferred, falsely, that no Marine was ever gay. Unless you have been a Marine, however, you will never know what it takes to become one, and I tell you from firsthand experience: sexual orientation has nothing to do with being a Leatherneck.

I chose to join the Marine Corps to be part of something greater than myself and because of a love of country and a sense of duty. Like most 18-year-olds who join, enlisting was also about the challenge to prove my salt as a man.

Being a closeted gay guy from Knoxville, Tennessee, reinforced my need to venture from the known world into the unknown world. There was promise beyond the gates of Parris Island—a promise to emerge as a Marine.

Marines sacrifice a lot of their freedoms to be in the ranks, and gay and lesbian Marines have been forced to sacrifice more. Like many gay Marines before me, I made the conscious decision to live a life of silence and secrecy so that I could serve a country whose ethos is freedom and equality. There were moments I felt the hypocrisy weighing on my soul but I was no longer an individual, I was a Marine.

Also, being a Marine allowed me to know that when I inevitably came out to my friends and family, despite what they might think a gay man couldn't do, being a

Marine wasn't one of them.

One year into my enlistment, I arrived at Marine Corps Air Station Miramar, San Diego, California. I was a boot helicopter avionics technician working on CH-53 Super Stallion helicopters.

In 2002, I began a yearlong tour with my squadron, Heavy Marine Helicopter 466 (HMH-466) in Okinawa, Japan, where I was introduced to an underground gay military culture. I established long-lasting relationships with service members from all branches. We had our own "family" and a place where we could talk about anything and lean on each other. Our exclusion from our units, by policy, had lead to the creation of a unit of a different kind.

The Marines in my squadron knew me as Corporal Fricke and all that came with my followership, leadership, and friendship. I could receive and execute orders, give guidance to others when needed, and stay true to the ethos of a Marine: no greater friend, no worse enemy.

One night I was working inside the belly of an aircraft, troubleshooting an issue with a friend and fellow Marine. All his talk of "chicks" pushed me to act on a decision I had been contemplating.

"You know I'm not attracted to women, right?" I said. In that moment, because of my anxiety, I expected the aircraft's wheels to collapse, the blades to fall off, the hull to split open, and the Commandant to snatch me up and toss me out of the Corps. I caught my breath. My senses returned.

"Oh?" he said. "No big deal."

No big deal? My being gay isn't that big of a deal? I thought I had made a courageous step toward liberation, and it was no big deal. I was still Corporal Fricke, who happened to be gay.

After deployment I returned to San Diego. I had a new outlook on being gay in the military: it was no big deal. The only ones who seemed to be affected were those writing policy in Washington, DC—those who had no knowledge of unit cohesion or the morale of my fellow Marines.

In California I met my best friend, the man who became my boyfriend and is legally my husband. With Brad beside me, my life was brighter, tastier—a bit more expensive—but greater. Yet even though I was awarded my first Navy Achievement Medal for excellent work, I couldn't talk about Brad at my workplace. I could relate to the Marines above and below me but could not share my love or pride. I couldn't relate and build the bonds that reinforce unit cohesion.

Service members fight for freedom, the freedoms gay service members could not exercise. In 2004 I went to Iraq and learned more about myself there in eight months than in the previous 20 years. Brad wrote to me faithfully, and I was in the same boat as the married Marines I fought beside except that I had to bottle up my affection because I was different. I missed my loved one, I cried, I was stressed. I loved also but I loved a guy, and policy nullified displaying my emotions.

I made it back to the land for which I fought. My fellow Marines were greeted by their families, husbands and wives, babies, and friends. I checked in my rifle and war gear, gathered my sea bags, and left base alone. Brad couldn't greet me on the tarmac, nor could my gay civilian friends. If they were there, that would have put me at risk of being outed. Seeing my loved ones in the hangar and being unable to hug and kiss them would have been more difficult than the entire deployment. My reunion with Brad took place out of view of the cameras and the command, but was just as sweet.

When I came out to colleagues before deploying, while I was in Iraq, and after leaving active duty, there was never a difference in the way we interacted. We accomplished our missions and maintained readiness. That is because we Marines are professionals. Since leaving active service I have worked with the Servicemembers Legal Defense Network (SLDN) in media, lobbying on Capitol Hill and in the White House, fundraising, encouraging, and holding discussions with those being discharged. I joined the SLDN board of directors in 2008 and am proud to have been a part of a movement to change the course of our nation's history.

My generation fights today to preserve the future of Americans tomorrow. The repeal of DADT ensures a closer, more unified service. A level playing field will come only when spousal benefits are offered to same-sex couples. Meanwhile, when a young lieutenant or a sergeant (such as I was) comes out—at his or her pace—each will be a leader of Marines. Period.

> *The highest obligation and privilege of citizenship is that of bearing arms for one's country.*
>
> – Gen George S. Patton, U.S. Army

"Buck Up and Serve Honorably"
by Justin H. Johnson

As a gay former Marine officer, I have followed the efforts to repeal the policy banning gay service members from serving openly but have kept a low profile about my views. By publicly adding my voice to those calling for repeal and sharing my experience, I hope I can assuage concerns and effect a change that will have an enormously positive effect on our military's fighting capacity and our country's commitment to human dignity, fairness, and equality.

I was commissioned a Marine officer through the Reserve Officer Training Corps at the University of North Carolina at Chapel Hill upon graduation in 2001. At this point I was still struggling to come to terms with who I was. Despite my efforts to safeguard my privacy and maintain the highest level of discretion, a constant fear hung over me that I would be outed by a jilted boyfriend or a disgruntled subordinate. Looking back, though I received feedback praising my abilities, the distraction this policy caused significantly impaired my ability to be as effective a Marine as I could be.

In 2004 I deployed with 2d Battalion, 4th Marines, 1st Marine Division to Ar Ramadi, Iraq. Our battalion faced fierce combat as the thousand Marines conducted stability and security operations in a city of more than 300,000. The honor with which the Marines served and the bonds I formed with my fellow Marines in combat continues to inspire me. The difficulty of this combat tour, however, forced me to confront my own mortality and make sense of what I experienced and what it meant. I made the difficult decision to come out to my family and to leave active duty when my period of required service expired in June 2005. I wanted to stay in the Marines but did not want to serve in an environment where my entire life and career could be upended because of who I am—regardless of my performance in the position. Additionally, it made little sense to violate two of the critical tenets of the Marine Corps, honor and integrity, to be a Marine.

After leaving the Marine Corps I came out to family, friends, and many of the Marines I served with between 2001 and 2005. I became more confident in my abilities and much happier with the honesty now present in relationships with family, friends, and colleagues. I remained committed to public service both because of my personal interests and my commitment to our country that was immeasurably strengthened by my experience in Ramadi.

In spring 2007, I was involuntarily recalled from the Inactive Ready Reserves for a tour in Afghanistan. I now faced a decision I had known was possible, given the stress on the military because of the surge in Iraq, but dreaded. Since I hadn't outed myself to the military in 2005 and simply allowed my four-year active duty service to expire, I was now faced with a decision to closet myself and deploy or out myself to the Marines, be honorably discharged, and consequentially not deploy. In effect, I faced a choice between maintaining my personal integrity or following through on my commitment to serve.

I reached out to friends, family, and Marines for advice. Surprisingly, the Marines with whom I served in combat were almost uniformly in favor of my deploying—despite my sexual orientation. Certainly, one or two were concerned about what might happen to me if I was outed, but the majority gave me characteristically blunt Marine advice: "Buck up, serve honorably. If you don't go, someone else will have to." They were saying you served honorably as a brother in arms with us; there is absolutely no reason you shouldn't do so again. So I deployed to Kabul, Afghanistan, in September 2007 until April 2008 without incident and with honor.

I have kept a low profile on this issue but can no longer abide the mischaracterizations made by politicians and conservative organizations, mischaracterizations that masquerade as arguments against open service. There are real concerns about training and discipline that must be addressed as this policy is repealed but the arguments put forth by many opponents are distaste and disapproval of homosexuality as opposed to genuine concerns about "readiness."

The Department of Defense's 2010 survey conducted prior to the repeal of DADT echoes my experience: 92 percent of those who have served with someone they knew or believed to be gay felt their unit's performance was better or the same as it was before. The combat-hardened Marines who I served with, respect, and love urged me to return to service. As my example demonstrates, although homosexuality may be "incompatible" with a person's moral code, it is not incompatible with military service. The repeal of DADT will contribute immeasurably to unit cohesion and national security, and is in keeping with our commitment to justice for all of our citizens.

A version of this essay appeared in the New York Daily News *in December 2010.*

After a First Salute to Two New Officers, Devastation

by Ed Luna

In the years leading to the termination of DADT, casual conversation about the topic was often lopsided.

Most Marines you spoke to agreed that gay people could not function and therefore did not belong in the military. Every so often you would hear a counter-argument, something along the lines of how some gay people are normal people and you would never know they were there. The rare voice of dissent was ambivalent enough to join the unanimous agreement that "DADT works," so why change it.

It is not difficult to identify and elaborate on the practical and moral faults of the implementation, application, and defense of DADT. At this time the only benefit of such a thing would be to make indignant gay people feel good about being on the right side of a historically significant issue. Instead of making a "what if" argument in my essay, I will limit myself to facts that anyone who wears the uniform can relate to, regardless of sexual orientation.

Apart from the use of the word "gay" as a negative descriptor and "fag" as a pejorative, I was a private the first time I got a full sense of the Department of Defense's gay policy. In 2003, one of my instructors at my Military Occupational Specialty school spoke to my class.

The topics were wide-ranging, from marriage to faith, deployments to boot camp. About a dozen of us junior enlisted students crowded around our mentor, listening in awe to his stories. When one of us inevitably asked about the instructor's experience in boot camp, he lamented about how the mothers of America had made the institution of Marine boot camp weak.

His example: a gay recruit had admitted his sexuality to his senior drill instructor (SDI). The recruit was kicked out of the SDI's office for trying to be a quitter and he was ordered to continue training. On the same night as his confession, the other recruits, including my instructor, had a "blanket party." The instructor described how they had held the recruit down and beaten him senseless, breaking his eye socket with a bar of soap in a sock. The instructor smiled as he explained how "they got him out of there real quick after that."

It would be dishonest if I claimed that I was concerned for my safety, primarily because I was not willing to let anyone find out that I had anything in common with the recruit in the story. But there was no doubt that I would have shared the recruit's fate if my friends found out who I really was.

For years the conversation with my instructor shaped my thoughts on being gay in military, and it simplified the issue of coming out. It wasn't possible.

Although I look back at those years with a sense of anger, at the time I used the reality I faced as a tool to convince myself that I could live a good life and have a successful career by ignoring my sexuality. I experienced other points of homophobia and learning but the one to shift my worldview occurred in 2006.

On my second deployment to Iraq, I worked for a master sergeant on the cusp of retirement. He had been the senior Marine of our detachment on my first deployment two years prior. At the time I considered him a mentor and a model of what a leader of Marines should be. As a result, I invested confidence in his advice.

During a conversation about the importance of attending the corporal's and sergeant's courses, he spoke to me about his experience at the advanced course—gunnery sergeants' PME (professional military education) school. He discussed a paper he had written about the insurmountable challenges of allowing homosexuals to serve.

His thesis was anchored in the belief that the essential element of gay-straight relations mirrored the cultural and sexual difference between men and women. Thus a military that allowed homosexuals in its ranks would, by virtue of American values, require privacy accommodations (berthing, bathroom facilities, etc.) for four distinct "genders." The confidence he expressed in his conclusion was not open to debate—at least not from me, a subordinate who looked up to him. He took pride that his instructor told him his paper would have been submitted to be published were it not for the controversial subject.

Again, the revelation that one of my leaders had such an opinion about people such as myself was not traumatic or devastating, but I remember feeling disillusioned about what the future would hold if I decided to continue serving as a Marine.

At this stage in my life I remained convinced that an asexual life, free of anything gay, was the most unselfish and patriotic path. This immunized me to the indignation or pain that I might have felt by what many would consider rejection or hate. To me, it was reality. I was numb to any other interpretation. However, this manufactured indifference proved to be unsustainable during the following years.

By 2010, I had come out to my family and closest Marine friends. My self-image was no longer separate from my opinion about "gay stuff." I had experienced several stressful episodes of DADT-related paranoia (related to my weighing the risks of coming out against the morale-crushing effects of refusing to do so) but had learned and become more myself.

That year I experienced one of the proudest moments of my life. Two Marine officers asked me to render the first salute at their commissioning ceremony. Never had I felt so honored as when they made that request. I dutifully obliged—and naturally ordered a round of drinks for us that evening.

Both Marines were close friends. But through them I gained an accurate sense of the full weight of the DADT policy.

Not long after I decided that I should be more honest with these dear friends, each dealt the hardest blows to my morale that I can remember.

One of them asked a friend of ours what he would do to his son if he turned out to be gay. The other one went on a tirade about a group of people being "a bunch of fucking faggots."

It felt as though they had shot across my bow—a harbinger of what would follow if I told the truth.

An articulate friend once said that we (humans) can never know the pain we cause to those we care about, because if we did we would be paralyzed by guilt. I know that neither of my friends had any idea I would be affected by their words, but the fact remains that such a situation was created by DADT.

For years I lived and acted according to the belief that mentoring aspiring Marines required that I respect the laws of the land and the policies that govern the Corps—even at the expense of my integrity and identity. Doing what was right for my Marines and my country meant corrupting myself and my values. I had always known this, so coming out to these two friends who held me in such high regard was inappropriate. It was simply not possible.

These anecdotes and incidents count for nothing if not put into context.

The purpose of service members—past and present—decrying the injustices inherent to DADT has not been to inundate the American people with sob stories in order to make the armed forces into an arena for social justice. It has been done to prove beyond doubt that sanctifying the virtues of integrity and honor on one hand, while forcing people to live an obscene lie on the other, is antithetical to the values of our military and our country.

To foster camaraderie throughout a brotherhood that willfully risks life and limb and then to contaminate those bonds by injecting distrust and dishonesty is not in keeping with what we stand for and defend. Our people hold their military in the highest regard and revere our service members. It follows that we—as a country—are simply better than a needlessly discriminatory policy such as DADT indicates.

We are better for having this blemish removed from our great military's reputation.

The Moral Dilemma of Honor and Deception
by Maj Alasdair B. G. Mackay, USMC

I have served in the U.S. military for more than 17 years: 5 in the enlisted ranks and 12 as a commissioned officer in the Marine Corps. During this time I have lied to virtually every single service member I have ever encountered, including commanding officers, peers, and Marines under my command.

I have been deceitful of who and what I am, including manipulating my personal image and the perception that others have of me. I have lived a double life in which I make up stories about where I have been and whom I was with. I have lived in constant fear of losing my job and being made an outsider in the organization to which I have dedicated my life.

I have served with honor, courage, and commitment, but I have lied to others and cheated myself. I have fought the battle of what is *right: right* for the Corps and *right* for my heart, soul, and well-being. Every day of my career I have compromised my values, my integrity, and my moral standards. I have been—knowingly and unknowingly—verbally abused, insulted, and berated. I have lived a personal life similar to a monk's—a life in the shadow of moral uncertainty. I am a professional Marine; however, I am also a gay Marine who has been allowed to serve freely, but not openly.

This essay attempts to provide an understanding of the moral dilemma of putting my profession as a Marine officer and my service to my country above my personal; moral; mental; and, sometimes, physical health as a gay Marine on active duty.

I have seen many Marines—subordinates, peers, and superiors—deal with professional and personal moral dilemmas. Some dilemmas are more complex and result in moral injury, and some are relatively simple and resolved in moments. However, my moral dilemma has not just lasted a few moments or a couple of days, but has been ongoing for more than a decade. *The Oxford Dictionary of Philosophy* defines "moral dilemmas" as "situations in which each possible course of action breaches some otherwise binding moral principle."

The courses of action that I have had open to me in my professional career, which have often led to an anxious moral and mental rollercoaster ride, were either to stay the course and continue to serve with the same commitment expected of all Marines, particularly Marine officers, or resign my commission so that I may work and live where and how I wish. There are several consequences to making either of these decisions.

If I stay the course, I face living with the moral dilemma each day—until DADT repeal's implementation, which will allow me to serve openly without the threat of discovery and potential discharge—of going against my and the Corps' moral standards, including "thou shall not lie." This doesn't include only the moral dilemma of lying about who I am, it also means being a moral hypocrite every time I make a recommendation or decision that results in the discharge of a fellow Marine who violates the DADT policy. On the other hand, if I leave the Corps, I face the mental anguish of throwing away my career, my retirement, and most importantly, a life of service to my country and the Corps.

When I encounter moral dilemmas in a professional or personal capacity, I usually take a pragmatic approach to solving them. I have always tried to stay focused on the positive of the end view (in my case, the end justifying the means), rather than to get bound up in moral contemplation or decision making. I am unsure whether this approach is inherent to who I am, or if I have unconsciously gravitated toward it partly as a coping mechanism for overcoming my never ending loop of moral dilemma.

What I know for certain is the extreme mental and sometimes physical strain that being in an endless loop has had on me. The RAND Corporation's report, *Sexual Orientation and U.S. Military Personnel Policy*, states there is "long-standing theory and some empirical evidence [to] indicate that concealing one's gay . . . orientation may have adverse psychological consequences." The report also points out, which I find poignant, that for many gay military service members, "keeping their secret requires constant information control—an endless series of decisions about whom to tell, when to tell, and when and to whom they should actively lie."* From a personal perspective, this moral dilemma has resulted in constant anxiety, depression, mental hostility, and decreased self-efficacy during my career. These by-products make an already demanding career even more challenging, particularly outside work.

RAND's report also states that many gay and lesbian service members said in the Department of Defense's 2010 DADT survey that they have had mental issues associated with the policy since it started in 1993. Many times I have contemplated the potential mental health issues that could be attributed to being required to live in a state of moral dilemma.

In recent weeks, I have considered the possibility of moral injury that I may have been subjected to under DADT. When I look at myself, I often feel that I have been morally scarred by having to lie so much for so long. If moral injury is determined by being required to make decisions that fall outside what is considered morally right by the individual, and, in my case, over a significant period, then I could probably be considered a wounded warrior of the DADT era.

Although the way ahead for the end of DADT is clear, the end to the moral dilemma, from my perspective, is not. The DADT policy forcibly told me not to tell or else face the consequences and receive a discharge.

The new challenge for me, and potentially many other gay Marines, is the decision of whether I should serve openly and face cultural stigma from many of my fellow Marines (I know the stigma exists; I have listened to it for the last decade) or continue to lie because lying is what I know and what I have become good at. Either way, this new moral dilemma will involve tough times dealing with those less accepting of us who are different from the norm, rather than our having to deal with the threat of losing our livelihood because of the "wrong" sexual orientation.

Whatever my decision, I will always put the Corps first, even if it puts me second.

---

* National Defense Research Institute, *Sexual Orientation and U.S. Military Personnel Policy* (Santa Monica, CA: RAND Corporation, 2010).

The End of Don't Ask, Don't Tell

Investigated 17 Times in 23 Years of Service
by Kristen L. Tobin

The military was and is my life.

At eight years old I was telling Mom I was going to join the Navy, and at 17 I came home from the recruiting office with one last hurdle to starting my dream—a permission slip from my mother. Since mom's own dream to join the Navy Nurse Corps was dashed by my grandparents, mom was a pushover.

Off I went to Orlando, but upon arrival I found that someone knew something about me that I did not know or was not able to understand: I was gay. Who knew? A lot of people, including a company commander who took "special interest" in me.

Even my boot camp company was called "Gay Company." Luckily I was home on leave when this nickname was achieved; I was not there for the removal of a couple of recruits who were found in the same rack. But the resulting scrutiny of our company caused fear and hiding, and so began my 23-year career in the U.S. Navy: loving what I did but hiding part of who I was. Despite hiding, there were 17 investigations into my sexual orientation. I laugh when someone says being gay is a choice. Believe me, no rational person would choose such harassment.

In my 17th year of service, President Bill Clinton and the powers that be did gay service members a favor and "allowed" us to serve. The catch? We could not say anything or act upon being gay. I was a senior chief and most of my investigations were behind me so I personally was not that affected by the stand-up of DADT. But I still had to hide who I was and be better than everyone else so the military's blind eye would protect me.

One time that I was not protected was when a sports team member (an officer) was discharged for being gay and for statutory rape; she really had chosen the wrong "little girl" that time. Once she was identified, Naval Investigative Service (NIS) smelled blood, and in their zealous interrogation, our coach turned all of us in as gay. Her list of offenders included straight women and her own sister.

The concept of DADT may seem to many a good comprise: you keep your job and we get your service. But to me the policy translated to this: gay members could serve (we already were), and government would act like the parent who knew but did not want to talk about it. What a great deal for the military and the Department of Defense (DOD): to "allow" gay members to serve, defend, and pay the ultimate sacrifice, with the condition of silence. Gay service members' ability to address harassment, prejudice, or ill treatment based on sexual orientation, or even to tell the truth, was now impossible without breaking the law.

As a senior female responsible for investigating and reporting rape/sexual assault cases, I would love for the DOD to investigate the number of sex-related crimes against service members that are deemed "consensual sex." Perhaps after the repeal, an out lesbian can dispute "consent" due to her sexual orientation, and gay men need not be persecuted by predators who are "gay while underway."

It is the inability to acknowledge our full selves and our families that cause the biggest negative impact on performance. Worrying every day about your job and your family because the DOD has abdicated its responsibility to take care of its own makes it much harder to give your all to the mission—although many gay members do in spite of the direct assault on who they are. I do not profess to be an expert on the legalities and nuances of DADT policy, but I know that the policy that intended to allow gay members to serve quietly resulted in or created other significant ramifications.

The acknowledgement of gay service members created a license to share hatred and a strong homophobic voice that were now permitted to be heard; there was no discrimination policy in that regard. Soon people I previously assumed cool with DADT were incensed with the notion of homosexuality in "their" military and were not going to stand for it. This viewpoint, provoked by or not effectively addressed by senior leadership (often senior leadership was the most vocal), gave confidence to individuals who would talk and take action, too; the number of assaults and gay bashings are evidence. Now gay members needed to not only serve quietly but also to listen to vocalized loathing (and even partake in it in order not to be targeted themselves). The early days were volatile and gradually the loud protests dissipated but the underlying anger and danger remained.

DADT, more accurately called "Don't Ask, Don't Tell, Don't Pursue," provided simple guidance—senior officials don't ask, members don't tell and don't pursue—and established requirements for initiating investigations. The media is full of reports about some of the 13,000 members who were discharged under the policy and most are reported to be a result of "telling." What we do not hear about is the "don't pursue" clause and later, a clause to prevent the harassment: "don't harass."

I can attest that while "don't ask" equated to not asking the obvious ("are you gay?"), the "don't purse" and "don't harass" clauses became highly discretionary. Senior leadership, lawmakers, and three administrations did not hold DOD to these provisions of the law, leaving many highly qualified and capable service members at the mercy of a policy that was not enforced to the letter of the law.

It would be interesting to determine the members who supposedly "told" but in reality never broke the law and instead were outed by a third party or coerced into naming names, and to determine the number of members who were tired of the battle and finally told due to integrity, frustration, and harassment, breaking the law but with extenuating circumstances. To say that DADT failed is an understatement.

I adamantly believe that allowing openly gay service members was not addressed by previous administrations not because of the morality issues presented by people such as Senator John McCain (R-AZ) but because of the fiscal impact. Full equality in benefits for gay members and their families (housing, exchange and commissary privileges, and health care) will increase costs.

However, investigations are costly, too.

In 2006 a University of California commission estimated the price of 9,488 discharges between 1994 and 2003 at 363 million dollars, including 14.3 million dollars for "separation" travel. While the amount is staggering, this figure does not include the investigative, legal, and salary costs (not to mention costs of replacing highly cleared personnel) of these early discharges. Look at just the case of Air Force Lieutenant Colonel Victor Fehrenbach. How much has the multiyear fight to attempt to discharge this pilot—selected to fly air coverage over the White House after the 11 September 2001 attacks—cost?

While not a monetary expenditure, one of biggest costs of DADT is the emotional impact to service members who are discharged, investigated, and/or harassed. Outstanding sailors, Marines, soldiers, and airmen lived in fear of getting caught for being who they are and were simply humiliated by the government. The stories are heart wrenching. One friend, a fourth-generation Navy pilot (select), days from graduation, was outed by a jilted civilian lover and had to call home and tell his grandfather and father that he was being discharged for being gay. He was top in his class and has taken years to deal with this.

As I said, the military is my life. I work at a military installation as a project manager, system engineer, and technical advisor, a job that is supposed to be filled by active duty personnel. (One of the ironies about DADT is that discharged personnel often take defense contractor jobs.) My life in the service made me who I am and I would do it all—even the investigations—again.

What we do matters, but we lessen our readiness when we fight among ourselves. As the only NATO country with an active ban against openly gay service members, the United States would have been best served by putting time, focus, and money into defending our country from those who wish us harm—instead of worrying about who we love.

A Legacy of the Holocaust, Normandy, and Vietnam
by Stacy J. Vasquez

I am a product of military service and its values, and my commitment to service and to veterans began early.

While serving in the U.S. Army in Europe, my adoptive grandfather went to Germany to adopt a little boy but the infant died before he arrived. However, a family friend had seen my mother, at the time a girl suffering from rickets, during a doctor's visit. (My maternal German grandmother had been taken to an internment camp after the Nazis discovered she had been feeding Jewish people.)

Because of the U.S. soldier's commitment to making a difference, the life of the little girl who became my mother was spared.

My earliest childhood memories involve holding my grandfather's hand and listening as he recounted 30 years of Army Air Corps service and the personal sacrifice of leaving my grandmother behind in Kentucky to go to war. I also recall my uncle recounting his horrible experience on the beaches of Normandy, but with little detail—as is common with veterans of his generation.

Like many military families, my family's service was generational.

I recall the departure of my father's ship from Pearl Harbor as he continued his duty after he had returned from Vietnam. After Vietnam, he was a changed man: paranoid, violent, and nervous. He paced the floors at home while chain-smoking cigarettes. Not much was known about posttraumatic stress (PTS), and as a result of the violence associated with the undiagnosed PTS, my mother, brother, and I sought refuge in battered women's shelters in our small town in Texas to escape the violence and death threats.

However, my family's service inspired me to join the Army at 17 in search of a brighter future, educational opportunity, adventure, and travel.

Most in the military were married or romantically involved. I was the opposite. I dated but never for any substantial length of time. I even married under the illusion that a fantastic friendship with a wonderful friend would be the equivalent of falling in love. Unfortunately, more than friendship is required to maintain a relationship with an intimate partner, and my marriage ended with the gradual realization that I did not feel affectionate in the way many others did.

I then focused on excelling in my military career as a means of filling the emptiness in my personal life. But career is no substitute for a relationship and, although I was successful, I was lonely. My mom began asking why I never brought anyone home. Men were interested but I was not, and the reason became clear as the years went by.

On occasion, I sat in a gay bar simply to be in the presence of lesbians, and I did not know where else to meet them. After becoming a recruiter and having more interaction with civilians, I began meeting people who were open about their sexuality. However, because I was conservative and my love of the Army took precedence, I knew I would not find love while I served. I sacrificed.

After 12 years of service, attaining the rank of sergeant first class and earning the distinction of honor graduate and top recruiter, my career crumbled when a colleague's wife told my commander that she saw me kiss a girl in a gay bar. He called me into his office to answer the allegation.

After outlining the investigative process and possible outcomes if the allegation proved to be true—to include Uniform Code of Military Justice punishment—he offered me the opportunity to sign an admission that would allow for my honorable discharge and retention of education benefits. I consulted with legal counsel and signed a statement admitting that I was gay.

I have been asked why I chose to sign the statement instead of going to a discharge board. The answer is not simple. However, I can tell you that I was not willing to compromise my integrity. If directly asked, I would not lie to a board of senior and noncommissioned officers.

During the discharge process my commander stated that although I should be promoted ahead of my peers and he wished the law were different, DADT mandated my discharge. He emphasized a "great loss" to the Army and said my exemplary performance should have been the deciding factor.

I felt that I had tarnished my family's legacy. Losing my retirement and career had a significant emotional effect on me. I was not prepared for life outside the Army, but I was determined to turn an unfavorable circumstance into an opportunity to excel. I returned to college on the GI Bill to complete my undergraduate and graduate degrees.

While in college, I interned for Annise Parker, currently the mayor of Houston, and interacted with her family. She taught me about being myself while maintaining some of my conservative fiscal views. Politics fascinated me, and I learned how to advocate for gay civil rights through the political system. I began participating in meetings with gay veterans who were also negatively affected by DADT, and local news media began asking me to discuss my experience with DADT.

Sharon Alexander, an Army veteran and lawyer at Servicemembers Legal Defense Network (SLDN), advised me about ways I could discuss my experience publicly. She connected me with people and resources through which I could discuss the repeal of DADT. In addition, she encouraged me to focus constructively. My negative feelings turned into positive endeavors. This led me to Washington, DC, where I worked for SLDN and had the opportunity to tell members of Congress the effect of DADT on my life.

After my graduation, Sharon advised me about a job with the SLDN law and policy team, and the opportunity allowed me to learn the law by working with clients. In 2006 I worked on the introduction of the House legislation to replace DADT with a policy of nondiscrimination.

However, I learned that I was not good at being gay all day for pay after being silent for so long, and the clients had a profound effect on me because their experiences were similar to mine—and would have the same outcome.

Simultaneously, SLDN and the Wilmer Hale law firm asked me if I would be interested in filing suit for reinstatement into the Army. I spoke with my family and agreed to join the case. *Cook v. Gates* became one of the primary legal vehicles through which the public was educated about the realities of DADT. For almost five years, 12 plaintiffs told their stories in the legal system. Being part of the case was hard because it gave me hope that I would be able to return to active duty. At times the hope of returning prevented me from moving on emotionally and letting go of the past.

In the end, we suffered disappointing losses in the courts. Because we knew our argument was valid, it was a difficult decision not to file an appeal with the Supreme Court. However, the landscape of the Court likely would have yielded a decision that would negatively impact several gay civil rights issues, leaving gay service members and veterans in a worse position legislatively.

My attention became laser-focused on legislative action. I spoke with any member of Congress who would listen. Every media interview or speaking event was an opportunity to change minds and garner votes in Congress. Some of the national media interviews were hard to accept because my government employer did not agree with my role as a civil rights advocate, but I did the interviews regardless. I tried not to let media coverage affect my career; however, when I applied later for the presidential management fellows and management positions, many doors were closed after my discharge paperwork, public profile, and suit against the Secretary of Defense became known.

I saw my service and sacrifice come full circle while I was standing next to members of Congress and hugging the president after he signed legislation repealing DADT. I was overcome with feelings of relief, happiness—and sadness that it had taken so long.

My previous shame faded and I was filled with renewed self-respect and an appreciation for the efforts that made the moment a reality. After years of fighting in court and in public, I realized the difficult public conversation had been necessary in order to affect change, not only in how others felt about gay Americans but also in how I felt about myself.

I now recognize that my service to my country was as valuable and honorable as that of my colleagues, even though I am lesbian. And I was honored to use my voice in the fight to ensure no other generation of lesbian, gay, bisexual, and transgender veterans and service members are forced to deny who they are while serving in silence.

A Time to Empower Gay Troops to Speak for Themselves

by Lara A. Ballard

As a female, newly minted second lieutenant in the U.S. Army, I received a fair bit of news media attention when our Patriot missile battery deployed to Kuwait City in support of Operation Southern Watch in 1992.

Every media visit to our tactical site resulted in either a photograph of me or an interview. My parents found out I had been deployed to Kuwait when they opened their morning paper one day to find a brief article about the deployment, which ended with my being quoted as saying, "It's hot."

One day, a fellow lieutenant suggested that I give some of the male troops some airtime. They wanted to get in front of the cameras and say, "Hi, mom," too. I am eternally grateful to my colleague for pointing this out to me, because while I certainly had not set out to garner any media attention (as a closeted lesbian, attention was the last thing I wanted), I was going to be resented for it just the same. Women in combat were enough of a novelty that photojournalists found them a virtually irresistible target, and I eventually took to hiding in the Scud bunker whenever the media came around.

This was my first clue that the way things play out in the news media does not always mirror the way they play out within the ranks of the military. The experience sensitized me to the perceptions of the people around me, who were probably working harder than me and for far less recognition. I hope that our first generation of openly gay, lesbian, bisexual, and transgender service members learn some of the lessons gleaned from years of hit-or-miss progress on integrating women into the services. Sometimes you have to keep a low profile.

This is not to say that gay service members should stay in the closet. Far from it. It's vital that they be out to their family, their colleagues, and their subordinates, some of whom will also be gay and for whom they will need to set a good example. But when the cameras come around and some gay people and the media insist on celebrating what is sure to be a succession of "firsts" in the coming years—the first openly gay man to command a battalion, the first open lesbian to serve in combat, the first person to invite her same-sex partner to an award ceremony—they need to remember that acceptance within the ranks is going to come about primarily from simply doing their jobs. Moreover, we need to give them the space to do that and not drive them into the Scud bunker.

This is going to be a sea change for gay activism. For 17 years, advocacy groups such as the Servicemembers Legal Defense Network and activists like myself took it upon ourselves to give voice to the voiceless, as those who were affected by DADT were the ones prohibited by statute from speaking out about it. It was important then to highlight the stories of gay service members such as Eric Alva (the first Marine to be injured in Operation Iraqi Freedom); discharged Arabic linguists; and my friend, the late Major Alan Rogers (the first known openly gay fatality in Iraq). But now we need to remember that our goal from the outset was simply for gay troops to be treated like everyone else. Several noteworthy activists who were discharged under DADT and then became effective spokespersons have made clear their intentions to reenlist. Somehow, we're all going to have to leave these now-familiar public figures alone as they get quietly back to work.

This isn't to say that we should abandon our activism and advocacy from the outside. Our work is not done. Transgender service members cannot serve openly. Discrimination based on sexual orientation and gender identity falls outside the mandate of the military's Equal Employment Opportunity programs. Same-sex spouses of service members are denied the benefits and recognition afforded to their heterosexual counterparts. But it does mean that those of us on the outside need to start taking our cues from those on the inside, and we should be empowering them to speak for themselves rather than presuming to speak on their behalf. Organizations such as Outserve and Servicemembers United will take on added importance in the coming years.

And again, let's keep in mind the end goal. A few years ago I reached out to a Canadian Army major who had been affiliated with a Canadian gay service members' group, to see if they would consider collaborating with one of our U.S. groups. He told me the group no longer existed. "Since we have all our rights now," he ex-

The End of Don't Ask, Don't Tell

plained, "we just didn't see any particular reason to be organized."

This was music to my ears. I never asked to be identified as a lesbian. I'm an Army veteran, a married woman trying to raise a kid, pay my taxes, and make ends meet like everyone else. The fact that I'm married to another woman is no more or less significant to the people in my life than the fact that I'm left-handed, and that's the way I like it. I suspect the majority of gay troops are the same way—not looking to make a fuss over themselves but wanting the same rights as everyone else so they can disappear into the fabric of American life. I'm going to be taking my lead from them from here on out and keeping a low profile.

The Knife Is Out of Their Backs
by Michelle M. Benecke

Being in the military was much more than a job. For me it was a calling, identity, community, duty, and honor. As an officer I was not afraid of being called to fight for our country but I was in fear of being found out as gay.

I served as an Army officer and battery commander during the 1980s, when women were integrated into traditionally male fields such as the Air Defense Artillery branch in which I served. At the time, I was told there were 26 women officers in a branch of 55,000 men. Likewise, there were only a handful of enlisted women.

I was among the first women to lead combat arms soldiers, serving in capacities within Hawk surface-to-air missile units as a platoon leader, battery executive officer, and assistant battalion S3 (for operations and training). I was selected early to start and command a new battery.

In most cases I was the first female officer to serve in my units. I worked hard to gain credibility. Before arriving for my first assignment, I earned both Airborne and Air Assault wings at a time when it was unusual for men to wear both badges.

As a new lieutenant, I landed in a field unit with leaders who treated me just as they would a male lieutenant. During my first year, our unit spent half the year in the field and my being a woman wasn't an issue. But when we were called up on alert, higher level officers wanted to replace me with a male. My commanders would have none of it.

Despite command support, the overall climate was hostile to women. Female officers in other units faced sabotage by their male peers and their careers were cut short. We dealt with harassment or efforts to undermine our role. And the majority of women officers serving in my branch were investigated for being gay, regardless of their sexual orientation. This was an era when witch hunts by the military's criminal investigators were rampant. With their resources and reach, one allegation could be leveraged into a dragnet.

My selection for a fellowship to law school—a prestigious program for which only 10 Army officers were selected each year—heightened the ethical dilemma I was experiencing, and I made the painful decision to resign my commission and forfeit the fellowship because of the military's gay ban. I could not return and prosecute other gay people, nor could I lie about who I was. I believed in the military's core values of honesty and integrity. The gay ban was antithetical to those values.

Shortly before my service ended, the witch hunts ensnared me. Investigators from the Army's Criminal Investigation Division (CID) removed two soldiers from our barracks late on a Friday night for interrogation. The agents pressured my soldiers to accuse me of being gay and to lodge false allegations that I had made advances toward them. When they refused, CID pointlessly interrogated them about their own sexual orientation.

I was on leave across the country and on Saturday morning, I received a call from my first sergeant. "Ma'am, you need to get back here. It's best we don't talk over the phone." My stomach dropped. CID was suspected of wiretapping phones during these investigations.

The first sergeant had been tipped off by another senior noncommissioned officer. Fortunately, I had time to think on the 1,900-mile drive to Fort Bliss.

When I arrived at base, I marched to headquarters and asked the battalion commander and command sergeant major why CID had been permitted into the barracks without my first sergeant's knowledge. My command's support temporarily protected me, and the commanding general put a stop to the CID investigation. In its place, however, he required a commander's inquiry to be conducted.

It was a nerve-wracking situation. I had been accepted to Harvard Law School but the Army would not release me to attend if I were under investigation. My contacts suggested CID's investigation was an attempt to pressure me into accusing others or lose my chance at attending school. I did not name names.

Finally, I was released, a bittersweet moment for someone who had wanted to be a military officer. I had vowed to start an advocacy group to repeal the gay ban and assist military members, and these experiences strengthened my resolve.

In law school, classmate Kirstin Dodge and I discovered that the gay ban was used by each service to drum women out of nontraditional fields. Our *Harvard Women's Law Journal* essay was circulated and, as a result, military members began calling me for assistance.

The calls made clear the need for an advocacy group. The opportunity opened when President William J. Clinton announced DADT.

DADT was supposed to stop the witch hunts but did not. Unable to seek help within the military, service members called the Campaign for Military Service (CMS), the umbrella organization that had supported President Clinton's attempt to lift the ban. CMS was a temporary effort, and as the organization closed, coworker C. Dixon Osburn and I stood at CMS headquarters and wondered aloud about the next steps.

No organization planned to seek repeal of DADT or assist military members. With Congress' moving to codify DADT, activists considered the fight to be over. If nothing were done, DADT repeal would fall off the table and military members would continue to suffer, their plight unknown to the public. With no seed money, Osburn and I launched Servicemembers Legal Defense Network (SLDN) the day after President Clinton announced DADT on 19 July 1993.

During my tenure as SLDN's codirector from 1993 to 2000, SLDN laid the foundation to overturn DADT, built a national movement, and provided direct legal assistance to thousands of military members. Our clients faced death threats, rape, beatings, harassment, and investigations, particularly in the early years. For example:

- At Camp Hansen on Okinawa in 1994, 21 Marines were questioned about their sexual orientation and about other Marines. One was imprisoned for a month. SLDN stopped the witch hunt before others were harmed.
- On the USS *Simon Lake* (AS 33) in 1995, Seaman Amy Barnes was accused of being gay after she rebuffed the advances of a male sailor. Up to 60 women were targeted before sailors came to SLDN. Barnes and another sailor were discharged.

- At Hickam Air Force Base in Hawaii in 1996, prosecutors agreed to reduce the sentence of an alleged rapist on the condition he accuse military men of being gay. He accused 17 men. Many were discharged and one faced court-martial.
- Private First Class Barry Winchell was murdered at Fort Campbell, Kentucky, in 1999. SLDN intervened after soldiers in Winchell's unit expressed concerns that officials were covering up the facts of Winchell's death. SLDN's investigation uncovered evidence of a hate crime and showed how verbal taunts escalated to violence when left unchecked by leaders.

By 2000, under SLDN's work, the witch hunts ended and selective criminal prosecutions waned. The Defense Department warned commanders away from investigating women as potential lesbians in retaliation for their reporting rape or sexual harassment, and instituted reforms that were intended to stem harassment.

Through these and other cases, SLDN chipped away at the foundation of DADT and brought the issue back to national attention. In 2005, Representative Martin Meehan (D-MA) introduced the first bill to repeal DADT, and repeal bills were filed in 2007, 2009, and 2010, the last under the leadership of Representative Patrick Murphy (D-PA). Finally, Congress voted to let DADT expire.

It was a privilege to lead such a momentous process and later, to help see it through to its fruition. I am honored to have worked with the thousands of military members and allies who came together to end DADT. On 20 September 2011, gay men, lesbians, and bisexual people had the freedom to serve.

Some will feel comfortable serving openly. Others simply want the "knife out of their back," as military members have poignantly described life under DADT. Finally they can be honest with family members or friends and not have to live in fear of being found out and thrown out.

Reactions from Indifference to Open Support
by SFC David Cogdill, USA

Born and raised in rural Montana, I was unaware of gay people except for what I saw in the mainstream media. My education indicated that this "behavior" was a choice, and my religious upbringing condemned the activity as an abomination before God, an activity practiced by sinners and deviants.

However, I was not concerned with homosexuality and believed that whatever you did in your home was your business—so long as those practices were not forced on me or flung in my face.

At boot camp in the early 1990s at Marine Corps Recruit Depot San Diego, initial shock gave way to dogged determination and then to the rush that goes with being greeted as a Marine for the first time. For a 20-something boy with no direction or purpose, graduation was a turning point. I ate, breathed, slept, and oozed Marine. To be anything less than a Marine was not acceptable.

This acceptance, strength, and newfound sense of belonging were shared with countless other "boots" as we trained and entered into the Fleet Marine Force. Our attention to detail served to feed our own insecurities as we measured ourselves against fellow Marines. Any weakness or perceived weakness was identified, catalogued, and often pointed out with all the finesse of an artillery barrage.

Common knowledge said that any homosexual activity was against regulations and was grounds for dismissal from the Corps. Homosexuality was viewed as different, and to the 20-something, insecure, heterosexual males with whom I served, homosexuality was viewed as weakness.

Anybody who engaged in homosexuality was obviously less than a man. Terms such as "fag, queer, homo, fairy, pole smoker, ass pirate" were tossed about in conversation. The popular perception was that a gay man couldn't be a Marine and that the other services (in particular, the Navy) were heavily populated with gay men. This perception was allowed—and often encouraged—by our superiors, who were building our confidence and courage and, often, arrogance and disdain for our "sister" services. The belief was that if we *felt* superior, we would *be* superior. On some levels the desired effect was achieved.

My first exposure to homosexual activity came in Okinawa, Japan. Individuals had set up a "glory hole" in a restroom at Camp Lester, and the Naval Investigative Service set up a sting operation. The operation resulted in the arrest of sailors and at least one Marine who were to be prosecuted and subsequently discharged.

Around this time, DADT was implemented.

To say that the policy was poorly received is an understatement. The perception was that DADT was the death knell of the Marine Corps as we knew it, and that the policy would be the first step in a series of changes forced upon the Marines, changes that threatened to unravel order, discipline, tradition—the foundation the Corps was built on.

Senior leadership stressed that despite the new policy, the Corps would conduct business as usual. Soon there were cartoons such "Clinton's Corps," which emphasized the changes we could expect—such as stylish new haircuts and uniforms with Spandex. It was tongue-in-cheek but there was an underlying sense of unease in the ranks. Some felt that the policy was the government's way of ignoring an issue, an issue that would magically go away.

In the mid-1990s while I was stationed at Parris Island, a Marine friend propositioned another Marine, a younger woman she believed to be interested in a relationship. Later, the younger Marine reported the incident. The command conducted an investigation and found the evidence needed to reprimand one Marine and discharge another. The Corps lost a good Marine simply because of her sexual orientation.

Meanwhile, more gay people, including celebrities, came out, and again the question of whether gay people had a right to serve openly became a topic.

In the ranks, many argued that allowing openly gay individuals to serve would be detrimental to order and discipline, cited the continuing struggle with acceptance of race and gender, and said sex in general was taboo.

I have heard Marines and soldiers state that if a gay man could shower in a room full of naked men then straight men should be allowed to shower in a room full of naked women. While absurd, this did sum up the position of many who would be uncomfortable living with an openly gay service member in the close quarters required by our profession.

With the official announcement about the end of DADT, I observed reactions from indifference to open support.

Why? Exposure and education. Service members have been exposed to same-sex relations in movies and television, and news reports of same-sex marriages and gay civil rights are in the news as much as any other world event.

And many service members, including me, have gay friends and have seen no ill effects of their sexual orientation reflected in their ability to perform in their professions.

Most service members I have spoken with agree there will be a period of adjustment while individuals are allowed to be honest about their sexual orientation. I am reminded that a similar period was observed when the armed forces desegregated and when women were allowed to serve onboard Navy vessels.

The policy has served as a bridge, a way to try and ignore a problem and hope it would go away, and a way to serve as a soft sell to the hard-liners—to allow them to get used to the idea that gay service members are and will continue to fight beside them.

Now we are able to move forward as a capable and professional force blind to race, gender, and sexual orientation.

The Law Magnified a Cultural Barrier
by Andrew Harris

Looking back at DADT so soon after its dismantling makes it tough to place exactly where it will fall in the record books of ill-advised military policy.

Nevertheless, it is already clear that the policy's corrosive effect extended beyond gay service members. By the time of its repeal, DADT was at the epicenter of a growing distance between U.S. society and the members of the military sworn to defend it.

My own history of military service—which began at a military college and culminated with combat service—demonstrates how much the general military attitude will have to change after DADT is a thing of the past.

I matriculated at the Virginia Military Institute (VMI) in fall 2000, a year before September 2001 when the world became radically different for the military. DADT was less than a decade old. I had not known any openly gay students in high school, and VMI was an unlikely place to expand my horizons. At VMI gay people were virtually nonexistent, an afterthought, not fit for the spartan environment in Lexington, Virginia. While many fellow cadets disapproved of homosexuality on religious grounds, I never heard anyone voice support for, or concern over, DADT. Homosexuals were simply "the other," perhaps seen during a visit home or on a trip to another school, but in a college dealing with issues of gender integration (women were admitted in 1997), the civil rights of gay men and lesbians rarely came up. This attitude of nonacknowledgement is laughable when you account for the law of averages and the fact that several of my fellow alumni have since come out. While I now appreciate the absurdity of this view from my time at VMI, I found the same story when I reported to duty with the U.S. Army.

While the active military is different than VMI, the attitude toward gay service members was of a strikingly similar mentality: utter denial. There were no gay soldiers in this mind-set; we were training to be supersoldiers with a deployment to

Iraq months away. When a male soldier in my unit was reportedly caught having sexual relations with a civilian man, he claimed drunkenness and insanity and was allowed to leave the Army under a "failure to adapt" discharge. Clearly, "drunk and possibly unstable" was more acceptable than "I'm gay." Just as with my experience at VMI, gay people did not exist in the artillery, infantry, and cavalry units I served in. In this environment, homosexuals were disparaged as not masculine, weak, and not manly enough for the ubermasculine lifestyle we inhabited.

When I arrived in Baghdad for my second and final deployment, I confronted a different work environment than that of the first four years of my career. I was transferred to a large division staff, doing routine work with the same people 12 hours a day on a tour slated to last 15 months. I got to know people and hear about their personal lives back home.

Near the end of my tour, I met my first gay service member. Her girlfriend was also in the Army, stationed at another base in Baghdad. Back in the States, they lived with a married couple in an apartment that they rented off post. This was a revelation to me not because there was a lesbian in my unit (this is inevitable with the law of averages), but because so many of my peers knew and did not think twice about it. I was also saddened by the thought that a soldier—a good soldier—was forced to put on a charade so that she could enjoy some of the most basic rights that I enjoyed as a straight soldier.

While I knew this young sergeant intended to leave the Army of her own accord, she was an example of those who served in the closet and who could have contributed more to our armed forces and our nation if we had given them basic acceptance.

After that second deployment, I left the military and took on the title I once applied only to grandfathers: veteran. "Veteran" outside a military context implies a degree of experience, but as I left Fort Hood, I realized that I had almost no experience interacting with or even knowing someone who is openly gay. This became clearer when I moved to Washington, DC, and experienced the opposite of what I had seen in the military. People seemed to have no problem saying they were gay. More importantly, being gay was not an issue. This was also my first opportunity to interact with nonmilitary members of my generation. I was struck by how angered they were by DADT and how closely they associated the law with the U.S. military.

My generation, the millennials, are as close to the military as one is to a distant cousin. Each knows the other exists but neither could tell you much else. For the military, the war is consuming, and my life had been dominated by deployments, timelines, friends' deployments, and by squeezing the most out of my precious time at home.

For the civilian millennial, the war is distant, remote, and something that other people do. Everyone has a distant connection to the military from a classmate or relative, but the wars are a low priority compared to the economy and potential careers after graduation. I was shocked that some of the first questions my civilian friends and classmates asked me centered around DADT. They could not fathom how someone seemingly normal like me would associate with an organization that tolerated systemic discrimination. My explanations about my limited experience with the policy did nothing to soften the criticism and condemnation of the military.

To the average civilian, a service member or veteran is a symbol of the entire military. Each issue in a decade of war—whether it be Abu Ghraib, DADT, or the killing of Osama bin Laden, for example—seems, to a civilian, as if every service member is directly connected to it. Unfortunately, DADT magnified this cultural barrier and may remain the lasting result of the failed policy.

After nearly two decades of a policy that forced gay service members to live a lie and allowed straight service members to deny their existence, it is time for the military to catch up with society. The DADT period of denial ran parallel with a period in which many in civilian society gradually embraced, destigmatized, and in the case of *Lawrence v. Texas*, legally endorsed the right of gay Americans to be open about who they are. Now that a new dawn is rising, individual service members must seize the opportunity to show that the military can accept those who are born gay. The country is right to expect a military that reflects its highest values, and the U.S. military is nothing short of duty bound to deliver.

Services Will Get On with the Business at Hand
by Brendan P. Kearney

As a native San Franciscan, I grew up in an atmosphere that exuded tolerance.

The Beat Generation was followed by the misnamed "Summer of Love," which was followed by the burgeoning gay civil rights movement and the flexing of growing political power, primarily focused in the San Francisco Bay area, from the mid-1970s to today.

For a Marine officer who came of age in the mid-1970s, what was going on at home meant little. Our society then, as now, was comfortably insular. Politics and religion were conversations one never entered into, either professionally or personally, within the context of our military family. Sex was something that was laughed and joked about. Among our Marines and sailors, sex was something that was alluded to with the wall locker displays of Playboy "art" that would be allowed or disallowed depending on the religious beliefs of regimental or battalion commanders. Homosexuality was never addressed, as it was acknowledged that "they" were not welcome in the Marine Corps and gravitated instead toward the Navy and Air Force. In short, homosexuality was somebody else's problem.

My first experience with a gay Marine was upon reporting for barracks duty in late 1979. As the new guy on the block, getting assigned the most recent investigation was an expected burden. My surprise was that this particular investigation was focused on a young corporal who had requested a discharge based on declaring his homosexuality.

What was particularly disturbing was his status in the barracks: NCO (noncommissioned officer) of the quarter for the entire Naval installation, multiple meritorious promotions, and—most importantly—the respect he received from his peers.

As a good officer, I fulfilled my responsibilities in a dignified and professional manner, as I had to interview the corporal and his gay civilian friends to ensure his seriousness and verify his eligibility for discharge. The bottom line is that he went out the door and left me behind. I was troubled at the prospect that a talented young NCO—in short supply—had just departed over an issue that had little real consequence.

Fast forward 15 years and the lieutenant was now a lieutenant colonel assigned to Headquarters, Marine Corps (HQMC) in the midst of the new Clinton administration and the turmoil over DADT.

My unease over gay Marines, frankly, had been set aside primarily because the issue had never come up again in the intervening 15 years. Not one disciplinary case, not one investigation despite my repeated tours in the Fleet Marine Force, a war in the Gulf, and serving with thousands of Marines. However, within the hallowed halls of HQMC, it appeared from listening to the discussions of senior officers that the Corps was bedeviled by what must be "hundreds" of incidents, all of which were having a profound adverse impact on the good order and discipline of our Corps.

Needless to say—as I found then and subsequently—these perceptions were not based on fact. There was no single incident of homosexual activity anywhere in the Corps that impacted unit morale. What did impact morale were repeated instances of officer or staff noncommissioned officer (SNCO) misconduct, often of a heterosexual nature (such as fraternization), that was directly linked to abuses of authority and resulting in command climates of mistrust and discouragement.

Subsequent tours in battalion and regimental command reinforced my overall impression that DADT was a policy in search of justification. With more than a dozen infantry battalions assigned to 4th Marines during my stewardship, there was not a single case that would have required invoking DADT. Not one. Each of those battalions, however, had leadership issues of officer or SNCO misconduct that did impact to a greater or lesser degree the good order and discipline of the units.

As my career wound down serving as chief of staff as III MEF (Marine Expeditionary Force) in Asia and MARFOREUR (Marine Forces Europe), DADT would periodically come up as a result of political discourse in the United States. Our European comrades were incredulous that the policy still existed. The Marines and sailors I served with never mentioned it, as they were seemingly disinterested in the issue of sexual orientation. It appeared to me that they simply did not care and were focused—rightly so—on professional competence.

Upon retirement and return to San Francisco, my former Marine sergeant son, at the time a law student, and I would wander the Castro neighborhood pushing my granddaughter's stroller. Invariably the two guys with a baby girl would draw appreciative comments from the locals.

Initially I was a bit put off and my son—a hard-nosed Marine NCO—took his old man by the stack and swivel and mentioned that my attitude, while tolerant, was out of touch. He challenged me to meet with Marines who were gay and then reevaluate my somewhat troubled, primarily ambivalent attitude toward gay people in the military.

During the succeeding years I took up my son's challenge. Getting Marines to open up—even to an old retired colonel—is not an easy thing, as the "oorah" response of simple agreement in order to get around tough issues and change the topic, is often difficult to overcome. The bottom line: I spoke to hundreds of Marines, gay and straight, and with virtually every single one—once they got past the party line—not one Marine cared about a fellow Marine's sexual orientation. Not one.

It just took about a year before I became completely convinced that DADT was a policy disaster for our military and had a profound, adverse impact on our country at large.

Considering the multiple complex challenges this country faces, a policy that overtly removes talented patriots from the military is nothing short of a self-inflicted wound.

I decided to speak out in my own way, primarily in news media opportunities and through the military advisory council of the Servicemembers Legal Defense Network.

What was harder, and discouraging, was a decision to engage those retired senior officers who I felt were misguided in their promotion of the status quo, i.e., the rigorous defense of DADT.

Almost all of these conversations proved difficult, as I could see the disappointment in their faces as I explained my position. Some of them took it on and others walked away, continuing to be convinced that our Corps was fighting for its life over the issue of gay Marines. Regrettably, I'm afraid there are a number of Marines my age and older whose attitude will change only with the passage of years. Their bitterness over the perceived challenge to the Corps will only be overcome with a realization that our younger generation of Marines will serve this country as well as they did. Sadly, there are those whose lives will be lived out with the conviction that the country, through the change in law, has mortally wounded their beloved Corps.

I don't pretend to see the future. But based on my experience and my profound confidence in this generation of Marines, I believe the demise of DADT will quickly become a nonevent, and the services as a whole will get on with the business at hand: defeating the enemies of our country.

My only regret is that I wish I had paid the issue greater attention and worked earlier to overcome a policy that has adversely impacted patriotic Marines, our Corps, and our country.

Appendix
Historical
Documents

They Are Already There
by Senator Jim Webb

Senator Webb (D-VA) is a decorated combat Marine, former Secretary of the Navy, and chairman of the personnel subcommittee of the Senate Armed Services Committee.

He opposed attempts to repeal "Don't Ask, Don't Tell" (DADT) before the completion of the survey of troops mandated by the Department of Defense because of his concern that "many members of the military would view as disrespectful a move to pre-empt the process." Following the study's release and before voting to repeal DADT, Webb gave this Senate speech on 18 December 2010. In lieu of a formal essay, Webb's office suggested that the text of his speech be published in this work.

I rise in support of the notion that we need to make adjustments to the "Don't Ask, Don't Tell" policy. I say this after many years of thought and consideration and also in light of the analysis that has been provided by the Department of Defense [DOD] to the Armed Services Committee on which I sit.

We need to, first of all, understand what this is and what it is not. The question is not whether there should be gays and lesbians in the military. They are already there. According to [Army] General [Carter F.] Ham, who conducted this extensive study, approximately the same percentage of the military is gay and lesbian as in our general population.

The question is not about whether anyone should be able to engage in inappropriate conduct as a result of this policy, because we will not allow that and we will be very vigorous in our oversight of the DOD to make sure that does not occur.

The question is whether this policy, as now enacted, works in a way that, on the one hand can protect small unit cohesion—or to sort that out—and on the other, allow people to live honest lives.

Here's what we have:

We have a secretary of defense who served in the Air Force and who implemented a policy of nondiscrimination when he headed the CIA, coming forward strongly and saying he believes that the alteration of this policy will work. I would remind my colleagues that he began as secretary of defense in the Bush Administration.

We have a chairman of the Joint Chiefs, who had an extensive career in surface warfare starting with small destroyers and up to commanding fleets, saying he believes the policy should change and that it can work. We have the vice chairman of the Joint Chiefs, a Marine, saying he believes this policy should change and it can work.

Most interestingly, we have General Ham, who conducted this study—an infantry officer and former enlisted Army soldier whose religious beliefs caused him concern about homosexuality—at the same time saying this policy can be changed and that it should be changed.

That is what we are seeing here. The question is whether a change in policy will create difficulties in small unit cohesion. That depends, as I mentioned during the hearings, on how the policy is implemented.

I wrote a letter yesterday to Secretary [of Defense Robert M.] Gates to reaffirm my understanding that this repeal would contemplate a sequenced implementation of the provisions for different units in the military as reasonably determined by the service chiefs, the combatant commanders in coordination with the secretary of defense and chairman of the Joint Chiefs.

He responded to me this morning saying, "This legislation would indeed permit" it and "The specific concerns you raise would be foremost in my mind as we develop an implementation plan."

Without this, Mr. President, I would not be voting to repeal this. I have spent my entire life in and around the military, including five years in the Pentagon. With this understanding and with the notion that we need to be putting a policy into place that allows an open way of living among people who have different points of view, I'm going to support this legislation.

What the Service Chiefs Said: Statements to the Senate

Service Chiefs' Statements at the Senate Hearing, 3 December 2010

General George W. Casey Jr., Chief of Staff of the Army

I've reviewed the final version of the working group report on the issues associated with the repeal of "don't ask, don't tell" and I want to be able to provide my informed military advice to the committee. I'll begin by relating how I see the military risks, the risks from a military perspective, and then I'll give you my views on the impact on the force if [DADT] is repealed.

First, I think it's important that we're clear about the military risks. Implementation of the repeal of [DADT] would be a major cultural and policy change in the middle of a war. It would be implemented by a force and leaders that are already stretched by the cumulative effects of almost a decade at war. It would be implemented by a force in which a substantial number of soldiers perceive that repeal will have a negative impact on unit effectiveness, cohesion, and morale, and that implementation will be difficult.

Further, the report clearly states that over 40 percent of our combat arms soldiers believe that the presence of a gay service member in their unit would have a negative impact on the unit's effectiveness, on the trust that the soldiers feel for each other, and on their morale.

As such, I believe that the implementation of the repeal of [DADT] in the near term will 1) add another level of stress to an already stretched force; 2) be more difficult in our combat arms units; and 3) be more difficult for the Army than the report suggests.

That said, if repeal is directed, the implementation principles in the report constitute a solid basis upon which to develop plans that will mitigate the risks that I just described. Properly implemented, I do not envision that the repeal of [DADT] would keep us from accomplishing our worldwide missions, including combat operations. We have a disciplined force and seasoned leaders who, with appropriate guidance and direction, can oversee the implementation of repeal with moderate risk to our military effectiveness in the short term and moderate risk to our ability to recruit and retain this all-volunteer force over the long haul.

I do believe that we will have to closely monitor the impact on our mid-level officers and noncommissioned officers as they wrestle with implementing repeal simultaneously with the other challenges that they're facing after nine years at war.

So it's my judgment that we could implement repeal with moderate risk to our military effectiveness and the long-term health of our force.

Let me close by saying that if [DADT] is repealed, the Army will work with the department and the other services to finalize the implementation plans and implement repeal in the same disciplined fashion that's characterized our service to this country for 235 years.

Admiral Gary Roughead, Chief of Naval Operations

Thank you for the opportunity to appear before you today to address the report of the Comprehensive Review Working Group and my perspective of the issues associated with the potential repeal of 10 U.S. Code 654.

I commend the working group for what they have accomplished and I applaud the professionalism and the seriousness of the men and women of the United States Navy as they participated in an unprecedented survey of our armed forces. I'm satisfied with the methodology and execution of the service member and spouse surveys and the extent to which the working group engaged sailors and their families.

I believe the appropriate policy issues have been researched, examined, and necessary courses of action have been considered. The responses helped me to assess the potential impacts to effectiveness, readiness, unit cohesion, and morale in our Navy. Seventy-six percent of sailors believe the impact on these force characteristics will be neutral or positive.

There will be issues to be addressed, especially in the period immediately following repeal. There's a sizable minority of the Navy, approximately 24 percent, who believe the impact of a repeal will be negative. Areas of greatest concern expressed in the survey include social cohesion, privacy in sleeping and showering facilities aboard ships and submarines and in certain training environments, and increased stress on the force during periods of high-tempo operations.

I believe these concerns can be effectively mitigated through engaged leadership, effective communications, training and education, and clear and concise standards of conduct. While we will engage all sailors regardless of their points of view, it is this minority upon which leaders must focus.

We all understand and appreciate the critical role of families in support of our sailors. The assessment of the spouses is important because of their support to our sailors and their role in reenlistment decisions that Navy families make. Of the more than 7,500 Navy spouses who responded to the survey, 81 percent told us they do not expect family readiness to be negatively impacted as a result of repeal.

Ten U.S. Code 654 is currently the subject of ongoing litigation and I cannot predict the outcome. I do believe any change in the law is best accomplished through the legislative process and not judicially. Legislative repeal affords us the time and structured process needed to effectively implement this significant change within our armed forces.

Should the law be repealed, the U.S. Navy will continue to be the professional; global; and effective, relevant force for the nation. Repeal of the law will not fundamentally change who we are and what we do. The U.S. Navy can implement the necessary changes to policies and procedures even in a time of war and increasing global commitments.

With the exception of the moderate risk associated with projected retention in some Navy irregular warfare specialties, I assess the risk to readiness, effectiveness, and cohesion of the Navy to be low.

Based on my professional judgment and informed by the inputs from our Navy, I recommend repeal of 10 U.S. Code 654. I have the ultimate confidence in the men and women of the U.S. Navy and in their character, in their discipline, and in their decency. Navy leaders will continue to set a positive tone, create an inclusive and respected work environment, and enforce our high standards of conduct throughout the Navy as we serve the nation.

Our sailors will continue to live by our core values of honor, courage, and commitment, which are fundamental to our character and our conduct.

General James F. Amos, Commandant of the Marine Corps

Thank you for the opportunity to appear before you to address the report of the Department of Defense working group that conducted a comprehensive review of the issues associated with repeal of Section 654, Title 10, United States Code, "Policy Concerning Homosexuality in the Armed Forces."

I would like to begin by stating for the record that the study conducted by the Department's Comprehensive [Review] Working Group is a valuable examination of the issues associated with repealing the policy concerning homosexuals in the armed forces and serves to usefully frame the perspectives of our service members and their families. I am grateful for the efforts of the Honorable Jeh Johnson and General Carter Ham. As team leaders, I believe they led their working group faithfully to uncover the attitudes and opinions of our service members.

The survey provides useful information about service member attitudes and issues regarding potential implementation of repeal across the Marine Corps. I would like to briefly share with you what this report says about our Marines' opinions concerning implementation.

Viewed holistically across the Corps, including all military occupational specialties, approximately 45 percent of Marines surveyed viewed repeal negatively regarding unit effectiveness, unit readiness, and cohesion. Five to 13 percent viewed repeal positively in those same categories. Of particular concern to me is that roughly 56 percent of combat arms Marines voiced negative concerns. Negative benchmarks for combat arms Marines range between 66 percent for unit effectiveness and 58 percent for cohesion. These negative perceptions are held almost equally by all ranks within the combat arms communities.

What the survey did not identify is the risk to the force should repeal be undertaken while the Corps is engaged in its ninth year of combat operations. With half of the Marine Corps operating forces either engaged in fighting in Afghanistan, returning from theater, or preparing to deploy to combat again, their readiness and associated focus are foremost in shaping my implementation assessment.

My experiences throughout nearly 40 years in uniform tell me that young men and women who volunteer to be Marines do so with honorable and patriotic intentions, and that even vast differences in backgrounds, beliefs, or personalities can be bridged. That said, if the law is changed, successfully implementing repeal and assimilating openly homosexual Marines into the tightly woven fabric of our combat units has strong potential for disruption at the small unit level, as it will no doubt divert leadership attention away from an almost singular focus on preparing units for combat.

I do not know how distracting that effort would be, nor how much risk it portends. I cannot reconcile nor turn my back on the negative perceptions held by our Marines who are most engaged in the hard work of day-to-day operations in Afghanistan.

We asked for their opinions and they gave them to us. Their message is that the potential exists for disruption to the successful execution of our current combat mission should repeal be implemented at this time.

In the final analysis, I'm faced with two questions. The first is, could we? Could we implement repeal at this time? The answer is yes. Despite the challenges I have briefly outlined above, at the end of the day, we are Marines. Should Congress change the law, then our nation's Marine Corps will faithfully follow the law. Marine Corps authorities, even its very existence in law, flow directly from Congress. I promise you that we will follow the law.

Chapter 13 of the study does a good job of articulating most of the elements of a successful implementation strategy. It will require and receive highly focused leadership at every level, beginning with me and the Sergeant Major of the Marine Corps.

The second question is, should we at this time? Based on what I know about the very tough fight in Afghanistan, the almost singular focus of our combat forces as they train up and deploy to theater, the necessary tightly woven culture of those combat forces that we are asking so much of at this time, and finally the direct feedback from the survey, my recommendation is that we should not implement repeal at this time.

Today your Marines continue to faithfully serve around the globe, partnered with our sister services and allies, defending our freedoms and our way of life. The focus of my complete energy is to ensure our Marines are properly led, trained, and equipped and that their families are cared for, so that our Marines can focus their energy on the vital task they are assigned. I can report to you that the combat effectiveness, readiness, and health and welfare of the Corps are as high as it has been in my nearly 40 years of service. Your Marines are accomplishing their many missions with professionalism and high morale, confident in the support of their families, fellow citizens, and elected leaders.

Finally, on behalf of all Marines, their families, and civilian Marines, I want to thank you for your continued and faithful support.

I know that the repeal issue has been difficult for all concerned.

I am grateful for the opportunity to represent our Marine Corps on this important matter.

General Norton A. Schwartz, Chief of Staff of the Air Force

Thank you for allowing the chiefs to offer testimony and our best military advice on the proposed repeal of 10 United States Code 654.

The DOD study confirms that Air Force attitudes run roughly 70 to 30 toward those who see positive, mixed, or no effect with respect to allowing open service by gay and lesbian airmen in the Air Force. The favorability distribution runs slightly higher for the spouse survey, at about 75 to 25, and lower for close combat Air Force skill sets, at about 60 to 40.

The study recognizes that there are a number of complicating factors—cohabitation, privacy, and universal benefits—among others. Each of these complicating factors will require focused attention and in time will be accommodated satisfactorily. Thus it is my assessment that the U.S. Air Force can accommodate the repeal of [DADT] with modest risk to military readiness and effectiveness, unit cohesion, retention, and recruiting of your airmen.

The Air Force will pursue implementation of repeal if the law changes thoroughly, professionally, and with conviction. Nonetheless, I do not agree with the study assessment that the short-term risk to military effectiveness is low. It is inescapable that our officer and NCO leaders in Afghanistan in particular are carrying a heavy load. While the demands of close combat affect fewer airmen in contrast to personnel of the other services, I remain concerned with the study assessment that the risk of repeal of military effectiveness in Afghanistan is low. That assessment in my view is too optimistic.

I acknowledge the findings of the study that under the pressures of combat, attitudes of our close combat skill personnel regarding [DADT] seem to moderate. After all, survival is a powerful instinct. Still, it is difficult for me as a member of the Joint Chiefs to recommend placing any additional discretionary demands on our leadership cadres in Afghanistan at this particularly demanding time. I therefore recommend deferring full implementation and certification until 2012, while initiating training and education efforts soon after you take a decision to repeal.

Finally, I would like to emphasize and add my strong endorsement to Secretary Gates' advice that legislative action on this issue is far preferable to a decision by the courts, from which we would enjoy much less latitude to properly calibrate implementation. Precipitous repeal is not—it is not—a place where your armed forces want to be.

Admiral Robert J. Papp Jr., Commandant of the Coast Guard

Thank you for inviting me and the Coast Guard to participate in today's hearing. I'm grateful for the opportunity to provide you with my views regarding the repeal's findings and the potential impacts of repealing [DADT] and the report's recommendations for implementation.

Let me start by saying I'm very proud of our Coast Guard men and women. They are individuals of extraordinary character and abilities who readily engage in the communities in which they live and serve. I'm particularly proud of the strong response by our Coast Guardsmen and family members in reply to the surveys put out by the report. Our active duty response rate was 54 percent, our Reserve response rate was 39 percent, and our spouse response rate was 39 percent, which demonstrates their understanding of the importance of this issue.

I concur with the report's recommendations on how to implement the repeal of the current law. Allowing gay and lesbian Americans to serve in the Coast Guard openly will remove a significant barrier to those Coast Guardsmen who are already serving capably and who have been forced to hide or even lie about their sexual orientation. Forcing these Coast Guardsmen to compromise our core values of honor, respect, and devotion to duty to continue to serve is a choice they should not have to make.

Now, I'm very respectful of the unique challenges facing each service, and I don't for a second suggest my circumstances and judgment would inform our very different responsibilities. My professional opinion is my own and comes from the two worlds in which I sit.

The Coast Guard is at all times a military service, governed by the laws this committee advances to ensure the effectiveness of our armed forces. Though small in numbers, we are integrated with our sister services around the world. But we're also tightly woven into the law enforcement and first responder communities in our nation. We work with federal, state, and local forces where gay and lesbian Americans serve with distinction and heroism. While I concur with the report's recommendations, prudence dictates that implementation must proceed with caution. I infer from the data relating to the Coast Guard that many Coast Guardsmen and their family members find gay and lesbian citizens in our service acceptable. However, minority views cannot be ignored. Moreover, there is no total force view. Views within our service communities vary to some degree. We must therefore fashion an implementation strategy that takes into account the attitudes that vary among our commands based upon where our people live and where they serve together.

Thus, I ask the committee to avoid inferring from the report that implementation of this rather significant decision will be easy. I describe myself as a pragmatist, which I define as an optimist with experience. My experience leads me to conclude that we must inform you, our civilian leaders, that implementation will not be achieved without encountering challenges along the course ahead, some of which, despite our best efforts, we cannot foresee and which will likely take considerable time and resources to overcome.

With that, I am absolutely confident that the Coast Guard leadership is prepared to implement any change that you direct. Moreover, I do not harbor the slightest doubt that Coast Guard men and women will be up to the task and will sustain their high levels of professionalism and effectiveness should the law change. They prove every day that they are among America's best, and I have unshakable confidence in their ability to weather change of this magnitude.

From the Commandant and the Sergeant Major of the Marine Corps, 28 January 2011

The following is a transcript of a video message by Marine Corps Commandant General James F. Amos and Marine Corps Sergeant Major Carlton W. Kent.

Amos: Marines, sailors, for the past decade we have engaged in constant combat operations. Today, we serve our nation at a critical time in its history. It's a challenging time, but we have been up to every task. Our fidelity to one another is our moral compass that guides us. It is the foundation of what being a Marine is all about. Above all else, we are loyal to the Constitution, our commander in chief, Congress, our chain of command, and the American people.

Kent: The repeal of "Don't Ask, Don't Tell" will take effect after our nation's senior leadership has determined an appropriate time line for implementation. Currently, we have an operational planning team working with the Department of Defense to determine the best way forward.

Amos: The Marine Corps exists to defend our nation. We are a nation of laws. We are committed by our oath and core values to obey these laws. Our success as Marines has always been grounded in the quality of our leadership, from general officers to small unit leaders.

Kent: Throughout the history of our Corps, Marines have always been professional, carrying on our warrior ethos and maintaining our core values. The Marine Corps is a diverse force and all have earned the privilege to wear the eagle, globe, and anchor. As Marines, we are confident that you will continue to treat each other with dignity and respect. The Commandant and I have trust in the great leadership of our Corps, from junior Marines to the most senior. As always, engaged leadership will be the key to implementation.

Amos: I want to be clear to all Marines, we will step out smartly to faithfully implement this new law. It is important that we value the diversity of background, culture, and skills that all Marines bring to the service of our nation. As we implement repeal, I want leaders at all levels to re-emphasize the importance of maintaining dignity and respect for one another throughout our force. We are Marines. We care for one another and respect the rights of all who wear this uniform. We will continue to demonstrate to the American people that discipline and fidelity, which have been the hallmarks of the U.S. Marine Corps for more than 235 years, will continue well into the future.

Certification of Readiness to Implement Repeal, 22 July 2011

Secretary of Defense Leon E. Panetta: Last December, this department began a careful and methodical process to prepare for the repeal of [DADT].

Since then, the Repeal Implementation Team has worked to coordinate the necessary changes to policy and regulations, and to provide education and training to service members. This effort, led by Undersecretary of Defense Clifford R. Stanley, was designed to ensure the smoothest possible transition for the U.S. military to accommodate and implement this important and necessary change.

Today, as a result of strong leadership and proactive education throughout the force, we can take the next step in this process. The president, the chairman of the Joint Chiefs of Staff, and I have certified that the implementation of repeal of [DADT] is consistent with the standards of military readiness, military effectiveness, unit cohesion, and recruiting and retention of the armed forces. This certification decision was carefully made after receiving input from the service chiefs, service secretaries, and from all the combatant commanders, who stated their views that the force is prepared for this change.

With this certification, and in accordance with the law, on September 20, [DADT] will be repealed. We will have taken the time necessary to get this done right and to ensure that service members are properly trained for a change that I believe is essential to the effectiveness of our all-volunteer force.

All men and women who serve this nation in uniform—no matter their race, color, creed, religion, or sexual orientation—do so with great dignity, bravery, and dedication. As secretary of defense, I am committed to promoting an environment free from personal, social, or institutional barriers that prevent service members from rising to the highest level of responsibility that their talents and capabilities warrant. They put their lives on the line for America, and that's what really matters. Thanks to the professionalism and leadership of the U.S. military, we are closer to achieving the goal that is at the foundation of America—equality and dignity for all.

Chairman of the Joint Chiefs of Staff Admiral Mike Mullen: I believe the U.S. Armed Forces are ready for the implementation of the repeal of [DADT]. I conveyed that opinion yesterday to the president and to the secretary of defense, and today we certified this to Congress.

My opinion is informed by close consultation with the service chiefs and the combatant commanders over the course of six months of thorough preparation and assessment, to include the training of a substantial majority of our troops.

I am comfortable that we have used the findings of the Comprehensive Review Working Group to mitigate areas of concern and that we have developed the policy and regulations necessary for implementation, consistent with standards of military readiness, military effectiveness, unit cohesion, and recruiting and retention.

Certification does not mark the end of our work. Ready though we are, we owe it to ourselves and to the nation we defend to continue to train the remainder of the joint force, to monitor our performance as we do so, and to adjust policy where and when needed.

My confidence in our ability to accomplish this work rests primarily on the fact that our people are capable, well led and thoroughly professional. I have never served with finer men and women. They will, I am certain, carry out repeal and continue to serve this country with the same high standards and dignity that have defined the U.S. military throughout our history.

Contributors (in order of appearance)

Nora Bensahel, PhD, is the deputy director of studies and a senior fellow at the Center for a New American Security in Washington, DC. She also teaches in the Security Studies Program in the School of Foreign Service at Georgetown University.

LtCol Thomas Dolan, USMC, completed recruit training in 1988, was commissioned in 1991, and was designated a naval aviator in 1993. He has served in billets ranging from forward air controller in an infantry battalion to commanding officer of a light attack helicopter squadron.

Cdr Randall J. Biggs, USN, was commissioned in 1990 and designated a naval aviator in 1992. He has served as a weapons and tactics instructor, Joint Special Operations Task Force fires officer, and commanding officer of a weapons school. He is currently an instructor at the Joint Services Command and Staff College at the Defence Academy of the United Kingdom. He coauthored his paper while a student at the Marine Corps War College in 2011.

Maj Darrel L. Choat, USMC, entered the Marine Corps in 1997 and is a student at Marine Corps University School of Advanced Warfare.

Maj Alasdair B. G. Mackay, USMC, graduated from Campbell University in 1997 after serving in the Navy from 1994–99 and was commissioned in the Marine Corps in 1999. He received a master's degree from Marine Corps University in 2011 and currently serves with the 1st Marine Division.

Col Michael F. Belcher, USMC (Ret.), was commissioned in 1983; is a veteran of Operations Desert Shield, Desert Storm, Restore Hope, and Enduring Freedom; and led 3d Battalion, 7th Marines, during the initial phase of Operation Iraqi Freedom. He subsequently commanded the 25th Marine Regiment. Until July 2011, he was director of the Marine Corps War College.

Justin Crockett Elzie joined the Marine Corps in 1982 and is the author of *Playing by the Rules*, a memoir.

R. Dirk Selland served on active duty in the Navy from 1990 through 1996. He is a chief judge with the Social Security Administration.

Vernice Armour enlisted in the Army Reserve in 1993 and entered Marine Corps Officer Candidate School in 1998. She left the Marines in 2007 as a captain. She is a motivational speaker and the author of *Zero to Breakthrough: The 7-Step, Battle-Tested Method for Accomplishing Goals That Matter*.

Kristen Kavanaugh graduated from the Naval Academy in 2002 and served in the Marine Corps from 2002 through 2007, attaining the rank of captain. She is the executive director of the Military Acceptance Project.

Julianne H. Sohn was discharged from the Marine Corps Reserve as a captain under DADT in 2008. She participated in the Call to Duty tour, is on the board of Service Women's Action Network, and works in public affairs for the federal government.

Antonio G. Agnone is a political officer in the Foreign Service assigned to Pakistan. He served on active duty in the Marine Corps from 2003 through 2007, attaining the rank of captain before being released from the Inactive Ready Reserve because of DADT.

Michael D. Almy served in the Air Force from 1993 through 2006, left as a major, and is a graduate of Marine Corps University. He works with a defense contractor.

David Hall enlisted in the Air Force in 1996 and was discharged under DADT in 2002. He is development director and information technology manager at Servicemembers Legal Defense Network.

Joseph Christopher Rocha served as a petty officer in the Navy from 2004 through 2007. He is a recent University of San Diego graduate.

Mark D. Faram served on active duty in the Navy from 1978 through 1987 and in the Navy Reserve from 2000 through 2006, leaving as a journalist first class. He is a senior writer at *Navy Times*.

Seth Moulton was a Marine Corps infantry officer and served four tours in Iraq. He is a recent graduate of the Harvard Kennedy School and the Harvard Business School. He is managing director for Lone Star High Speed Rail.

Maj Dirk Diener, USMC, enlisted in the U.S. Army Reserve in 1988 and in the Marine Corps in 1994.

Brian Fricke enlisted in the Marine Corps after high school, served from 2000 through 2005, and attained the rank of sergeant at the end of a tour in Iraq in 2004. He works as a civilian employee of the Navy in Washington, DC.

Justin H. Johnson served in the Marine Corps from 2001 through 2005 and from 2007 to 2008. He is currently a presidential management fellow in the office of the Secretary of Defense.

Ed Luna enlisted in the Marine Corps in 2002, deploying twice to Iraq. In 2011, he graduated from Tufts University and was commissioned as a second lieutenant.

Kristen L. Tobin retired from the Navy as a chief warrant officer 2 in 1998. She is a project manager at a military installation.

Stacy J. Vasquez served in the Army from 1991 through 2003 and was discharged at the rank of sergeant first class.

Lara A. Ballard served in the Army Air Defense Artillery from 1991 through 1995 in Germany and Kuwait and left at the rank of captain. She is a special advisor for privacy and technology at the Department of State.

Michelle M. Benecke served in the Army from 1983 through 1989 and left as a captain.

SFC David Cogdill, USA, served in the Marine Corps from 1991 through 1995 and in the Army National Guard from 1995 through 2003. He entered the Army in 2003 and served in Iraq.

Andrew Harris graduated from Virginia Military Institute and served in the U.S. Army for five years, departing as a captain in 2009. He is a senior consultant at Deloitte.

Brendan P. Kearney joined the Marine Corps Platoon Leaders Course program in 1971, was commissioned in 1975, retired as a colonel in 2006, and is an independent consultant.

About the Editors

J. Ford Huffman is an editor, writer, educator, designer, and artist whose nonfiction book reviews appear regularly in the *Military Times* newspapers. His articles have appeared in *USA Today, San Francisco Chronicle, Hindustan Times,* and Carnegie Corporation's *Reporter* magazine.

Tammy S. Schultz, PhD, is the director of the national security and joint warfare department and professor of strategic studies at the Marine Corps War College. In 2010, she won the Dr. Elihu Rose Award for teaching excellence at Marine Corps University and was the 2011 nominee from the Marine Corps War College. Dr. Schultz also teaches in the Security Studies Program at Georgetown University.